PERGAMON INSTITUTE OF ENGLISH (OXFORD)

Language Teaching Methodology Series

New Directions in Language Testing

Other Titles of Interest

ALDERSON, *Evaluation* (Lancaster Practical Papers in English Language Education, vol. 6)

CARROLL, *Testing Communicative Performance*

See also: SYSTEM, The International Journal of Applied Linguistics and Educational Technology

ESP Journal, An International Journal of English for Specific Purposes

Free sample copies available on request

New Directions in Language Testing

Papers presented at the International Symposium on Language Testing, Hong Kong

Edited by

**Y. P. Lee, Angela C. Y. Y. Fok,
Robert Lord and Graham Low**

University of Hong Kong

PERGAMON PRESS

Oxford · New York · Toronto · Sydney · Paris · Frankfurt

U.K.	Pergamon Press Ltd., Headington Hill Hall, Oxford OX3 0BW, England
U.S.A.	Pergamon Press Inc., Maxwell House, Fairview Park, Elmsford, New York 10523, U.S.A.
CANADA	Pergamon Press Canada Ltd., Suite 104, 150 Consumers Road, Willowdale, Ontario M2J 1P9, Canada
AUSTRALIA	Pergamon Press (Aust.) Pty. Ltd., P.O. Box 544, Potts Point, N.S.W. 2011, Australia
FRANCE	Pergamon Press SARL, 24 rue des Ecoles, 75240 Paris, Cedex 05, France
FEDERAL REPUBLIC OF GERMANY	Pergamon Press GmbH, Hammerweg 6, D-6242 Kronberg-Taunus, Federal Republic of Germany

First edition 1985

Library of Congress Cataloging in Publication Data

International Symposium on Language Testing (1983 Hong Kong)
New directions in language testing.
(Language teaching methodology series)
1. Language and languages—Ability testing—
Congresses. I. Lee, Y. P. II. University of Hong
Kong. III. Title.
P53.4.I58 1984   428′.0076   84-1082

British Library Cataloguing in Publication Data

International Symposium on Language Testing
(*1982: Hong Kong*)
New directions in language testing—.
(Language teaching methodology series)
1. Language and languages—Ability testing.
I. Title II. Lee, Y. P. III. Series
418′.007 P53.4

ISBN 0-08-031535-6

Printed in Great Britain by A. Wheaton & Co. Ltd., Exeter.

Acknowledgements

The Editors wish to thank the British Council for providing sponsorship for two of the keynote speakers and for undertaking some of the coordinating work on behalf of the Organizing Committee of the International Symposium on Language Testing. They would also like to thank those who willingly and generously accepted key roles: Kenneth Topley, former Secretary for Education in Hong Kong, who opened the Symposium; Alan Brimer, Dean of the Faculty of Education, University of Hong Kong; Francis Johnson, Chairman of the Department of English, Chinese University of Hong Kong, and Oliver Siddle, Representative of the British Council in Hong Kong, who chaired the Plenary Sessions; as well as the many others who chaired the working sessions: Peter Barnes, Nelson A. Berkoff, James D. Brown, Evelyn Cheung, William Cheung, Peter Falvey, Anne Hilferty, John Hunt, Keith Johnson, Randall Jones, Rex King, Helen Kwok, Teresa Leung, Alan Maley, Elaine Marshall, Michael Milanovic, Alan Moller, Pauline Rea, John Read, Douglas Stevenson, Merrill Swain, Tsao Feng Fu, Christine Wright and Arne Zettersten. Nor would they want to overlook the great deal of painstaking labour that went on behind the scenes in making the International Symposium a success: Amy Lam for her work as Treasurer to the Organizing Committee; Christine Wright, Evelyn Cheung, Cynthia So, Caroline Lo, Helen Yeung, and Irina Lau, who took care of the details of the programme and registration; Matthew Leung, Amy Lam, Cheng Ngai-lung, and Ip Kung Sau, who provided information and planned the amenities; Tsao Feng Fu, who was the Translation Adviser; and Joe Sing He and Edward Leung, who provided technical and audio-visual assistance. Our especial thanks, finally, to Connie Kwok who typed the final draft.

Contents

List of Contributors   ix

Editors' Introduction   xi

1. Language Testing and the Curriculum   1

Follow my leader: Is That What Language Tests Do?   3
ALAN DAVIES

Language Testing and the Communicative Language Teaching Curriculum   15
PAULINE M. REA

2. Large-Scale Testing   33

Large-scale Communicative Language Testing: A Case Study   35
MERRILL SWAIN

A Test of Swedish as a Second Language: An Experiment in Self-assessment   47
TIBOR VON ELEK

The English Proficiency Test Used in China: A Report   59
YANG HUI ZHONG AND GUI SHI CHUN

Experiments in Large-scale Vocabulary Testing   67
ARNE ZETTERSTEN

3. Testing Oral Proficiency   75

Some Basic Considerations in Testing Oral Proficiency   77
RANDALL L. JONES

Simulating an Academic Tutorial: A Test Validation Study   85
DONALD M. MORRISON AND NANCY LEE

Testing Oral Proficiency: A New Approach   93
NELSON A. BERKOFF

OLAF N. 73: A Computerized Oral Language Analyser and Feedback System   101
THOMAS M. PENDERGAST, JR

4. Validating Language Tests   109

Pop Validity and Performance Testing   111
DOUGLAS K. STEVENSON

How Shall a Test be Referenced?   119
GRAHAM D. LOW AND Y. P. LEE

Language Proficiency and Related Factors   127
ANGELA C. Y. Y. FOK

Investigating the Validity of the Cloze Score   137
Y. P. LEE

The Use of Latent Trait Models in the Calibration of Tests of Spoken
Language in Large-scale Selection-placement Programs   149
PATRICK E. GRIFFIN

Bibliography   163

List of Contributors

NELSON A. BERKOFF, The Hebrew University, Jerusalem.

ALAN DAVIES, University of Edinburgh.

ANGELA C. Y. Y. FOK, University of Hong Kong.

PATRICK E. GRIFFIN, University of Hong Kong.

GUI SHI CHUN, Institute of Foreign Languages, Guangzhou.

RANDALL L. JONES, Brigham Young University, Utah.

NANCY LEE, University of Hong Kong.

Y. P. LEE, University of Hong Kong.

GRAHAM D. LOW, University of Hong Kong.

DONALD M. MORRISON, University of Hong Kong.

THOMAS M. PENDERGAST, JR. Osaka University of Foreign Studies.

PAULINE M. REA, University of Dar Es Salaam.

DOUGLAS K. STEVENSON, Universität Essen.

MERRILL SWAIN, Ontario Institute for Studies in Education, Toronto.

TIBOR VON ELEK, University of Göteborg.

YANG HUI ZHONG, Jiaotong University, Shanghai.

ARNE ZETTERSTEN, University of Copenhagen.

Editors' Introduction

In December 1982 Hong Kong hosted an International Symposium on Language Testing. Its organizers, drawn from the Language Centre of the University of Hong Kong, chose two themes which have been, in microcosm, of central concern to teachers and testers in the Language Centre and, in macrocosm, to language testers the world over. The two themes chosen were: *direct* or *performance* testing, and *large-scale* testing. Hong Kong offers a common focus for these two areas of language testing, which otherwise could seem disparate and none too obviously related.

In recent years there has of course been a general shift in emphasis in approaches to second or foreign language teaching, with a language being increasingly perceived as a tool to be used in a purposeful and controlled manner. With this shift have emerged new ideas about language testing and new ways of evaluating the performance of second language learners. A concern with measuring how well language is used within certain contexts and as a means of establishing aspects of context has therefore become one of the main features of this new direction. To date, a good deal of work has been devoted to identifying and formalizing the required target behaviour of learners at the end of their courses, and to constructing viable formats with which to test what one might call "proficiency in action". Until recently there has been relatively little published work examining the data that results from such tests; for example, the construct and predictive validity of such data, and ways of maintaining reliability.

Hong Kong shares with many other multilingual societies the problem that the medium of instruction is not the first language of the vast majority of its school population. As a direct result of this, second language achievement, and the evaluation of second-language achievement play a crucial role in educational planning. Language attainment needs to be carefully assessed at every stage, and students' ability to use the second language for learning carefully monitored. Without a detailed knowledge of the students' ability to make use of the medium of instruction, no appropriate plans for improvement and development can be formulated. It is for this reason that, in exploring new directions in the design of language tests, the validity and reliability of the testing instruments need to be established with particular care. On the other hand, such procedures can be time-consuming and this has to be balanced against practicability, which tends to mean simplicity of test administration and ease of scoring, especially when the tests are administered to very large groups.

It was our hope that the shared experience and aims of participants in the Symposium would lead to new ways of producing suitable tests to evaluate the language behaviour of the student population as well as shed new light on some of the perennial problems besetting our various educational systems.

The participants came from 16 different countries. The Symposium consisted of papers, workshops and demonstrations, and included four plenary sessions with invited speakers: Alan Davies (University of Edinburgh), Randall Jones (Brigham Young University, Utah), Pauline Rea (University of Dar Es Salaam), and Merrill Swain (Modern Language Centre, Ontario Institute for Studies in Education, Toronto).

The Opening Ceremony included addresses by the Hon. K. W. J. Topley, then

Secretary for Education in Hong Kong, and Robert Lord, Director of the Language Centre and Chairman of the Symposium Organizing Committee.

This book consists of an edited selection of 15 of the papers presented, and includes all four of the papers presented at the Plenary Sessions. The papers have been reorganized to form four sections, which differ slightly from the three sections of the Symposium. Since virtually every paper is concerned with the question of performance testing, it seemed more sensible to remove this as a separate section. On the other hand, so many papers were concerned with questions of test validity, that it was decided to group these together under the general heading of *Validating Language Tests*. This section is organized from the more general to the more mathematical and the last paper in particular, that by Griffin, is clearly mathematical in orientation. It contains recent work on virtually every major dimension of validity: predictive validity (Low and Lee, Fok), face validity (Stevenson), and construct validity (Lee). Papers on content validation (e.g. Morrison and Lee) have been included in other sections. Similarly, von Elek's discussion of the possibility of validating self-assessment tests has been placed in the section on *Large-scale Testing*.

The section devoted to *Large-scale Testing* has been retained and contains attempts to solve the problem of how to reconcile recent ideas on communicative testing with the reality of large numbers of students and the little time and or money available for testing each individual student. Swain considers the case of classroom teachers wishing to evaluate the effectiveness of their bilingual education programmes (here French and English) in Canada and the development of a package involving simulated tasks which is administered by classroom teachers. Von Elek discusses recent work on the long-running project to develop self-assessment tests for adult learners of English in Sweden, particularly adult migrants. Zettersten discusses work done in Denmark to develop large-scale tests of lexical skills, with a special focus on ways in which such tests can be computerized. Yang and Gui, in a similar spirit, discuss recent work on the development of a national language proficiency test (of English) for young adults in China.

The section *Testing Oral Skills* begins with an overview of the situation by Jones, who cites numerous examples of recent, particularly American, work in the area. This is followed by three case studies. Both Lee and Morrison, and Berkoff give details of attempts to construct and validate tests aimed at measuring the oral skills of university students by means of a group testing approach. The paper by Pendergast is of a rather different nature and has closer links in many ways with the large-scale testing section; it is a summary of work done over the last few years in Japan in developing a very rapid (2–3 minute) test of oral ability where the examiner is aided by a "testside" computer.

We have taken the two plenary sessions which were most general in scope and put them at the front of the book to form a readable though detailed introduction to the current language testing scene. Both are concerned that testing should not be seen as something divorced from language teaching. Davies focuses particularly on a number of recent errors of philosophy or judgement, while Rea is concerned to develop a method of handling test types which is usable by the classroom teacher.

We hope, therefore, that the papers published here will be of interest and use to a wide variety of readers, from research workers attempting to develop new ways of designing and validating tests, to language teachers who would like to know what has been going on over the last few years and who would like a framework for dealing with the multiple variations on the theme of communicative or direct or performance testing which have been appearing in the literature.

1

Language Testing and the Curriculum

Follow my leader: Is That What Language Tests Do?

ALAN DAVIES

An Agony* in Eight Fits

Fit the First

"Just the place for a Snark! I have said it twice:
That alone should encourage the crew.
Just the place for a Snark! I have said it thrice:
What I tell you three times is true"

In disciplines where data reveal themselves to consistent view and leave no case to appeal, where objectivity, what Melville called the level log and line, holds sway, in scientific disciplines such as medicine, what students learn is, we recognize, true. It may be that in different medical schools there are varying emphases such that a young surgeon from one medical school may be more practised with the knife while one from a second school may be more into computers and data banks. But we are confident that they share a common core such that the diagnosis of an ailment will be identical whichever surgeon makes it.

And yet how true is this? Our emotional selves may want to believe that medical opinion is not only consistent but true as well, but our rational selves, and our experience when we listen to it, reminds us that the commonsense world is a hit-and-miss affair, even in rubbery hard sciences like medicine. What doctors do, in fact, in order to overcome the subjectivity and unreliability of their diagnoses is to establish very strong consensus and to ensure that their apprentice youth are firmly socialized into that consensus. Thus, it does not matter in medicine to be wrong, what matters is to be odd. And since being wrong has probably no useful meaning, since we do not know what being right would be, even if we take a realist position, patients, potentially all of us, are no doubt grateful that consensus validity can be achieved, promising at least some small kind of content or concurrent validity.

Paul Atkinson (1981) describes the socializing into consensus of young doctors in the Edinburgh Medical School. Atkinson discusses his fieldwork as part of a critique of young medical students during the clinical phase of their training. As he points out, "clinical" phases of training rest on the assumption that the trainee is to gain practical knowledge and experience through some form of exposure to, immersion in, and some sort of "practice" on "real" settings (p. 115). What he tries to show is how this clinical reality is socially organized, achieved and managed.

" . . . The medical reality to which the beginning student is exposed is by no means straightforward. There is nothing natural about such 'reality'. Like any other it is a matter of

---

* *Agony* is glossed by Carroll as a struggle that involves great anguish, bodily pain or death. It is possible that Carroll also had in mind the "woeful agony" that periodically seizes Coleridge's *Ancient Mariner*, forcing him to tell to strangers his "ghastly tale".

social construction. What novitiate students are introduced to, then, is not the practical reality of some essential clinical medicine. Rather, they encounter the dramatic enactment of a particular form or version of medical work. . . . I found myself identifying, at least tentatively, a style of teaching I labelled 'thaumaturgical' (wonder working). The patients and medical students would find themselves recruited partly as audience, partly as stooges, partly as props in displays of clinical expertise and diagnostic skill. The effect of such displays, and of less dramatic teaching too, is to produce vivid firsthand reconstructions of the logic and rationality of clinical medicine. It is as audience to these performances that the students gain their first clinical experiences."

In clinical teaching what we have, says Atkinson, is a mock-up in which the "facts of the case" are determined and legitimized by reference to the procedural rules of "correct" and "methodical" enquiry. And he goes on to suggest that this is true of all science, reminding us of the structure of scientific thinking T. S. Kuhn has described, in which what is at any time "true" is only so because, or if, it fits into the currently accepted paradigms. No doubt Kuhn, and his followers, like Atkinson perhaps, would as empiricists have been delighted to read the 1901 parody version of *MIND* (published as *MIND!*) in which the pragmatist philosopher F. C. S. Schiller provided a mock-serious commentary on Lewis Carroll's *The Hunting of the Snark* which, Schiller insisted, is a satire on the Hegelian philosopher's search for the Absolute. It is from *The Hunting of the Snark* that I take my texts for this talk. No doubt, in philosophy, empiricism is a comforting refuge, for there no patients die, no bridges fall down, and no languages remain unlearnt. But in the world of applied (social) sciences in which we deal we are genuinely concerned that what we do should somehow be in pursuit of some external validity represented by consensus, and that validity should not be solely a matter of internal and therefore self-justifying consistency.

Fit the Second

"Come, listen, my men, while I tell you again
The five unmistakable marks
By which you may know, wheresoever you go,
The warranted genuine Snarks"

If we accept that reality is thus socially constructed even in hard sciences, how much easier it is to agree that in the softer social sciences and, in the quicksands of Applied Linguistics and Language Teaching, facts (like snarks) keep changing shape.

"Reality" for most language learners *is* socially constructed. However reconstructed the syllabus, the teaching and anything else may be, what the students' gaze (and the public's) is fixed on is the test, no matter how unreconstructed that may be. And, understandably, learners are grateful for the social rather than individual reassurance, because what they want is the reassurance that can only come from consensus: thus it would be possible to contemplate a complete mismatch in which the individual succeeds communicatively, interactively, but is dissatisfied because he does badly on the test which is out of phase with "true" measures. Eventually, such a mismatch represents a lack of agreement as to what stands for the language. Examples of such a mismatch are found for example in situations where the syllabus and the teaching may be wholly concerned with the language, may be communicative, but where the test is still dedicated to literature. A student who is unprepared for such a literary test (which is institutionalized in the educational system) will not be grateful for a syllabus and a teaching method that make it possible for him to communicate with ease. He has not been able to unsocialize his view of what language learning goals in his situation are – they are literary and have to do with some kinds of language-*like* behaviour rather than with language behaviour.

I want to go on to some specific examples of such mismatches and the harm they do.

Fit the Third

"*'That's exactly the method', the Bellman bold*
In a hasty parenthesis cried,
'That's exactly the way I have always been told
That the capture of Snarks should be tried!'"

A test situation such as the one just described is not satisfactory. Such situations fall into two main problem categories: problems of excessive conservatism or problems of unthinking radicalism.

First, two conservative examples. One of these is a historical example which illustrates how a language test can become ritualized and irrelevant except in a symbolic way. The example is that of the *neck verse* which is defined in the Shorter Oxford Dictionary as

"Neck Verse 1450. A Latin verse printed in black-letter (usually the beginning of Psalm 51) formerly set before one claiming benefit of clergy by reading which he might save his neck. Now only Historical" (sic!)

(Psalm 51 – for those who wish to put something aside in the hope that they can, if it ever proves necessary, preserve their necks – begins "Miserere mei, deus", or in our present vulgar or doric "Have mercy upon me, O God, after thy great goodness: according to the multitude of thy mercies, do away mine offences.") The neck verse may be "only *Hist*.", but we do still make judgements on similarly ritualistic foundations, e.g. the language question in the UK Census presented in Wales and Scotland: "Do you speak Welsh/Scots Gaelic?" (only recently added to by the secondary questions: "If so, do you read/write it?"). Or, for example, this item from a questionnaire carried out in Bedford and reported in Sutcliffe 1982 (*British Black English*). Sutcliffe was interested in the variability of English among the younger black community in Bedford. His questionnaire attempted to find out what percentage of the sample was able to speak Broad Creole.

"The test sentence used was the Jamaican Creole: *mi asks di man fi put mi moni iina him pakit* (I asked the man to put my money in his pocket). Subjects were asked to translate it and were asked: 'Do you sometimes speak like that?' A surprising number . . . said they did – 78 % . . . Similarly, over 90 % . . . reported using at least some Creole" (p. 151).

It is not surprising that Sutcliffe's results have been challenged – as he himself admits. It is difficult to see *what* conclusions could be drawn from so unsatisfactory a test item.

My second conservative example comes from Saudi Arabia (personal information, Alan Beretta, 1982) in the British Aerospace English Language programme, where what is required is to obtain a "pass" in the English Comprehension Level (ECL) examination. The only course materials used are the American Defence Language Institute's ALC (American Language Course). Over the years there have been complaints about and criticisms of this course but, I am assured, while it might have been possible to modify it in practice, the rigidity of the ECL examination does not allow for any change. Not only do the authorities forbid any change in the examination, but the students themselves know exactly what is demanded, and insist that no changes in the course be made.

Approximately 70 % of all items test the students' capacity to associate tenuously related lexical items, e.g.

> *Stem:* A *pioneer* was a tough man.
> *Choices:* tradesman, colonist, cowboy, foreigner

where the correct answer is *colonist*. The effect of such rigid testing is that *pioneer, settler, colonist, explorer* are taught as synonymous (known as *same-same* to the students), and that much of the teaching consists of similar vocabulary lists. My informant concludes that the format of the test means that there is no teaching of writing, speaking, reading of more than sentence-length, or listening to anything of more than sentence-length. He provides this science-fiction scenario of a "typical" teacher-student interchange:

Teacher:	pick up the book
Student:	pick up same-same collect same-same take away
T.	start the next sentence
S.	start same-same begin same-same take up same-same commence
T.	OK that's enough of that
S.	enough same-same adequate same-same sufficient
T.	keep quiet
S.	keep quiet same-same shut up same-same quit it, same-same can it, buddy . . .

The neck verse test and the same-same test both have residual validity. Those who were both poor and illiterate would not have been priests and would, in the absence of any kind memorizer, have failed the test. Similarly, the same-same test keeps close to the ALC syllabus. What disturbs us about both is precisely the conservatism that characterizes them. They *ought* to have been changed, to relate to more valid ideas of literacy, to help revise the ALC course in such a way as to prevent what, my informant tells me, happens every course end where students cheerfully proceed to the next phase of training, linguistically incompetent in English after a year (or often 2 or 3 years) of intensive study. No doubt it is a virtue of achievement tests to stick close to the syllabus – as has often been said, their job is to sample, and the validity issue is one for the syllabus. But without change in the syllabus that virtue of the achievement test is a recipe for disaster: the teachers alone just cannot generate enough power to bend those institutional bonds.

> *Fit the Fourth*
>
> *"For the Snark's a peculiar creature that won't*
> *Be caught in a common-place way,*
> *Do all that you know, and try all that you don't:*
> *Not a chance must be wasted today."*

Let me now take my two unthinking radical examples. The first comes from Malaysia where some years ago the Curriculum Development Centre (CDC), concerned to integrate the two language-medium systems, English and Malay, as quickly as possible, introduced a new Communication Syllabus for English into the secondary schools. The idea was that what secondary school graduates needed was the ability to communicate in English, particularly in spoken English, and of course by communicate was meant that rather special *communicative* view which involves the capacity to cope adequately with the English of every possible situation. I think it is now recognized that such a view is one kind of vague description of what the native speaker can do. Schools were provided with the new syllabus which was mandatory: it consisted largely of sociologically described situations, e.g. in a tourist office or hotel, with no indication of what language was relevant or necessary. There were no textbooks. The Examinations Syndicate, a separate organization from the CDC, were unwilling to radicalize their school certificate type examination to bring it in line with the new syllabus. The result was a grotesque mismatch in which the syllabus was in large part unteachable because it properly required, in part, the competence and the intuition of a native speaker teacher and the examination did not in any case test the syllabus. Failure was severe except among those from the more élite English-medium schools; many average English-medium students and most of the Malay-medium students failed. Remember that the purpose of the new syllabus was to help those very Malay-medium students who had had no access to English medium, and that English medium was then on its way out. Twenty-five per cent of the new syllabus was intended for spoken English, again to encourage the use of spoken English among those with least opportunity in school to use it. The Exams Syndicate refused to give more than a token share of the examination percentage to oral English. The CDC had acted with brave but foolhardy zeal: it was right to be concerned about promoting appropriate use of English, but wrong not to check with its sister, but separate, examinations institution, and with the teaching profession. Change is essential but it needs a fabian lead.

The same comment can be made on my second unthinking radical example, this time from West Africa. In the 1960s, D. W. Grieve wrote an excellent report on English examining in the West African secondary schools. He was then asked to rewrite the examinations, and at that point things began to go wrong. Grieve's interest in linguistics, an interest which had helpfully informed his critique of the existing school certificate (modelled on the Cambridge overseas school certificate), dominated the new examination which he constructed. Whether or not the new examination was piloted I don't know – if it was, it can only have been in the main urban centres, a warning to us all when we are sampling whole educational systems. But although syllabus and text books were redrafted and revised, the change was too great and the teachers could not cope. Of course all systems have inertia and some way round the problem of mismatching is typically found, if only, as in Singapore, by insisting with the weight of authority, on reverting to a traditional school certificate type of examination so as to encourage (by backwash) in the schools continuous writing in English which, so it seems, was being dropped after the introduction into the examination of a more objective-type approach.

Change in language teaching must be possible; that is, there must be some way of responding to new ideas and demands. It is best if the change comes in through the syllabus and the examination and the teacher. If a choice has to be made among these in order to move quickly, then undoubtedly the test/examination is the most sensitive; it is the most controllable, it acts overall, it is most difficult (*pace* W. Africa) to ignore, it has most certainty in terms of its goals. The test/examination is a major and a creative influence for change and development in language teaching, and if there is a need to choose, then that is what should always change first. *But* the influence for good that the test/examination can have (and I would cite here the work of the Royal Society of Arts of London on its language teachers' examinations, its communicative test of EFL, its new examination in ESL; the Joint Matriculation Board Test in English (Overseas); the

ARELS oral examination; to some extent the developments in the Cambridge examinations; the work of the Assessment of Performance Unit (APU) at the Department of Education and Science in London; and the English Language Testing Service of the British Council (ELTS) test) this influence must not be abused by moving too fast so that the syllabus – or for that matter the teacher – lose their horizon. Teaching shares with other professions a lack of innovative interest and is very quick to reject what it regards as theoretical, academic or airy-fairy. Some 15 years ago in Scotland a far-sighted administrator introduced a "new" O Grade examination in French and German, which was largely oral/aural, to meet what he regarded as the new wave of interest in and enthusiasm for spoken language, for oracy as the important communicative mode. Those examinations still exist, still admit candidates, but very few. The soul of French or German is still claimed by the quite traditional literacy examining, and teachers have not leapt to the bold new opportunities.

Most testing – in terms of bulk – does of course follow its leader: the syllabus, the teaching, in the sense that most testing is a check on achievement; it is achievement testing. But creative and innovative testing, starting often in a proficiency guise, charts a slight detour, not a whole new terrain, and in doing so can, quite successfully, attract to itself a syllabus change or a new syllabus which effectively makes it into an achievement test. Indeed, it could be said that the proper accolade for a good proficiency test is that it allows itself to be outdated – it becomes the achievement test for a teaching syllabus and thereby permits a new proficiency test to be constructed, more appropriate for developing ideas of language teaching and learning. In my own case that is the way in which I see the replacement of the English Proficiency Test Battery (EPTB) by ELTS.

Fit the Fifth

"The method employed I would gladly explain
While I have it so clear in my head,
If I had but the time and you had but the brain –
But much yet remains to be said."

I am now half way through my Agony and, so far, I have been talking about education, teaching and some aspects of language examining. I seem to have been saying nothing about real language testing. But language examinations are not categorically different from language tests: they inhabit the same world and face the same demands, and must admit to the same limitations. No doubt it is true that language examinations are more a large-scale activity (though consider TOEFL or the MLA Coop. Tests or the ELTS) and, equally, that language tests are more obviously at home in research and development in second language learning (but consider the harsh practicality of classroom testing). However, I do now move into a more obvious applied linguistic mode in order to discuss the relationships that language testing enters into there.

In the introduction to his latest book, S. D. Krashen (1982) provides a useful diagram showing the relationships, as he sees them, between *Applied Linguistics*, *Second Language Acquisition Theory*, and *Language Teaching Practice*. (He also has a box labelled *Ideas and Intuition*, but I will not consider that at this time). I recognize that diagrams are unsatisfactory because they are static – they force us into discrete relationships while what we want to show is a whole range. Even so, I wish to raise two objections to Krashen's model: the first is the directionality of his arrows, all (in the ideal model) leading into *Language Teaching Practice*, none leading out; the second is that he has no *Language Testing* category at all. My own view is that relationships with *Language Teaching Practice* should be two-way; and that Second Language Acquisition and Applied Linguistics should be merged. If it is necessary to show them separately, then my predilection would be for Second Language Acquisition as a subordinate of Applied Linguistics. But my real preference is Occamian: a major contribution of John Oller has been to argue for the importance in its own right of Language Testing both as a research activity and for its influence on Applied Linguistics. In a Krashen model this could lead to yet another equal superordinate alongside Second Language Acquisition, Applied Linguistics and (in his case) Ideas and Intuition, and now Language Testing, all dominating Language Teaching Practice. I am for as simple an explanation – or metaphor at least – as possible, and would be happy for Applied Linguistics to incorporate both Second Language Acquisition and Language Testing. Then I would like to see a two-box model with Applied Linguistics and Language Teaching Practice with dual directional arrows, each informing the other; because that is, in my experience, what actually happens.

Normal relations between Applied Linguistics and Language Testing (now treating them as apart) are probably those of "pull", i.e. that the test represents some form of practical demand or outcome which requires a development within Applied Linguistics in, for example, determining the content of a proficiency test. An identical duality can be indicated for the Applied Linguistics/Language Teaching relationship. Work on *contrastive analysis*, for example, can be cited as interesting to Applied Linguistics, not in its own right, but because of the insistence by language teachers on the importance of error analysis and the salience of the mother tongue. Applied linguistics has never been quite sure what to do with contrastive analysis. In spite of the vast amount of work in the field, S. P. Corder concluded in his *Introduction to Applied Linguistics* (1973) that "it looks . . . as if, in the present state of linguistic knowledge, between the message and its physical expression in sound, there is a fundamental lack of common categories and relations available for really adequate comparison between two languages" (p. 255). And yet at one time contrastive analysis was the whole of applied linguistics and in some places it still is. With hindsight we could argue that contrastive analysis was in part a "pull" from language teaching, in part a "push" from descriptive linguistics, but most of all an attempt to provide some theoretical underpinning for the technique of error analysis, a method that has existed for a long time and has lacked explanation. Indeed, what happened after the decline of contrastive analysis has been that the technique of error analysis has continued to flourish, but now as a methodology for second language acquisition and inter-language studies.

If the contrastive analysis episode shows "pull" from Language Teaching, then "push" from Applied Linguistics is well illustrated by the growth of the *communication* construct over the last 10 or 15 years, which has been very much fostered by those working in applied linguistics; often, it has seemed, as an antidote to the strong psycholinguistic views of the early transformationalists (and, to some extent, trends in second language acquisition studies). Whether or not that antithesis explanation is correct, sociolinguistics has been heavily influential in applied linguistics in this last period – during which time, interestingly enough, there has been a lessening of activity in aptitude testing, almost as though that was an improper area of investigation during a largely interactionist phase. Language is, of course, for interaction – but not only so: like all heresies, the communicative construct has exaggerated its uniqueness and there are signs that it is already on the wane. But what is, I suggest, clear, is that communicative language teaching as a method – or was it a goal? – was not created because it was what language teachers wanted, but because it seemed like a good idea to applied linguists.

As far as the relationship between language testing and applied linguistics is concerned, the "pull" has been to get applied linguists to take an interest in language testing – very much on the periphery until recently, except for the semi-psycholinguistic work in language aptitude (see Carroll and Sapon, 1959; Pimsleur, 1966; Davies, 1971; Green, 1974–5; and most recently Skehan, 1982). The "push" from applied linguistics to language testing has been to make language testers more interested in, for example, communicative language teaching and therefore testing, and in, for example, the establishing of proficiency levels, which is both a practical and a theoretical issue, raising such questions as: what does to "know" a language actually mean? Then there are various attempts to define "oracy" or to delimit language abilities factorially (as in the work of Oller, 1974; Bachman and Palmer, 1981; Vollmer, 1981; Hughes and Woods, 1981). As I have suggested elsewhere,

> "language testing does seem in recent years to have come of age and is now regarded as a methodology that is of value throughout applied linguistics . . . Language testing is now better known and more widely appreciated and what we have in fact been seeing is greater acceptance of the role of construct validity such that the approach of, for example, John Carroll to aptitude testing, which furthered our understanding of language, has now been extended to proficiency testing" (Davies, 1982).

If we now return to our two-box model and consider the relation between Language Teaching and the Language Testing part of applied linguistics, then, as has been said earlier, the "normal" relation between language teaching and language testing is the "push" from language teaching to language testing, i.e. the demand to set up achievement tests. But the argument of this paper is that all such relationships are two-way affairs and that language testing can lead language teaching and does not always have to follow – with the caveat we made about language examining, that the tests and the teaching must not be too far apart.

Fit the Sixth

"They sought it with thimbles, they sought it with care;
They pursued it with forks and hope;
They threatened its life with a railway-share;
They charmed it with smiles and soap."

What I now want to do is to refer to three pieces of testing research which I think show the proper relation between testing and teaching. They all have both theoretical (i.e. applied linguistic) and practical (i.e. language teaching) "pull" and "push". Furthermore, there is a bridgeable gap between theory and practice in all three. The first is the multitrait multimethod oral testing research of Bachman and Palmer reported for example in Read (1981) under the title "Basic concerns in test validation". Bachman and Palmer describe their investigation of the hypothesis

> "that two language-use skills, speaking and reading, which differ both in direction (productive vs. receptive) and in channel (aural vs. visual) are psycholinguistically distinct and can be measured independently of each other. Three different methods of testing (namely, interview, translation

and self-ratings) were used to investigate each of two hypothesized traits (namely, 'communicative competence in speaking' and 'communicative competence in reading')".

Six tests were used. The results of the various factor analyses indicated support for the partial divisibility model of language competence, i.e. two separate factors of speaking and reading – plus a general factor. Now apart from its theoretical interest, there are useful practical outcomes. For example, we can accept that our commonsense approach to teaching in separate skills is still sound, and that the traits do indeed differ, when method is controlled. It may be true that, as Horatio said to Hamlet, "there needs no ghost, my lord, come from the grave to tell us this" – and yet research does have more of an effect than researchers often realize. Witness the pervasive influence of Bernstein's code distinction, or, nearer home, the value given to Oller's claims for cloze and dictation tests.

The second piece of research has only recently been published and is a pilot study by J. C. Alderson and A. H. Urquhart: *The Effect of Student Background Disciplines on Comprehension: a Pilot Study* (1983). Theirs is a testing approach to ESP; much needed in view of the enormous industry generated worldwide on behalf of ESP. They looked at reading comprehension among non-native-speaking university students in the UK and hypothesized "that students reading texts in a familiar content area, that is, related to their area of study, would perform better than students unfamiliar with that subject". As they point out, this again spans a theoretical interest (language variation, language varieties) and a practical one (the teaching of ESP and attempts through the ELTS test, for example, to test it.) Four groups of students from different academic disciplines were tested, the disciplines being: development administration, engineering, maths-physics, arts and social science (of course – as again they note – specificity does not disappear as a problem when the language is divided into registers for specific purposes; indeed it may become more of a problem). The measures were cloze tests on texts in each subject discipline given to all students. The results indicated that

"the hypothesis was supported that students from a particular discipline would perform better in tests based on texts taken from their own subject discipline than would students from other disciplines. That is, students appear to be advantaged by taking a test on a text in a familiar content area".

Again this has theoretical interest precisely because it contradicts the unitary competence hypothesis – and, incidentally, favours *at least* the Bachman-Palmer partial divisibility conclusion. The practical implications are urgent and do not require dwelling on.

Fit the Seventh
" 'Leave him here to his fate – it is getting so late!'
The Bellman exclaimed in a fright.
'We have lost half the day, Any further delay,
And we shan't catch a Snark before night!' "

My last example comes from some only partially published work of my own on language aptitude. In the 1960s and early 70s, we carried out a large-scale investigation into language aptitude for modern foreign languages in UK secondary schools, testing in due course over 5000 subjects. Our main findings were not dissimilar from those of others, notably Carroll and Sapon, and Pimsleur. We were able to carry out a longitudinal study over 4 years of schooling. Our results indicated that at the beginning, at the start of learning a foreign language, general ability is as good a predictor as anything – and general ability itself can be determined by grade-point average or its equivalent, by an intelligence or verbal reasoning test or by a language aptitude test such as Pimsleur's Language Aptitude Battery. But in the second and subsequent years of learning, both in the continuing language and in a second foreign language (e.g. German added in the second year to French), more specific abilities did seem to emerge in our study. Let me describe that part of the study involving the addition of German in the second year of the secondary school. Those children selected for additional German had consistently higher mean scores than the rest of the sample on the predictors. It might be concluded therefore that general overall performance is what decides selection (by the school or by the pupil) for a second foreign language. However, the German group was not just better on the IQ test – it was *very* much better (almost 1 SD above the total sample mean). But in the French tests at the end of the year the German group's superiority was minimal. In other words, the German group was not significantly better than the sample from which they were drawn in French *and yet* they were selected for the second foreign language. What selects is their IQ performance: they were recognized as "clever" children. Now when we look at the correlations we see that the best predictor of German proficiency (in the second year) is *not* IQ but French proficiency. What this evidence suggests is that existing language performance (in this case in French) is much the best predictor of future language performance in another language. This finding is borne out by a further longitudinal study, over 4 years, of children's French. There, across a range of schools and different kinds of language criteria, after three more years of learning French, the best predictor of success at the end of the 4 years is performance at the end of Year 1 in French. Other predictor variables including IQ, a language aptitude test, or more exotic ones – creativity tests, interest inventories – do contribute, but not as much. Our conclusions from this research were that language aptitude is something that takes time to develop and needs a good deal of encouragement and patience.

The practical conclusions are that everyone should be given the opportunity to start a first foreign language (at the appropriate age, i.e. on the basis of local decisions) and that, while those likely to succeed at first are those who will succeed in other academic subjects, this will not necessarily continue in later years. The optimistic conclusion here is that it is worth persevering, for those who do not do so well in, say, the first year. The pessimistic conclusion is that there is inevitable self-selection on the grounds of verbal fluency at the initial stages and that thereafter this general ability ceases to matter very much. Our data did not suggest that different teaching methods are more or less likely to be successful with some groups than with others: learning a language is learning a language, whatever the method by which it is supposed to be taught. Schools should accept that, however they try to teach a language in the early stages, it is still being *taught* in a *school*. General ability still dominates. Selection of any kind, for first or second foreign language, should therefore be delayed as long as possible. Otherwise what is partially a skill is treated entirely as an area of knowledge.

Those were the conclusions when the report was written some years ago. There seems no reason to change them. The problem with institutional language learning is that it may be the *institutional* modifier that dominates rather than the *language* one. No doubt it is this that Krashen attempts to point out to us.

So, finally:

Fit the Eighth

"In the midst of the word he was trying to say.
In the midst of his laughter and glee,
He had softly and suddenly vanished away —
for the Snark was a Boojum, you see."

Language Testing and the Communicative Language Teaching Curriculum[(1)] *

PAULINE M. REA

Introduction

Evaluation is universally accepted as one of the basic tenets of any curriculum design, yet an examination of commercially available language teaching texts reveals, sadly, that language testing is infrequently attributed any useful function within the teaching and learning process. It would appear that, for researchers in applied linguistics, syllabus designers, materials writers and language teachers alike, the main goal of language teaching is to develop in the learner an ability to communicate efficiently and effectively through the medium of the target language. It should follow from this, therefore, that the measurement of student progress towards this shared aim will be an important feature of the communicative language teaching and learning context.

The purpose of this paper is threefold. Firstly, it will examine the role assigned to language testing within the teaching syllabus, as evidenced by a sample of commercially available language learning materials. It will then briefly review the state of the art of communicative language testing and outline proposals for the classification of test items within the context of the communicative teaching of English. The final section outlines dimensions of "language testing for teaching purposes", with an overview of assessment procedures, integrated within one of the Communication Skills in English courses offered at the University of Dar es Salaam.

The paper is written with the intention of bridging the gap between the work of the applied linguist, with an interest in language testing, and that of the language teacher, whose main concern is the implementation of appropriate language programmes designed to develop communicative abilities and the administration of valid tests to monitor student progress and assess student performance.

The Role of Language Testing Within the Teaching Syllabus: 3 Case Studies

In current curriculum models, it is commonplace for four dimensions to be specified with evaluation seen as a central and integral part (Taba, 1962, Hamilton, 1976, Kelly, 1977). However, this view is little reflected in the writings of applied linguists concerned with language curricula (but see Shaw, 1975, Breen and Candlin, 1980).

At the level of syllabus design, Richterich and Chancerel (1980) maintain that "assessment should be an integral part of the learning material. . . . " Perry (1976) posits a five-phase model of language training of which "evaluation" and "validation" are essential parts. Shaw (1977), on the other hand, in his survey article on foreign language syllabus development excludes "evaluation" at the level of syllabus design, despite the

---

* Superior figs refer to notes at end of chapter.

fact that it is included within his definition of the curriculum. No reason is given for this omission. I find it surprising that the majority of otherwise excellent publications in the area of syllabus design and communicative language teaching rarely address issues of evaluation in any detail (Howatt, 1974, Wilson, 1975, British Council, 1977, Brumfit, 1980, Littlewood, 1981, Johnson, 1982; but see Brumfit and Johnson, 1979). My own impressions are confirmed by two recent surveys. Robinson's (1980) useful reference book on developments in ESP has only four articles cited under the heading of testing and evaluation. The EST Clearinghouse Bibliographies (1981, 1982), out of a total of more than one hundred and forty eight entries, have only two for testing.

Although the role of testing and evaluation is seldom made explicit in any systematic and integrated way in handbooks for teachers (but see Valette and Disick, 1972, Valette, 1977, Cohen, 1980, Heaton, 1982), it is still mentioned as an important dimension for materials' writers, i.e. at the level of syllabus implementation.

In the next section, I have selected Teachers' Manuals for three recently published language teaching texts: *Reading and Thinking in English* (1979, 1980), *Nucleus General Science* (Bates and Dudley-Evans, 1982), and *Challenges* (Candlin and Edelhoff, 1982), for a closer examination of the ways in which testing and associated issues are incorporated and implemented into course design. These materials have been chosen for three main reasons. Firstly, according to their authors, they are concerned with the "communicative" teaching of English; secondly, they are all intended for an audience at an "intermediate" level of instruction; and thirdly, they represent, for me, better examples of commercially available language learning materials of their kind.(2)

The 1979 edition of *Reading and Thinking in English* has a concise yet comprehensive introduction to the course in the Teacher's Manual. It contains information for the student who wishes to take a self-study approach to the materials, and the teacher receives information on the rationale of the series, information about the organization and structure of the units, and suggestions for using the learning activities. In the self-study guide, the student is introduced to the concept of self-monitoring in the learning activities and is presented with a detailed flow chart of the way in which this may be done. The Teachers' Guide contains only three references to testing. The first refers to criteria for the evaluation of written work. The Guide says that "it is particularly important when testing students that their accuracy in writing should not count for more than, say 10%" (1979, p. xvi). This implicitly contrasts the linguistic accuracy of an utterance with the overall ability to convey and interpret messages which relates, I suggest, to a more "global" approach to testing. Later, it is asserted that "it is better to test students on the final aim of comprehension than on their mastery of all the means of getting there" (1979, p. xvii). This appears to recognize a distinction between "product" and "process" and between the assessment of enabling skills on the one hand and global (integrated) skills on the other, thus raising the issue of test strategy. The final reference (1979, p. xviii) takes up the role of the teacher in the assessment process, as a monitor of "students' progress", as a designer of tests, and as an administrator of tests, and would seem to introduce the notion of formative assessment through the monitoring of students' progress, thus relating directly to the teacher's purpose for testing. No further details are provided on the design and content of tests, on their aims, or on the evaluation criteria to be used. Perhaps, one wonders, this mirrors the rather unhelpful view of the Associate Editor of the series that "following the communicative approach, testing is not a normal activity. Imposing tests on learners, therefore, may have the effect of compromising the naturalness of behaviour which the communicative approach aims to promote" (Widdowson, 1977, p. 51). Although this is indeed a correct view, it has to be recognized that testing *is* an inevitable part of the teaching and learning process and that brushing the issue aside in this manner does not, unfortunately, move us towards a solution to the very real problems facing the language teacher.

I turn next to the recently published *Challenges, Teacher's Guide* (Candlin and Edelhoff, 1982). The teacher is assigned three main roles of which one is that of "evaluator", and it is encouraging to read of the pivotal role that evaluation plays in the learning process, with the assertion (1982, p. vi) that "learners learn most when they are quite precisely aware of . . . how their efforts are to be judged and evaluated". Learners are seen as "co-determiners" of evaluation criteria and, together with their teachers, are involved with the evaluation of learning goals "evaluated by a set of mutually determined criteria" (1982, p. vi). The teacher is also informed early on that the learning goals are "exhaustively indicated in the guides to the teaching of each unit" (1982, p. x), which for me sets up the expectation that the interdependent roles of learner and teacher in the assessment process will be expressed in a similarly explicit manner. But, unfortunately, this expectation is not fulfilled. At several points throughout the manual, there is reference to a "two-way process of observing and evaluating", but it is not made clear to the reader what this involves. It is even less clear what is meant by " 'a natural grading system', which is feedback . . ." to the learner (1982, p. 30). More tangible reference is made to the formative nature of assessment: "Teachers and other learners must be given the opportunity of offering feedback to this process of communicating, identifying and where appropriate remediating success and error" (1982, p. 34), with a promise that this specific aspect will be addressed in subsequent discussion. The question is indeed posed: "Can learners suggest their own ways of evaluating an activity and their own performance at it?", but the promise remains unfulfilled in that the only answer provided states: "We would hope that, in various ways, the CHALLENGES materials provide an affirmative answer. . . ." (1982, p. 38). In short, there is ample evidence in the *Challenges, Teacher's Guide* that the authors strongly sense the importance of assessment in the process of learning, and they make specific reference to formative assessment for diagnostic purposes and to teacher-learner cooperation. However, the manual fails to document systematically the roles of testing for communicative language learning, to provide details on test methods, test format, test content, and to give any guidelines on the assessment criteria that might be used for the evaluation of communicative performance. Since there is a positive recommendation for testing running throughout the manual, I am left to assume that it is not because of some insurmountable practical problems associated with evaluation activities that the issue is left hanging in mid air.

In striking contrast, the *Nucleus General Science Teacher's Manual* (New Expanded Edition, 1982) consists of incisive statements on the way in which testing is incorporated within the *Nucleus* course of instruction and on the way in which it is to be implemented. Three types of test are identified: initial proficiency check and placement, progress (diagnostic) and achievement, and a final check for overall achievement/proficiency. The format, content and item designs for each test are clearly specified and so are the weighting details for each of the parts of the tests. Explicit instructions are provided to the teacher for the administration of the tests, and for marking, grading, and interpreting the test results. Further, the author of the manual's test section (Shelley Vance) recognizes the need for a flexible approach to assessment and therefore provides very clear instructions for teachers who may wish to construct additional tests for administration at intervals in the course different from those already specified.

Comparing the *Nucleus* and *Challenges* approaches it is observed that both sets of authors recognize the motivational value of testing and its diagnostic potential integrated within the process of learning. Both see testing as one way in which learners may be sensitized to the materials and learning objectives. One of the most noticeable differences is that *Nucleus* tends towards a more traditional methodology, with the teacher as the sole executor of the tests and their grading and interpretation, whereas in the *Challenges* course we would expect to see joint co-operation (teachers and students) in defining the evaluation criteria and in the diagnosis of areas of difficulty[3]. If this last point is seen as a criticism of *Nucleus*, then it should be counterpointed against the great value of the series in actually providing concrete tools for the teacher for implementation in the classroom. With the testing programme already mapped out, teachers will have a far less onerous task of incorporating flexibility and shared responsibilities within the testing process than those who have to select their testing territory and to specify their routes.

It should be clear that a good number of important issues in testing for language teaching purposes have been raised in these three coursebooks. These include the role of testing for pedagogic purposes (formative) and/or classificatory (summative) purposes; the issue of assessing discrete and/or integrated skills; whether testing should be the sole responsibility of the teacher, or whether it may be efficiently and effectively handled as a joint responsibility, by teachers and students.

There is scant evidence, unfortunately, that language testing has been systematically incorporated within communicative language learning programmes. Although materials writers have assigned importance, in varying proportions, to the process of assessment, one is left with an impression that this is the result of an afterthought. There is a strong element of "vague puff" about many statements on "testing for teaching", which are of doubtful value to the (overworked) practising teacher, who has then the task of interpreting this "puff" in the form of a coherent testing programme which involves, minimally, the selection of tests and item types appropriate to the purpose(s) for testing.

There are, of course, a variety of reasons why insights from language testing have not been applied to foreign or second language education, in any rigorous way. It is not my intention to explore these reasons here but it does seem quite reasonable to conclude that part of the answer derives from the state of the art of language testing in general, and communicative language testing in particular. It is to a discussion of the latter that I now turn.

The State of the Art of Communicative Language Testing

The belief that communicative language testing is something novel (Morrow, 1979, p. 151) is, I feel, misguided. In his survey article on language testing Davies (1978) indirectly recognizes that this is not the case. I also agree with Davies' further claim (1978, p. 223) that the assessment of communicative competence is "largely programmatic"[4]. This situation is somewhat surprising when we consider specific comments from language testers over the last 20 years.

Firstly, the frequently discussed distinction between language competence and language performance has been drawn, albeit implicitly in some cases, by a large number of language testers (Carroll, 1961, Spolsky, 1968, Cooper, 1968, Jakobovits, 1970, Brière,

1971, Clark, 1972). Carroll (1961, pp. 35–36) contrasts "*knowledge*" (his emphasis) as "what the individual has learned" with "integrated performances which call upon the candidate's mastery of language as a whole . . .". Spolsky (1968, p. 90) focuses on the need to assess "a student's ability to speak naturally on a topic . . . other than those he has been trained for".

Secondly, the need for situational relevance has been matched with concerns of situational appropriacy of utterances and communicative realism. Clark (1972) high-lighted the pragmatic value of language learning and referred to "real-life competencies" for specific purposes. Carroll (1961) also pointed to the need for test content to relate to the kinds of situations in which examinees will find themselves on successful completion of a test. Moreover, such factors have an effect on the types of criteria for the assessment of student performance which, it has been suggested, should not be restricted to linguistic accuracy but should include other criteria which relate to the effective communication of ideas. According to Clark (1972, p. 120) student performance should be analyzed "in terms of the adequacy with which students can communicate in specified language-use situations", and this criterion of quality was incorporated in the empirical research conducted by Savignon (1972) and Schulz (1977).

Innumerable other considerations now commonly associated with communicative language testing have been aired over the last decade and a half. By making reference to the steps the "non-native speaker of the language can himself take . . . to minimize or bypass areas of linguistic weakness in a given communicative situation" Clark (1972, p. 119) introduced the notion of strategic competence, more recently associated with the work of Canale and Swain (1980a). Discussion has also focused on "direct" versus "indirect" testing (Clark, 1972); as also on the criterial features of "performance" and "competence" tests (Carroll, 1961, Clark 1972), on "integrative" versus "atomistic" approaches to assessment (Carroll, 1961) and on the validation of performance tests by reference to the real world (Carroll, 1961, Spolsky, 1968).

A major issue in the current debate on communicative language testing concerns the nature of the theoretical base on which language tests are constructed (Morrow, 1977, Davies, 1978, Carroll, 1980). The need for "theoretical" insights in the production of language tests led to a distinction between concerns of construct validity on the one hand, and those of content validity on the other. The former is reflected in the work of Carroll (1961) and Cooper (1968), with the latter stressing the inadequacy "of a linguistically undifferentiated view of the target language as a single code" (1968, p. 60). Influenced by the work of Hymes on communicative competence, Cooper posited two sets of competencies which are essential to effective communication, namely "linguistic" and "contextual" competence. This concept was also elaborated by Jakobovits (1970). Upshur (1971, p. 436) on the other hand, raised the question of content validity with reference to performance theory, and argued that "a major reason for the stagnant state of foreign language proficiency testing has been the absence of an adequate model of language creativity, or the communicative use of language".

It would be grossly misleading if I were to represent the view that language testing has remained static for the last 15 years. This is clearly *not* the case. There have been significant developments in the field, especially in research into the construct of language competence and on techniques for evaluating this construct (Oller and Perkins, 1978, 1980, Palmer and Bachman, 1981, Sang and Vollmer, 1980, Vollmer, 1981). A glance at the very comprehensive Lange and Clifford Bibliography (1980) provides ample evidence of a high level of activity in language testing generally. This is also borne out by the number of papers delivered at international conferences and symposia. In the UK, in the specific area of proficiency testing, there is a noticeable trend to update existing proficiency tests to reflect current concerns in communicative language teaching, in both English language and foreign language education. Aside from developments in the testing of English proficiency for general communicative purposes (RSA, ARELS)[5] significant work is now in progress in ESP testing, especially in English for Academic purposes (ELTS[6], Weir, 1984, Gove, 1984). All these examples are evidence of a widespread interest in the assessment of communicative language skills.

In the teaching context, however, in spite of the pioneering work of Savignon (1972) and Schulz (1977) and discussions on the nature of communicative competence and communicative syllabus design (Trim *et al*. 1973, van Ek and Alexander, 1975, Munby, 1978, Canale and Swain, 1980a, Johnson and Morrow, 1981, Littlewood, 1981, Johnson, 1982), considerations of communicative language testing for teaching purposes have not received as much attention as might be expected, or been regarded as desirable. And I would still wish to agree with Davies (1978) that communicative language testing is largely programmatic. The majority of language tests commercially available for classroom use are predominantly structure-based (Archer and Nolan-Woods, 1976, McCallum, 1979, Fowler and Coe, 1978, Allen, 1982). Excluding the exceptions already cited, language teaching coursebooks and teachers' manuals incorporate few insights from language testing research; and teachers' handbooks on testing have tended to focus either on isolated aspects of testing which are not subsequently viewed interdependently, or on theoretical issues which are, at best, one remove from the immediate (practical) concerns of the classroom teacher. In particular, I feel a definite lack of guidance on (i) the relationship between types of tests and the different purpose(s) for testing; (ii) the design of item types suitable for inclusion in communicative language teaching programmes; and (iii) the appropriate selection of specific test formats and item types at different stages in the (communicative) teaching and learning process.

This situation may be traced back to the existence of a number of ill-defined criteria abundant in the literature on language testing. As an example, I refer to the frequently cited distinction between competence and performance. Whilst I have little problem in maintaining a theoretical division of knowledge of rules on the one hand, and the application of these rules on the other (Morrow, 1979, p. 149, Canale and Swain, 1980a), I have to admit to confusion at the level of practice, by references to "competence-oriented" tests, "performance" tests, and "actual performance", and comments such as "one would . . . not want to ignore performance tests completely in a communicative testing programme even if more competence-oriented tests that correlate highly with actual performance were developed" (Canale and Swain, 1980a). It is not clear to me what a "competence" test would look like. I am left to assume that it is held in contrast in some way with a performance test. But what are the criterial features of each? To what does actual performance refer? Does it include or exclude language behaviour elicited in a testing situation? There is implicit in many discussions an assumption that communicative language testing equates with direct (oral?) performance testing (Morrow, 1979, Carroll, 1980), but what are the implications for testing from the notion of "directness"? How is performance defined? And what is the relationship, if any, between the two?

In my view, the issues do not appear as clearcut as some would have us believe (Carroll, 1978, 1980). Neither do I feel that they are as overwhelmingly complex as others would suggest (Davies, 1978). In the next part of the paper I raise four problems, related to testing strategy and the classification of test items, that require clarification if advances are to be made in making language testing for teaching purposes less problematic. These are the relationships between "competence" and "performance", "discrete" and "global", "integrative" and "non-integrative", and "direct" and "indirect" approaches to testing. It would also seem to me desirable and helpful to examine what relationships and interactions exist in practice between these four issues. Are these parameters best described as dichotomies independent one from the other, or do they constitute clines (Davies, 1977, Morrow, 1979, Alderson and Hughes, 1981) which interact in some systematic way with each other? The next part of this paper considers possible answers to these questions and discusses the implications they have, independently and inter-dependently, for the practice of testing communicative abilities in the classroom.

Classifying Language Tests: Competence and Performance

I take as my starting point the view of communicative competence taken by Canale and Swain (1980a). I also assume that the ultimate objective of communicative language teaching is to get someone to perform his competence and, thirdly, that a prerequisite for performance is a basis of competence, no matter how minimal. Nonetheless, I find misleading the view that language testing involves discovering both how much a learner knows about using a language (competence) and how this competence is realized in performance. Is it in fact possible to maintain this theoretical distinction in practice? In what way can "competence" be assessed as distinct from "performance"?

Firstly, it is clear that we are dealing with two different levels, as Table 1 shows:

Table 1. *Competence and performance model for testing*

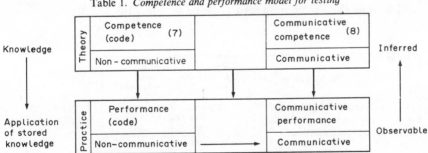

On the other hand, there is "competence" which may be defined as knowledge stored in an individual's mind. As an abstract system, this knowledge cannot be assessed in any direct way. "Performance" on the other hand is something which an individual does with this stored knowledge. As observable language behaviour it is open to direct assessment.

Secondly, according to the model just proposed, I suggest that all linguistic behaviour, whether it involves phoneme recognition, assigning a meaning to a single lexical item or, at the other end of the spectrum, interpreting stretches of discourse, constitutes instances of performance. From this perspective, therefore, competence *per se* cannot be subjected to direct assessment as it is only through performance that one may infer levels of competence. I am, therefore, attempting to refute the commonly held distinction between "competence-oriented" tests and "performance" tests and am arguing for a single category in practice, that of "performance".

As a first step in the refinement process, I suggest that "communicative" language behaviour may be contrasted with "non-communicative" performance.[9] Consider items (1) and (2) below:

(1) Stop ar- gu-ing you two   (Ingram, 1964)
     ( ) ( )( )( )   ( ) ( )

(2) How . . . . . milk have you got?
     (a) a lot; (b) much of; (c) much; (d) many

                                        (Clapham, 1975)

The first item, at the level of the phonological code, is presented aurally and the testee is required to recognize the syllable which carries the tonic of the sentence. Item (2) on the other hand requires manipulation of the grammatical code; and the recognition of *milk* as a mass noun to be matched with the quantifier *much*. In my terms, then, having rejected "competence-oriented" tests, examples (1) and (2) have the objective of evaluating performance at the level of "well-formedness", as applied to isolated aspects of the language code, through a discrete-point approach to testing. As such, these represent instances of "non-communicative" performance. It is worth noting here that, within the context of communicative language teaching, limited occasions will arise for this exclusive manipulation of the code in this manner.

However, the position is rarely as clear-cut as the first examples suggest, and a more sensitive criterion has to be found. Consider the following examples:

(3) ". . . to Tanzania in April, but I'm not sure."
     (a) I'll come (b) I'm coming (c) I'm going to come (d) I may come

(4)
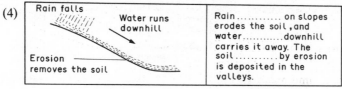

                                        (CSU, 1981)

In (3), the testee has to demonstrate the "competence" to match the modal *may* with the meaning "possibility", as realized by *I'm not sure*. According to the position I have just taken, (3) is an instance of "performance" (through which "competence" is inferred) but it is not the same kind of item as the previous two examples. Items of the type exemplified by (3) are concerned with grammatical accuracy but, in the selection of the acceptable response, they require attention to more than mere collocational constraints of well-formedness, as they involve relating form to meaning.

(4) is of a different order again. In common with the previous examples, the main focus is on the grammatical code but it contrasts with them in that it requires the selection of the appropriate participle phrase. Further, the appropriate linguistic form is selected for its

function within a text (in this case accompanied by a diagram). This task involves a non-mechanical response which, in turn, also involves decisions about the overall function of the text itself, in this case a "description".

So far I have suggested that the main difference between items (1) and (2) and between (3) and (4) seems to be that the former pair require manipulation of the language code as an abstract system, whereas the appropriate syntactic response for the latter pair is dependent upon the meaning assigned to the sentence or text. Thus, I draw a distinction between item-types that are meaning-independent, (1) and (2), and those which are meaning-dependent, (3) and (4).

Table 2. *Criterial dimensions of "non-communicative" performance (1)*

	Non-communicative performance		Communicative performance
	Meaning-independent	Meaning-dependent	
Application of stored knowledge	(1) (2)	(3) (4)	

Yet, this is useful only up to a point. There is, for example, as noted above, a definite difference between (3) and (4) which is not accounted for so far. Let me clarify what I mean by considering a further three examples:

(5) *Doctor:* (Show me where it hurts)
      (a) seeking information
      (b) asking a question
      (c) making a statement
      (d) making a suggestion

(6) *Sister:* When is Mr. *Bright* having his operation?
      (a) I know about the other patients
      (b) At what time on what day?
      (c) He's already had the preliminary tests
      (d) I know he's supposed to be going home next week

(7) *Patient:* I was in the kitchen getting lunch, and I cut my finger
    Doctor: (a) "You've bruised it, have you?"
          (b) "Was this last night?"
          (c) "Where were you at the time?"
          (d) "With a knife, was it?"
                      (10)

Item (5) is an example of a function recognition task in a medical context. The testee has to identify the function of a doctor's utterance which is relayed on tape. Here, an interaction between "grammatical" and "sociolinguistic" competencies may be observed, with the grammatical category "imperative" matched with the communicative category "seeking information". Additionally, the test candidate will make use of knowledge derived from the context of situation in decisions on the overall appropriacy of the functions. (6) is seen as an example in which the "phonological" code interacts with sociolinguistic competence. Both (5) and (6) clearly refer to use. With the last example, however, it is impossible with any precision to isolate that aspect of competence which is activated for the comprehension of the patient's utterance and for the selection of the appropriate doctor's response. The essential feature is that successful performance reflects an interaction between grammatical, sociolinguistic, strategic, and other competencies. Thus, as an instance of "integrated" performance, I would place example (7) at a higher point on the continuum than the other items previously discussed.

Returning to the classification of item (4), we note that it has two features in common with (3). Firstly, it is concerned with well-formedness at the level of (grammatical) usage. Secondly, it is meaning-dependent. When (4) is then compared with (5) and (6), it is considered similar to the extent that selection of the appropriate response is dependent upon details provided by context. In other words, the acceptability and appropriacy of the responses are retrievable from a correct interpretation of the communicative intention(s) implicit within a given communicative context. In this sense, the response is defined as context-bound. Additionally, it can be claimed that responses for (4) to (7) all require an integration of linguistic knowledge with meaning which simulates more closely the processes involved in the natural use of language. However, to the extent that (4) focuses on "usage" rather than "use", it is best positioned on the boundary between "non-communicative" and "communicative" performance, as indicated by the wavy line in Table 3.

Table 3. *Criterial dimensions of "non-communicative" performance (2)*

	Non-communicative performance			Communicative performance
Application of stored knowledge	Meaning-dependent	Meaning-dependent		
			Context-bound	
	(1) (2)	(3)	(4)	

The position I have taken draws a distinction between "non-communicative" and "communicative" performance. Within the former category three types of item are placed, all of which relate primarily to "usage". Those of the first type are straightforward and refer to items which are meaning-independent, for example (1) and (2). Items of the second type are meaning-dependent but, because of the indeterminacy of the context provided, they typically force a mechanical response which does not demonstrate an ability to use the appropriate forms as the "real-life" context requires. This is illustrated by item (3). The third class, comprising items exemplified by (4), are also meaning-dependent but they differ from (3) in that they stimulate a context-determined response.

The "communicative" category includes, by definition, meaning-dependent items relating to language use. In common with (4) (and it is for this reason that (4) is positioned on the borderline between "non-communicative" and "communicative" performance) items in this category require decisions on the appropriacy of responses with reference to the context in which the items occur.

There remains, however, the question of distinguishing between those items which focus on clearly identifiable aspects of communicative performance and those which focus attention on instances of integrated communicative performance, as in item (7).

Table 4. *Criterial dimensions of "non-communicative" and "communicative" performance*

Non-communicative performance	Communicative performance		
	Meaning-dependent		
		Context-bound	
Meaning-independent		Gr Comp Soc Comp Str Comp AO Comp	Gr + Soc + Str + AO Competencies
Atomistic			Global
(1) (2)	(3)	(4)	(5) (6)	(7)

This leads to a further confinement of the model which incorporates the dichotomy of an "atomistic" versus a "global" approach to "communicative" performance testing.

The Problem of Integrative and Discrete-point Tests

At this point, there are two common confusions which are associated with the concept of "integrative" language testing. The dichotomy "global" and "atomistic" has sometimes been merged with issues of "integrative" language testing, and a polarity is often drawn between "integrative" tests on the one hand and "discrete-point" (i.e. "atomistic") tests on the other (Davies, 1978, p. 222). These are, however, two separate issues.

Firstly, an "atomistic" approach is illustrated by items (1) to (6) above (see Table 5) in which an attempt has been made to isolate individual elements or aspects of the target language that have been taught (in the case of achievement or diagnostic testing) and to assess them one by one. This contrasts with the "global" approach which, at its purest, is unconcerned with individual items but requires an integrated performance on the part of the test taker (see example (7)).

As a second and *separate* issue, it is useful to isolate an "integrative" approach to assessment from a "decontextualized" approach. This distinction I advocate contrasts a "contextualized" test item, (see example (4)) with one that is presented in an "isolated sentences" format (examples (5) to (7)). It follows from this, therefore, as Table 5 shows, that the distinction "integrative" versus "decontextualized" cuts across the "global" and "atomistic" axis.

Thus, the distinction between "integrative" and "decontextualized" test formats on the one hand and the distinction between "atomistic" and "global" on the other are to be viewed not as two sides of the same coin but as two separate dimensions.

Table 5. *The "atomistic" and "global" dichotomy and communicative performance*

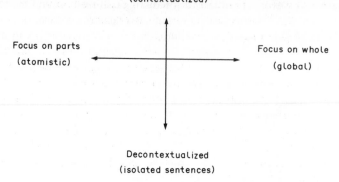

Directness in Language Testing

I now come to the final point I wish to raise in connection with the "global" assessment of performance. This is the notion of "directness" which has considerable implications for the testing of "communicative" performance. It is particularly important because of its relationship with concerns of validity which remain, after all, *the* criteria by which we may establish the adequacy of our tests.

A test may be defined as "direct" to the extent that it requires the integration of linguistic, situational, cultural, and affective constraints which interact in the process of communicating. In assessing "communicative" performance, the emphasis, therefore, will be on conveying meanings, i.e. on comprehension, in contexts relevant to the purposes for which the language is being, or has been, taught. "Directness" is therefore crucially concerned with situational and communicative realism. A prime example of a "direct" test is the FSI Oral Interview[11] which has been in operation since 1956 (Wilds, 1975). By way of contrast, the traditional cloze format, although "integrative" in approach and an example of "global" assessment, may be cited as an "indirect" measure of communicative performance. Thus the FSI Oral Interview would be positioned at the extreme right of the "global communicative" performance box in Table 4 while a cloze test would appear to the left of this box.

There is a discernible sense of urgency in developing "global" and "direct" performance measures. I assume that this is what Morrow is referring to in his comment: "If the purpose is proficiency testing . . . then it seems . . . incontrovertible that performance tests are necessary." Why should this be the case?

Firstly, "direct" measures have popular appeal to face validity. In other words, the more a test looks as if it is testing what it is intended to measure, the better it is. Secondly, in the absence of an adequate theoretical model of communicative competence, construct and content are assured to the extent that a test mirrors dimensions of performance,[12] the features of which are derived both from observation of performance and from the significant amount of information available in the literature on communicative syllabus design and needs analysis (Trim *et al.* 1973, van Ek and Alexander, 1975, Munby, 1978, Carroll, 1978, 1980, and Richterich and Chancerel, 1980). However, the concepts of "global" testing, to a lesser extent, and that of "direct" testing, in particular, do pose a number of problems which require serious attention (for useful contributions, see Morrow, 1979, Canale and Swain, 1980a, Alderson and Hughes, 1981). As a first comment, I maintain that pure direct testing is by definition impossible (I presume that this is what is meant by Widdowson's comment, cited earlier). "Naturalness" criteria can only be satisfied up to a point: thus all testing procedures will require compromises on this criterion. Secondly, "direct" performance testing rates low on practicality criteria (expense and administrative feasibility) for large numbers of students. For this reason, again, further compromises will have to be accepted. It should also be recognized that the type of language samples from students in a "direct" test will be restricted, thus raising the crucial question of making valid inferences from isolated samples of students' language. Given these serious constraints, it would seem to be a *sine qua non* that "indirect" measures of "communicative" performance will have to be implemented, and this will have a direct bearing on the extent to which tests will measure "global" or "atomistic" student performance.

The final modification to the testing model developed in this paper would be to add a continuum "indirect" and "direct", running from left to right within the "communicative" performance category. Of course, this continuum could be extended across the entire model but it makes no sense to do so since "non-communicative" aspects of student performance and "atomistic" assessment of "communicative" performance are, by definition, "indirect".

To conclude this section – and this is a point rightly emphasized in Alderson and Hughes (1981) – a question: Do we have any empirical evidence to confirm the superiority of direct tests over indirect ones, in terms either of the amount of information or of the quality of information elicited on these tests in relation to learners' actual communicative abilities in natural performance situations?[13] It is clear that future research efforts must take up as a matter of priority the relationship that exists between "indirect" and "direct" measures of student performance. As a related issue, we shall need to discover which level of directness is most appropriate to the different purposes for which teachers design and use language tests in the classroom. In the next and final part of the paper, I outline the roles of language testing for teaching purposes and suggest one approach towards integrating communicative language testing and teaching.

The Design of Testing Programmes Appropriate to Teaching/Learning Situations

I shall first identify the main features implicit in the design of any testing programme which has as its objective the evaluation of student progress and achievement. There are at least ten key features, as raised by the following questions.

1. *Why* test?
2. Whose *Responsibility?*
3. *What* is tested?
4. *How* do we test?
5. What is the *function* of the tests?
6. What *feedback* will there be from the tests?
7. What are the *evaluation criteria?*
8. How are the test results to be *interpreted?*

Answering these questions will involve decisions on, for example, the purpose for testing, on the function of the tests (classificatory or pedagogic), and on which strategy to use. In Table 6, I summarize these dimensions of "language testing for teaching purposes".

Table 6. *Key features of language testing for teaching purposes*

	Initial	In progress	End
Purpose ↕	• Selection / placement • Motivation • Sensitization	• Achievement • Progress • Motivation • Sensitization	• Achievement • Proficiency • Maintaining standards
Function	• Classificatory • Pedagogic	• Pedagogic • Classificatory	• Classificatory
Whose responsibility? ↕	• Teacher • (students)	• Joint : teacher and student	• Teacher
Strategy ↕	• Tests • Self-appraisal	• Tests • Self-appraisal • Record / diary keeping • Observation • Peer assessments	• Tests • Self-appraisal
Nature	• Formal	• Informal • Formal	• Formal
Knowledge ↕	• Non-communicative • Communicative	• Non-communicative • Communicative	• Communicative

Content ↕	• Product
	• Global
	   (+/-direct)
		• Process
		• Global /atomistic
		   (+/-direct)
			• Product
			• Global
			   (+ direct)

Evaluation criteria	• Objectives-based	• Responsive	• Objectives-based
How ?	• Integrative • (Decontextualized)	• Integrative • (Decontextualized)	• Integrative
Feedback	• Quantity • Pass / fail • Immediate	• Quality • Immediate	• Quantity • Pass / fail • Delayed

I find it useful at the same time to isolate three stages in the teaching and learning process. Within the first "initial" stage, three main purposes are identified. These are testing for selection and/or placement purposes, which takes place immediately prior to a course of instruction. Student assessment may then be introduced at the start of a course, as a means to stimulate in the learner an awareness of the teaching and learning goals (Rea, 1980), and it may also serve to increase motivation. Whilst the course is "in progress", the main purpose for testing will be to determine achievement and to monitor progress. As in the initial stage, assessment techniques play "motivational" and "sensitization" roles. At the third stage, i.e. at the "end" of a course, students may be tested on their overall achievement, referenced to the teaching syllabus. Or, the purpose may be to assess proficiency levels, referenced to criteria external to the course. End-of-course assessments will also provide information essential to the maintenance of overall standards.

In my view, evaluation at the beginning and end of a teaching programme has received most attention. However, it is frequently divorced from the main stream of teaching in the form of a pre-and/or post-test. For this reason, in suggesting a framework for integrating testing within a programme of instruction, I have chosen to highlight aspects pertinent to student assessment whilst a course is in progress.

The Communication Skills Unit (CSU) at the University of Dar es Salaam is primarily concerned with helping students reach an adequate level in English communication skills for academic purposes. Our situation is probably not atypical, in that most of our courses are credit earning and, thus, examinable. As a result, there is potential conflict between the purposes for testing determined by the wider context of the University on the one hand, and those internal to the ELT context, i.e. within the CSU, on the other. There are, therefore, two important distinctions to be made.

The first contrasts "summative" with "formative" evaluation. When information is used mainly for classificatory purposes, then the assessment may be defined as summative. Thus, all coursework assignments, projects, and examinations which contribute towards the overall grade awarded to students at the end of their course of instruction may be classified as largely "summative" (terminal), "formal", "external" to the learning process and "product-oriented". This contrasts with the situation when the outcome of a test is used as input for pedagogic purposes. In this case, the assessment is said to be formative. Within a teaching and learning programme, teachers need to be informed of the extent to which their students have mastered the skills practised in the course. Their aim is to assess the "process" of learning – what are the changes taking place during the course, which are the areas of student weakness/strength? – so that suggestions for improvement and supplementary work may be made. Thus "within course" assessments are largely "formative" (pedagogic), "diagnostic", and "process-oriented". Outcomes will be qualitative and descriptive rather than quantitative and prescriptive. Further, feedback to students will be immediate rather than delayed.

The next set of descriptors which require definition are "evaluation", "assessment" and "appraisal". The first refers to testing activities which are formal and satisfy requirements external to the teaching situation. Assessment and appraisal activities are, on the other hand, internal to the ELT programme. The former generally implies assigning a grade to a piece of work whilst the latter does not. Table 7 illustrates the way in which these three activities may be combined during a course of instruction. Downward arrows indicate summative assessment procedures whereas arrows pointing to the right indicate formative assessment procedures.

Experience at the University of Dar es Salaam has shown how essential it is to integrate testing procedures to suit both internal and external purposes of student appraisal, assessment, and evaluation. The procedures established for one of our courses are indicated below.

Although the example is taken from a university teaching context, it is hoped that it will have wider applicability.

Testing strategies for purposes of formative assessment will include self-appraisal, peer-group observation, and record and diary keeping[15]. It will be noted that student participation is largely confined to appraisal activities whereas assessment in the form of tests will be largely the domain of the teacher.

Table 7. *Formative and summative assessment within the teaching and learning process*[14]

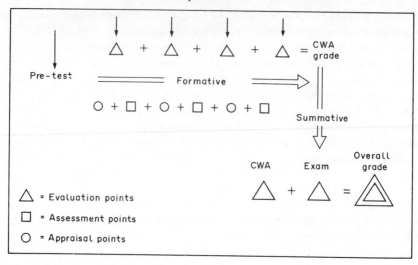

△ = Evaluation points

□ = Assessment points

○ = Appraisal points

Table 8. *Internal and external coursework requirements*

A.   To satisfy internal (pedagogic) requirements

   (1)   Check points (assessment and appraisal) are integrated into the main stream of the course, in the form of tasks designed to determine:

      (a)   Whether target language learning objectives (global / atomistic) have been acquired;

      (b)   (In the case of inadequate performance) the extent to which these objectives have / have not been realized so that appropriate remedial action may be implemented.

   (2)   Student performance at assessment check points are graded (not scored) : excellent, good, pass, marginal fail, and fail. Further advice and supplementary practice activities are made available for students who do not reach the acceptable pass standard.

   (3)   Tutors use full range of grades available.

B.   To satisfy external (University) requirements

   (1)   Four tests are set: two in term 1 and two in term 2. In each case, the first test of the term is usually after approximately five weeks tuition, when students are settled in the course ; the second test is scheduled towards the end of each term but allows sufficient time for marking, before the end of term.

   (2)   Student performance is scored according to the guidelines laid down by the University.

   (3)   One repeat performance only is allowed; for subsequent failure, a fail grade is recorded.

The content of the tests themselves will, of course, be defined with reference to the teaching syllabus. The selection of test items will be guided by interim and terminal course objectives which have been matched with the item-classification system outlined earlier in this paper, in Table 4. In other words, when the focus rests, for example, on well-formedness, then items of the meaning-independent type will be used. At the other end of the spectrum, when the focus is on integrated performance, requiring interaction between the different competencies posited in the Canale and Swain model (1980a), then a global approach will be selected. It follows from this that attention will sometimes focus on assimilation of individual teaching points and that, at other times, it will focus on the global aim(s) of a unit, or series of units. In the CSU, the most appropriate type of test draws together various skills in the completion of a series of related study-skills tasks which requires the processing of aural and/or written input materials, in a variety of styles.

Conclusion

I would now like to conclude by drawing together the four main strands of this paper. Firstly, it is unlikely that anyone would wish to dispute the fact that testing is an integral part of the teaching and learning process. However, a survey of language teaching texts will quickly reveal that testing does not feature as an operational component of the learning syllabus. It has also been suggested that communicative language testing is something novel (Morrow, 1979). This does not appear to be the case since a historical overview of language testing reveals quite clearly that the main issues associated with communicative language testing today have, in fact, been discussed at various intervals over the last 15 to 20 years.

Although we are aware of significant advances in the field of language testing, there is a definite lack of information filtering through to the language teacher, especially on the ways in which student performance may be assessed. In part, this may result from the general "fuzziness' which currently shrouds communicative language testing and, in an attempt to clarify what is, for me, one of the main issues, I have put forward a classification scheme for test items within the framework of the communicative teaching of English.

But this is only a partial solution. What is also required is a systematic analysis of all the possible dimensions of a testing programme and of the way in which these dimensions will be appropriately integrated at different stages within the teaching and learning process. In the final part of this paper, I have given some indication of the dimensions that would be included in such an analysis, and highlighted the need for more attention to be addressed to issues of formative student assessment.

In the area of testing for teaching purposes, it is all too obvious that communicative language testing is still problematical. But this is an unduly pessimistic note on which to conclude this paper. In my view, more research is needed, and it would be on the basis of an increased understanding of the problems and issues involved in assessing language as communication that we shall then be in a position to make other than programmatic pronouncements on the state of the art. Finally, I consider it to be of the utmost importance for these research findings to be conveyed in a systematic, coherent, and helpful manner to the practising classroom teacher.

Notes

1. Special thanks to my colleague Sarah North for her insightful comments on an earlier version of this paper, and for finding time to discuss these with me.
2. They are, however, dissimilar in that the first is directed towards a general EAP audience, the second oriented on a specialist subject base, in this case General Science, with *Challenges* aimed towards a "general English" audience.
3. For innovative work in this area, see Henner-Stanchina and Holec, 1977.
4. My interpretation of Davies is that the testing of communicative abilities is still at an experimental stage: it is largely problematic, and its feasibility is not assured.
5. The Communicative Use of English as a Foreign Language, administered by the Royal Society of Arts (RSA) Examinations Board; and the ARELS Oral Examinations, administered by the Association of Recognised English Language Schools Examinations Trust (ARELS).
6. The English Language Testing Service (ELTS) of the British Council, London.
7. Syntax, phonology, lexicon.
8. Grammatical plus sociolinguistic, discourse, strategic (and any other) competence (Canale and Swain, 1980a).
9. The distinction between "non-communicative" and "communicative" performance is identical to that made by Widdowson (1978, p. 3) between "usage" and "use": "Usage is . . . one aspect of performance, that aspect which makes evident the extent to which the language user demonstrates his knowledge of linguistic rules. Use is another aspect of performance: that which makes evident the extent to which the language user demonstrates his ability to use his language of rules for effective communication."
10. These examples were developed in connection with the General Medical Council's T.R.A.B. examination (now renamed P.L.A.B.) by C. M. Clapham (1976) University of Lancaster.
11. As Low rightly points out (personal communication), the FSI test has almost zero realism or communicativeness for anyone except US (or other) diplomats.
12. For discussion of criterial features of communication, see Morrow, 1977 and 1979.
13. Unfortunately, when writing this paper I was not aware of the recent research on direct testing by Low (1982) and Lee and Low (1982) at the Language Centre, University of Hong Kong.
14. See also North and Rea, 1980.
15. For discussion of self-assessment procedures to promote student participation in the teaching and learning process, see Candelier *et al.* 1975 and 1976, Rea, 1980, Fok, 1981a. See Bruton *et al.* 1981 on peer-group assessment.

2
Large-Scale Testing

Large-scale Communicative Language Testing: A Case Study

MERRILL SWAIN

In Canada we are experiencing an increasing demand from English-speaking communities for schooling that will produce bilingual individuals. The motivations for this demand are varied, but minimally they are both social and economic. Recent political events in Canada have heightened awareness of the needs and demands of Canada's French-speaking peoples. As a result, there has developed a genuine desire on the part of some English-Canadians to learn French in order to be able to interact with French-Canadians in their own language. These same political events have also resulted in establishing bilingual proficiency in French and English as a highly desirable or, in some cases, a required qualification for employment. Clearly, then, what was needed in these circumstances were school programs that could provide students not only with a formal knowledge of the second language, characteristic of traditional second language teaching programs, but also with the ability to *use* the second language as a communicative tool.

A variety of programs have been initiated in Canada over the last decade aimed at turning out English-French bilingual students. Although these programs differ with respect to the grade level at which they begin, the length of the program and the proportion of the school day taught in each of the two languages, they all have in common the exclusive use of the second language, French, as a medium of instruction for all or most of the school day for several years. These programs, referred to in Canada as immersion programs and considered as experiments in bilingual education, have been monitored to evaluate the students' first and second language development, as well as their academic achievements in content subjects taught to them through the medium of the second language (e.g. Lambert and Tucker, 1972; Swain and Lapkin, 1982).

Assessments of the immersion students' second language proficiency have included the use of French achievement tests standardized on native speakers of French, word association tests, cloze tests, tests of general listening and reading comprehension, as well as oral and written production tests. However, with the exception of several isolated and small-scale studies (e.g. Genesee, Tucker and Lambert, 1975; Harley, 1982; Harley and Swain, 1977; Szamosi, Swain and Lapkin, 1979), there has been little attempt to assess the immersion students' ability to use French as a communicative tool through directly engaging them in communicative activities. With the intention of filling this gap, several of us [1] in the Modern Language Centre of the Ontario Institute for Studies in Education have undertaken the development of "testing units" to be used in province-wide assessments of the communicative performance of immersion students.

The purpose of this paper, then, is to describe the testing unit we have developed for students at the secondary school level; that is, for students who are fifteen years of age or older. I intend to describe the testing unit in the following way: first, by outlining several general principles of communicative language testing which guided our test development; and secondly, by discussing briefly the process we are following in developing scoring procedures for the test's large-scale administration. Overall, this paper describes aspects of the development of valid and viable communicative language tests, using one specific example of a test that we have developed to assess the communicative performance of immersion students at the grade 9 level, in order to illustrate this process. My intention is to provide an educational/pedagogical viewpoint on the development of communicative language tests rather than a measurement point of view. Having said this, I would add that I see no necessary long-run incompatibility between the two approaches.

Before turning to a discussion of the general principles of communicative language testing that guided our test construction, it will be useful to describe briefly the actual components of our testing unit. The central component is a 12-page student booklet entitled *A Vous la Parole*, which can be roughly translated as "the floor is yours". The booklet presents information about two summer employment possibilities for youth. Included in the booklet is information about job qualifications, the nature of each job, the location of each job, remuneration, working and leisure time, and living conditions. The student booklet also contains a list of government offices which offer, or organize, special programs for the summer employment of youth, and it encourages the students to write for more information if they are interested.

The second component consists of a series of six communicative tasks commonly required of a native speaker of the language: four involving writing, two involving speaking. The four writing tasks consist of writing a letter, a note, a composition and a technical exercise. The two speaking tasks consist of an informal discussion among three or four students at a time, and a formal job interview with an adult. More details about the nature of these tasks will be given below.

The third component consists of a *Teacher's Guide*, which outlines the objectives of the testing program, explains how to organize and administer the test unit, and instructs on scoring procedures appropriate to each communicative task. We are in the process now of completing the writing of the *Teacher's Guide*.

General Principles of Communicative Language Testing

A considerable literature now exists on communicative language teaching and communicative language testing. I have no intention of reviewing that literature here. Rather, what I would like to do is highlight four general principles that we found highly relevant when faced with the practical problems of developing a communicative test of speaking and writing that could be administered on a large scale, and which could be sensitive to a wide range of proficiency levels. The four principles are:

(1) start from somewhere
(2) concentrate on content
(3) bias for best
(4) work for washback.

(1) *Start from somewhere*

The first principle – start from somewhere – is intended to suggest that from both a theoretical and practical viewpoint, test development should *build from* existing knowledge and examples. Practically, of course, starting from somewhere saves reinventing the wheel. But I think there is much more at stake in this principle than the somewhat superficial interpretation of simply saving time and energy. What I consider to be at stake is the gradual and systematic growth in our understanding of the nature of the communicative competence.

Several years ago, Michael Canale and I had the opportunity of reading much of the then existing literature on communicative language teaching and testing. We found that the literature contained quite different conceptions of communicative language teaching (Canale and Swain, 1980a). We attempted to bring together the various viewpoints into a coherent, linguistically-oriented and pedagogically useful framework, arguing that communicative competence minimally includes four areas of knowledge and skills: grammatical competence, sociolinguistic competence, discourse competence and strategic competence (Canale and Swain, 1980b). The assumption is that learners may develop competence in any of these areas relatively independently, that learners and native speakers will differ in their relative mastery of these skills, and that the skills are involved in different degrees in specific language tasks.

Grammatical competence is understood to reflect knowledge of the language code itself. It includes knowledge of vocabulary and rules of word formation, pronunciation/spelling and sentence formation. Such competence focuses directly on the knowledge and skills required to understand and express accurately the literal meaning of utterances.

Sociolinguistic competence addresses the extent to which utterances are produced and understood appropriately in different sociolinguistic contexts, depending on contextual factors such as topic, status of participants, and purposes of the interaction. Appropriateness of utterances refers to both appropriateness of meaning and appropriateness of form.

Discourse competence involves mastery of how to combine grammatical forms and meanings to achieve a unified spoken or written text in different genres such as narrative, argumentative essay, scientific report or business letter. Unity of a text is achieved through cohesion in form and coherence in meaning. Cohesion deals with how utterances are linked structurally to facilitate interpretation of a text. For example, the use of cohesion devices such as pronouns, synonyms, ellipsis, conjunctions and parallel structures serves to relate individual utterances and to indicate how a group of utterances is to be understood logically or chronologically as a text. Coherence refers to the relationships among the different meanings in a text where these meanings may be literal meanings, communicative functions or social meanings.

Strategic competence refers to the mastery of communication strategies which may be called into action either to enhance the effectiveness of communication or to compensate for breakdowns in communication due to limiting factors in actual communication or to insufficient competence in one or more of the other components of communicative competence. (For further discussion of the nature of these components, see Savignon, 1983.)

The point of reviewing briefly these four proposed components of communicative competence is not to argue for or against them, but is rather to indicate our starting point for the development of the *A Vous la Parole* testing unit. Other theoretical frameworks (see also Cummins and Swain, in press) might have equally well provided a starting point for our test development.

Having a theoretical framework to start from is crucial. In a practical sense, its constructs guide the development of the stimulus material, the tasks to which the test-

taker must respond, the scoring procedures and the subsequent analyses and interpretation of the data. However, even more is at stake. With regard to accomplishments in
standardized testing from 1927 to 1977, Buros (1977) states: "Except for the tremendous
advances in electronic scoring, analysis, and reporting of test results, we don't have a great
deal to show for fifty years of work" (p. 10). Shoemaker (1980) argues that

> "improvements will not be brought about by further refinements of what generally has been done
> in achievement testing to date, nor in the development of more elaborate statistical procedures for
> analysing data, nor in the expanded use of computer systems. . . . advances in the state of the art
> of achievement testing are directly related to advances in the conceptualization of the skill
> domains on which student achievement is assessed".

We think there is merit to Shoemaker's claim in the area of communicative language
testing, and that only through the specification of a theoretical framework will, as
Michael Canale (in press) recently stated, "the current disarray in conceptualization,
research and application in the area of communicative language pedagogy" disappear.
Competing claims about the efficacy of communicative language teaching programs, for
example, cannot be verified unless we can agree upon what is meant by communicative
competence and performance. In proposing the constituent components of communicative competence (Canale and Swain, 1980a) and a general outline of communicative skills
involved within each component (Canale and Swain, 1980b), we were proposing a starting
point. What has been proposed are constructs that need to be validated. In fact, in a
separate study on the development of bilingual proficiency being undertaken at the
Ontario Institute for Studies in Education[2], we are specifically testing the model using a
multitrait, multimethod design (See Bachman and Palmer, 1981, 1982 for discussions of
this approach to language test validation.) Although the data from *A Vous la Parole* will
not be sufficient for a complete trait-method analysis, they can, however, provide a
separate, albeit limited, validation of the theoretical constructs. Starting from somewhere
assumes that a "scientific" rather than an "evaluation" model underlies test design and
implementation. Starting from somewhere allows one to build and refine one's concepts;
starting from nowhere may mean another 50 years of little progress.

(2) *Concentrate on content*

The second principle refers both to the content of the material used as the basis of
communicative language activities and the tasks used to elicit communicative language
behaviours. The content of the material used as the basis for generating communicative
activities – the *A Vous la Parole* booklet in our case – must be sufficient to generate each
component of communicative performance. Similarly, the specific tasks – the composition, letter, note, technical exercise, informal peer discussion and formal interview in
our case – must in their entirety provide the opportunity to use each component of
communicative language behaviour. The necessity of the first principle, start from
somewhere, becomes all the more obvious in this context: the "somewhere" provides the
framework which guides material and task development.

In order to ensure that our materials and tasks are capable of generating language that
includes sociolinguistic, discourse, grammatical and strategic performance, we considered that the content needed to reflect at least four characteristics: it needed to be
motivating, substantive, integrated and interactive in nature. These are essential

characteristics from the learners' point of view; that is, the materials need to be motivating, substantive, integrated and interactive for the testee. What, for example, is motivating in content for the learner, may not be for the test-maker.

I would like now to illustrate how these characteristics are reflected in our testing unit of *A Vous la Parole*.

(a) *Motivating in content*. In order to provide content that would be motivating for the target student population, we could have carried out a needs-assessement-type survey. But we had neither the time nor the resources to do so. Instead we made contact with several high-school students from immersion and francophone programs for input into the topic of the materials. In informal sessions with these students which took place both within and beyond the school walls – over lunch in a restaurant, in fact – project staff explored topics of greatest personal relevance and interest to these students. Recurrent themes in these discussions included travel, summer employment, care of animals, camping, cycling and music. Topics such as roller-skating and student exchange programs were considered to be too boring, too old hat.

After these consultations with students, the project staff went away to work on a booklet which would incorporate as many of these themes of interest as was feasible. Developments of the materials focused on two possible summer employment opportunities: one was to work on a rock-concert series to be organized in one francophone locale, Sudbury, in the province of Ontario; and the other was to tend vegetable gardens and farm animals in the historic francophone park of Fort Louisbourg in the province of Nova Scotia.

Early drafts of the *A Vous la Parole* booklet and tasks were pretested in classes containing some of the same students who had provided input in the design stages. Most students were thrilled to see their opinions in print. Since then the materials have been pilot-tested with a number of students who had not provided input to the content of the materials, and their feedback has been overwhelmingly positive. Thus, while we cannot claim to have hit on two topics of interest to all youths of this age, it is clear that the themes are interesting and relevant to the large majority of the students we have tested.

A second aspect to the provision of content that would be motivating for the students is in the actual presentation of the materials. We therefore tried to present the material in as attractive a format as possible, subject to budgetary restrictions. As a result, the *A Vous la Parole* booklet includes a comic strip, cartoons, drawings, maps, photos and the use of bright, cheerful colours.

A third aspect to the provision of motivating content is in the nature of the communicative tasks the students are required to undertake based on the stimulus material. We felt the tasks should reflect contexts for writing and speaking that do not end when education comes to an end; that is, activities that would represent real uses of French by those who may or may not be continuing their studies. For this reason, the tasks of writing a letter, a note for a bulletin board, a factual paragraph, an opinion composition, and of conversing with peers and participating in an interview were used. Thus, although the tasks were not truly authentic in the sense that they were performed in school rather than in the actual setting, they represented tests of the students' ability to use their second language in situations reflecting real situations of interest to them.

(b) *Substantive in content*. A second characteristic of the content is that it be substantive. By this is meant not only that information is presented to the students, but that some of it is new information for them. There are several reasons for presenting substantive content, some of which is new to the learner. In part, the presentation of new information should contribute to the motivation of the learner to read the materials carefully. Already known content can be boring and provide little incentive to consider the content thoughtfully. Additionally, the presentation of new information ensures that "real" communication can occur. That is to say, real communication frequently occurs as a function of an *informational gap*.

For this reason, the *A Vous la Parole* booklet contains information about the two locales of the job opportunities being proposed. In the case of Sudbury, the students are informed that approximately a third of the population is French-speaking, that there is a bilingual university situated there where some courses taught are unique in Canada; that there is a rich and dynamic cultural life with theatres, orchestras, choirs, festivals, museums and an art gallery; that Sudbury is in the north-east part of Ontario, close to a lake offering exceptional facilities for swimming and water-skiing, and so on.

In the case of Louisbourg, the students are given a brief history of it as a French fort set up to protect French possessions, which later became an important fishing port and active commercial centre. The fort was later destroyed by the British and the town was abandoned. Recently, in 1961, the Canadian government decided to reconstruct Louisbourg, and in so doing relieved some of the hardships of unemployment caused by the closing of the coal mines in Cape Breton. Today the fort stands as a monument to the life and times of the 18th Century where, during the summer, approximately 200 people are employed to live as the colonists did, growing and preserving their own food, making their own clothes, etc. In the case of both Sudbury and Louisbourg, maps, photos and illustrations support the text.

This information, much of which will be new to many students, provides the context of the tasks they will be required to carry out. In order that the students consider this new information without feeling anxious or threatened by the test situation, we begin *A Vous la Parole* by indicating to the students that "the authors of this booklet have tried to propose some new ideas to you in a form that pleases you and will encourage you to learn and think about them".

From our point of view, then, presenting content that is substantive fulfils three criteria for communicative language tests. First, it provides a context for the tasks the students will be required to carry out. Secondly, it is potentially one of the few means by which the students' attention can be focused on content rather than form, which represents one way of approximating real communication in a test situation. Thirdly, to the extent that some of the content is new for the learner, the test material fulfils a genuine communicative function by responding to an informational gap between the learner and the materials.

Additionally, and perhaps more an issue of pedagogy or ethics than of communicative language testing, by presenting substantive content some of which is new, the test-taker will not go away empty-handed – or, should I say, empty-headed. He or she should have gained some new ideas or knowledge, or even some new linguistic insight by having taken the test. To put it another way, in taking a communicatively-oriented test, the testee should have the experience of being communicated to, and of being able to communicate. The "meta-test" of this is that the testee has learned something from the experience of being tested.

We have discovered that to translate these criteria into practice means being prepared to spend considerable time collecting relevant and accurate information, and translating this information into age-appropriate textual material. In fact, this phase of test development was equivalent to the development of curriculum materials for use in schools by our target population. I will return to this point below in the discussion of the principle of work for washback.

(c) *Integrated in content*. Neither the characteristic of being motivating in content nor being substantive in content implies that the content be integrated: integrated, that is, in the sense of dealing with one theme around which *all* information and activities are centred. In the case of *A Vous la Parole* the central theme is summer employment for youth. This theme provides the central focus for all the tasks which the students are asked to do. It is, as the criterion for substance in content implies, like a lesson the students might encounter in class.

Although integrated content may not seem particularly radical for those who have been working on communicative language test development, when one compares the text and tasks of *A Vous la Parole* to a typical language test, the differences are profound in this respect. Even in the communicative test items that were developed by us several years ago as part of an item bank for the Ontario Ministry of Education to test French as second language communicative skills (Ontario Ministry of Education, 1980) the contexts established were minimal – limited to sentences or short paragraphs. And, to a large extent, each test item involved a new context. In traditional discrete-point tests of language proficiency little attention was paid to context, let alone to integrated situational contexts.

Integrated content is essential to communicative language testing because it gives clues to meaning: the more context, the more clues. When a test item can be responded to correctly on the basis of the immediate linguistic environment alone, to that extent the task is unlikely to be reflective of the communicative aspects of language behaviour.

(d) *Interactive in content*. The fourth characteristic of the content of a communicative test is that it should foster interaction. This can be accomplished in part by providing new substantive content so that the learners may be stimulated to ask questions. Perhaps more important, though, in fostering interaction is the provision of content which includes opinions or controversial ideas. This offers the possibility of an exchange of opinions, or of the expression of one's own ideas and opinions on the topic.

For example, to start the students thinking about the topic of *A Vous la Parole*, we reproduced a letter written by Eric Martin, a Montreal student of the same age as the students tested. The letter reads as follows:

"Dear friends,
  I would like to give you my point of view on the subject of the life of today's adolescents. I am 15 years old and I am shocked to see the ignorance and the lack of respect that is shown us by adults. For adults, we are inferior beings and of little importance. For example, in stores and restaurants, adults are served before us even if we were there long before them.
  What I find the most annoying is that adults also have priority over adolescents in the work world. It's always difficult for students between the ages of 15 and 17 to find a summer job, or a full-time job after graduation, and this will be even more serious this year. Contrary to what most adults think, adolescents are more conscientious and open than those of the same age in the 1960's and 70's. We have a big contribution to make to the work world.
  The preoccupations of the adolescent of the 80's are not only the threat of nuclear war, the depletion of our energy sources, and the political divisions in our country. There is also a problem we don't talk much about at school: unemployment. It turns out that we are not well-prepared for the labour market. What a shame! So much money and time wasted.
  Adults judge our situation and make decisions for us without asking our advice. Then, when these decisions don't meet our needs, they ask why! Since they don't want to consult us . . . let's speak for ourselves . . . à nous la parole!
                                                                                  Eric Martin"

In the associated task, the learners are asked to write a letter to Eric, giving their opinions about what Eric said. The students are specifically asked to say whether they agree or disagree and why, giving examples from their own experiences or the experiences of their friends. They are reminded that Eric is also a student of their age, in order to indicate the tone and style in which their letter is to be written.

Similarly, the *A Vous la Parole* booklet describes, among other aspects of the summer jobs, the living conditions for the students: seven to ten students will live together in a large house along with two adults. Each one will have his or her own bedroom, but will share bathroom, kitchen and living room. In the associated task, the students, in groups of three or four, are asked to discuss such questions as: what difficulties might occur when living together like this with others they don't know; what solutions might be sought in face of these difficulties; what they would do if two people in the house didn't get along at all; and so on.

Thus the content of the stimulus material can set the stage for some form of interaction and the tasks provide the opportunity for the interaction to occur. Together they help the student to determine the tone, the style and even the format of the interaction. This is important if one is to be able to judge the learners' socio-linguistic competence.

(3) *Bias for best*

The third principle we have used in guiding our communicative test development is bias for best. By this is meant do everything possible to elicit the learners' best performance. There is a good reason for this from the point of view of test interpretation: if the testee does well, then it can be said with some confidence that the learner can do what is expected of him or her when given the opportunity. However, if the testee does not do well, then it is not clear whether this occurs because the testee cannot do what is expected, or is prevented from doing it because of distracting factors, or whatever. In other words, it is important to minimize the effect of the measurement technique on the test-taker's performance.

In *A Vous la Parole* we introduced several procedures into the testing situation to bias performance positively. Recognizing that individuals work at varying paces, the testees are given more than adequate time to complete the task assigned for the day. In addition to being allowed to work at their own speed on the written tasks, they are given an opportunity each day to review the work they have previously completed and are encouraged to make any changes they wish (Odell, 1977). Furthermore, they are given access to reference materials such as dictionaries and are explicitly encouraged to make use of them. While the task is being done, the test administrator is expected to check that everyone is following the task instructions correctly.

In addition to these procedures, we decided that we could bias results for best performance by, in some cases, informing the students of what was being tested. Thus, in the introduction to *A Vous la Parole*, the students read that "this short booklet serves as a basis for a series of exercises in order to evaluate your written and spoken French". In the technical exercise, where the students are required to take the point from a description of the tasks to be performed in the summer jobs and write them up in a paragraph written in the same style as the rest of the text, it is explicitly stated that "the goal of this exercise is to be able to evaluate your ability to produce complete sentences".

In a similar vein, students are given suggestions as to how to go about the task as, for example, in writing the composition, where they are advised "to express their ideas clearly". In some cases the students are given suggestions of points to include in their written work or discussion, and are explicitly told who their audience is and therefore the style, or level of formality, they should adopt. For example, in the note-writing task of *A Vous la Parole*, the students who choose the Louisbourg project are given the following instructions:

> "In this exercise, we are asking you to write a note to other young people your age. The style should therefore be informal. In order to do this exercise, you must imagine that you are already a participant in the Louisbourg project. Imagine the following situation: you have been in Louisbourg for several weeks now and you would like to visit Halifax next weekend. You decide to post a note in French in the cafeteria in order to find someone who can drive you to Halifax at that time. In your note, mention that you will share expenses for the trip and that you have a driver's licence. Leave your telephone number or indicate where you can be easily met. Don't forget that you are writing to someone your own age."

Thus, to bias for best is to provide the test-takers with useful suggestions as to what and how to respond, to provide adequate time to complete the task and, in the case of written work, to have access to dictionaries or other reference material as well as to have the opportunity to review and revise their work.

(4) *Work for washback*

The fourth and final principle guiding our test construction is to work for washback. Washback refers to the effect a test has on teaching practices. It has frequently been noted that teachers will teach to a test; that is, if they know the content of a test and/or the format of a test, they will teach their students accordingly. This is not particularly surprising, given the frequent use made of tests by educational administrators to form, legitimately or not, judgements of teacher effectiveness.

Recognizing that neither teacher nor administrative behaviour is likely to change in this regard, and believing that teaching practices, especially in the higher grade levels of immersion programs, could profit from some changes, we have tried to build teacher involvement into the development of the test, its administration and eventually into its scoring. Before discussing how we have done this, I would like to digress briefly to comment on the suggestion that some changes in teaching practices might be appropriate in the higher grades of immersion education.

Immersion education has two goals: one is to foster the development of high levels of second language proficiency; and the other is to do this at no expense to mother tongue development, cognitive growth or academic achievement. These goals are accomplished essentially through the teaching of academic content in the second language. Although at later grade levels more class time is used for the teaching of French *per se* (Swain, 1981) the emphasis is on teaching content. The result, typical of many classroom settings, is that the teacher talks and the students listen. Student responses are typically short and elliptical. In other words, individual students are given relatively infrequent opportunities to make use of their second language, especially in extended discourse or in sociolinguistically variable ways. As might be expected in this situation, the students develop native-like comprehension skills (Swain and Lapkin, 1982) but their spoken French has many non-native features in it (Harley and Swain, 1978, Harley, 1982). We think that the sorts of materials and related activities that form the *A Vous la Parole* testing unit exemplify teaching units which may help students to overcome these weaker aspects of their second language proficiency. Incidentally, there is no suggestion being made by this that *all* teaching be activity-oriented and student-centred. Rather, the implication is that communicative activities form a legitimate and significant part of the teaching-learning process for both the acquisition of language and content knowledge.

To return then to the main point, that of working for washback, we have for this reason involved teachers in the development of *A Vous la Parole*, first by establishing an advisory panel which includes teachers as well as Department of Education (Saskatchewan) officials to comment on this and other test units we are producing while still in the development stage; secondly, by holding a workshop to explain the test and its purposes to teachers whose classes were involved in the pilot-testing of *A Vous la Parole*; thirdly, by asking these same teachers to help in the supervision of the students being tested; and fourthly, by informally discussing with these teachers their reactions to the test unit and their perceptions of the students' reactions to it. In general, their reactions have been both positive and thoughtful, with many excellent suggestions made for revisions, which have been incorporated in the present version of the testing unit.

Practically, in order to administer a test like *A Vous la Parole* on a large scale, teachers must be involved in its administration and scoring. It is simply too time-consuming and therefore too expensive to hire the additional personnel necessary for its administration. Moreover, for the very reason of working for a washback effect, we consider it to be advantageous that teachers be involved in test administration and scoring. To this end, we have begun the writing of a *Teacher's Guide* which explains the purposes of the testing unit, a step-by-step guide of how to administer the test including the specific wording of the information and instructions which the teachers will give to the students, and a description of how to score the exercises, including a brief theoretical and empirical rationale for the scoring criteria as well as many illustrative examples.

Through these means of involving teachers in the development and/or administration and scoring of the test, then, we hope not only to change aspects of what is taught, but also to suggest alternative teaching-learning strategies.

Scoring

Although *A Vous la Parole* was developed for use in a large-scale, summative evaluation of immersion education, it could also be used for formative program evaluation, or for the evaluation of individual student performance. The scoring procedures developed should reflect the use or uses the test is intended for and the theoretical framework which initially guided the test's construction.

We began the development of scoring criteria with the view that each task would reveal aspects of communicative language performance; that is, that each task could be scored for grammatical, sociolinguistic, discourse and strategic aspects of communicative language performance. We did not, however, attempt to predetermine the specific aspects of each component that would be scored. Rather, we worked from the data gathered during the pilot-testing phase to determine what specifically would be scored in each task and what scoring criteria would be used. By proceeding in this way the scoring scheme was able to reflect the most salient aspects of each task response and the full range of responses observed for any specific aspect. Neither could have been fully known prior to an examination of the data.

Our approach in developing scoring procedures has been to begin comprehensively, using a mixture of objective counts and subjective judgements. Scoring the note to be posted on the bulletin board, for example, included counting the number of word-order errors, anaphora errors and omissions, homophonous and non-homophonous morphological errors, and the points of information provided. Additionally, judgements were made on a three-point scale about the use of attention-getting devices, the overall appropriateness of lexical register used, the persuasiveness of the note, and the physical organization and appearance of the note as a note.

For purposes of large-scale testing, our intention is to reduce the number of aspects scored, based on analyses carried out with the pilot data. Several factors will determine the final set of features to be scored.

One factor will be the ways the data cluster in correlational and factor analytical analyses. We anticipate, for example, that the analyses of the written data will reveal clusters of variables that correspond to the theoretical constructs of sociolinguistic, grammatical and discourse competence. (Strategic performance was not scored in the written data.) Preliminary analyses on a partial data set are suggestive of these components, but also revealed a fourth cluster of variables having largely to do with vocabulary knowledge. Our plan is to select several variables from each cluster of variables.

Which variables are selected will depend in part on the face validity of the variables. Additionally, however, their selection will depend on patterns of systematic and interesting variability. For example, the data suggest systematic differences between early immersion students (those starting an immersion program at age 5 to 6) and late immersion students (those starting an immersion program around age 13) in their ability to write homophonous morphology correctly. Early immersion students tend to make more homophonous morphological errors (e.g. tu *a* dit; les enfants *pense*) than late immersion students, reflecting perhaps the stronger oral base of the early immersion students' language learning experiences.

Thus the steps we pursued in developing scoring procedures for large-scale testing – one which is not yet complete for us – involves the selection of variables from a much larger set, the larger set being determined by the nature of the responses to each task. By proceeding in this way, the criteria reflect the range of possible responses and the task responses will have been exploited to their fullest in contributing to theory and practice.

Summary and Conclusions

Four principles useful in guiding the development of communicative language tests have been discussed using the testing unit of *A Vous la Parole* as illustrative material. The four principles – start from somewhere, concentrate on content, bias for best and work for washback – assume a pedagogical function to language testing as well as a scientific approach to language test design and implementation. Although some may foresee inherent conflicts between these assumptions and those of measurement theory, I do not see any necessary long-run incompatibility.

Additionally, the process followed in developing scoring procedures and criteria has been discussed. The process has involved moving from maximum detail and comprehensiveness to the selection of key variables, which still permit comprehensiveness in the measurement of the components of communicative performance. It has also involved working from the testees' responses to each task. This has ensured that the scoring criteria reflect the range of possible responses and that the salient component features elicited by each task are considered. What is still not known, however, is the feasibility of large-scale administration and scoring of *A Vous la Parole*. We think it is possible and some Departments of Education think it is possible for purposes of *program* evaluation. Its feasibility for individual student assessment on a large scale remains uncertain owing primarily to the testing time involved. The testing unit is well suited, however, to use by classroom teachers as a teaching unit through which the communicative language performance of individual students can be assessed.

* * * * * * * * * * * * *

I would like to thank Michael Canale, Daina Green, Jill Kamin, Sharon Lapkin, Sandra Savignon, Nina Spada and Peter Tung for their time and thoughtfulness in commenting on an earlier version of this paper.

Notes

1. Actively participating in this project are Valerie Argue, Suzanne Bertrand, Jim Cummins, Daina Green, Gila Hanna, Jill Kamin, Sharon Lapkin, Laurette Levy and Merrill Swain.
2. The principal investigators for this project are Patrick Allen, Jim Cummins, Raymond Mougeon and Merrill Swain.

A Test of Swedish as a Second Language: An Experiment in Self-assessment

TIBOR VON ELEK

The purpose of this paper is to present a preliminary version of a self-assessment test of Swedish as a second language. It is being developed at the Language Teaching Research Centre, University of Göteborg, as part of project sponsored by the National Swedish Board of Education. The test is meant to serve as a self-diagnostic instrument for adult migrants studying Swedish as a second language. It is hoped that the test will provide a model easily adaptable to other second or foreign languages.

Background to the Project

During the 1970s the teaching of Swedish to migrants developed into a school subject which in scope is second only to English among modern languages taught in Sweden. The rapid development of Swedish as a second language has led to acute needs for teaching aids, teacher-training programs, and, of course, various test instruments.

The urgent need for placement and achievement tests has mainly been met by tests constructed by teachers. To a certain extent these tests are also diagnostic instruments in that they give the teacher some information about linguistic areas within which the student needs to improve his ability. The majority of these teacher-made tests could probably be classified as "pre-scientific" or "traditional" types of tests in Spolsky's terms (1976).

A proficiency test which presumably would qualify as representative of Spolsky's "psychometric-structuralist" or "modern" period was developed at the Language Teaching Research Centre in 1974–75. The test was to a certain degree modelled on the TOEFL, and it was primarily developed for the labour market training schools where large numbers of adult migrants attend courses in Swedish. Scores from this test are "translated" into proficiency levels on a rating scale defining, in quite general terms, the testee's global proficiency in Swedish. These test results often underlie decisions about the student's admission to professional training or to additional courses in Swedish. The test has been described in detail in a report which also presents the findings of a quite extensive investigation into the migrants' proficiency in Swedish as measured by means of the same test (von Elek, 1977).

A common complaint on the part of adult migrants attending courses in Swedish as a second language at labour market centres and awaiting subsequent professional training or retraining, has been that they lack information about their actual Swedish proficiency as well as about the level they are supposed to achieve in order to qualify for and be able to cope with the job or professional training they are aiming at. What they have in mind is not a vague and general description of these proficiency levels but quite concrete and

47

explicit information on their own proficiency profile in relation to the language proficiency they ought to achieve – or at least approach – in the course of their studies. Such information, they believe, would make their coursework more goal-oriented and would consequently motivate and stimulate them in their efforts to make up for obvious shortcomings.

These expectations imply that in the teaching of a second language to migrants, especially adults, conventional achievement tests and end-of-course tests are of limited value. Instead, emphasis should be put on the development of instruments that will enable the students themselves to diagnose their weak areas and organize their studies with a view to satisfying individual needs.

The guiding principle in our assignment within the project has, therefore, been to try to provide migrants with the type of instrument that would correspond to their expectations mentioned above. It was also decided that this instrument should be constructed in accordance with self-assessment principles. There are several reasons for this.

Experiments with self-assessment conducted at the Language Teaching Research Centre by Balke-Aurell (1977), von Elek (1978), and Oskarsson (1980), as well as elsewhere by Wangsotorn (1981), Bachman and Palmer (1981), Fok (1981a), and Rea (1980), to mention but a few, have shown that adults are fully capable of making reliable judgements about their own mastery of a foreign language, provided they have access to adequate instruments. Therefore, there is good reason to give adult students an opportunity to assume greater responsibility in the evaluation process and thereby to contribute to their autonomy. Apart from these psychological and motivational aspects, the engagement of students in self-assessment has also some practical implications. It allows the development of tests with more substantial, more varied and, consequently, more valid content. It also reduces the teacher's burden of marking, an activity that does not contribute to anybody's learning and can therefore be regarded as a waste of time.

We also wish to see our assignment as an opportunity to take a step away from the "modern" period towards Spolsky's third, or "post-modern" period: the "sociolinguistic-psycholinguistic" one. Thus instead of over-emphasizing test reliability we are trying to give priority to high validity. This we hope to achieve partly by providing sub-tests in all skills, including the productive ones, and partly by playing down the role of discrete point items in favour of integrated tests. This also means transferring the emphasis from linguistic ability to communicative competence.

Finally, by introducing our test, which we should like to classify as a representative of "the gentle art of diagnostic testing", we hope to show that testing does not necessarily have to be a dramatic and formal event in a tense atmosphere of teacher authority and student anxiety. It will probably not be possible to eliminate formal tests altogether in the future, or at least as long as we need test results underlying end-of-term statements, grades or ranking. We should, however, like to see them used in alternation with informal, student-centred tests that can be taken as relaxed classroom activities or homework, and in which the teacher's role is that of a helper and partner assisting the learner to make the best possible use of the information provided by his self-assessment.

In summing up, it can be said that the aim of our work is to develop an instrument which will enable the target group – adult migrants studying Swedish in order to become fully-fledged citizens in their new country,

(1) to assume greater responsibility in the evaluation of their proficiency and progress,

(2) to diagnose their weak areas and obtain a realistic view of their general proficiency as well as their skills profile,

(3) to see their actual proficiency in relation to the level they wish to achieve in order to qualify for a certain job or training program, and consequently

(4) to become more motivated and goal-oriented in their further studies.

Design, Format and Use of the Test

Our test consists of a large number of items (1,500) arranged into content areas (hereafter: skills) on the one hand and into difficulty levels on the other. The grid in Fig. 1 illustrates the structure of the entire battery. It falls into six skills (vocabulary, grammar, listening and reading comprehension, oral and written production) and within each of these skills into ten difficulty levels. Thus the battery encompasses a total of 60 sub-tests or units, each of which comprises 25 items. A test of these dimensions is only practicable if it can be self-administered and self-scored. To make this possible the items are presented in sections headed by questions like: Do you understand the word underlined? Can you give the opposite of the word underlined? Do you understand this sentence/passage? The student is asked to give his answer by checking one of the following alternatives for each item: (1) Yes, absolutely, (2) I think so, (3) No.

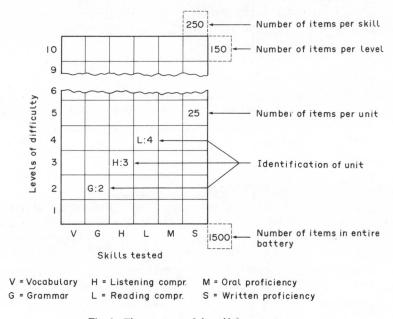

V = Vocabulary   H = Listening compr.   M = Oral proficiency
G = Grammar   L = Reading compr.   S = Written proficiency

Fig. 1. *The structure of the self-assessment test*

Normally the student starts at the lowest level or, if he is not a beginner, at some other suitable level. He is supposed to do all six units at the same difficulty level before he proceeds to the next one. If he has checked alternative 1 for a minimum of 80% of the items (i.e. 20 out of 25) in a unit, he can consider himself to have passed the level in question. If his "yes-answers" are below 50 % in a unit there is no point in going on to the next level within that particular skill.

In Figs 2 and 3 we present the results of an imaginary student's self-assessment at levels 1–5. Figure 2 shows the percentage of items answered with "yes" within each unit. In Fig. 3 the units with 80 % or more of such answers have been shaded so as to make the student's skills profile more apparent. In this particular case the student seems to be comparatively poor at grammar and writing, but these weaknesses are compensated for by a high level in oral skills. His average proficiency corresponds to level 3, which is two levels short of the student's imaginary goal-line at level 5. The most important information gained from the outcome of this assessment is that our student ought to concentrate on grammar and writing, areas in which the distance between the actual and desired levels is greatest.

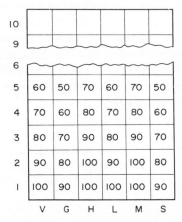

Fig. 2. *Items answered with "Yes" (percentages) in an imaginary student's self-assessment*

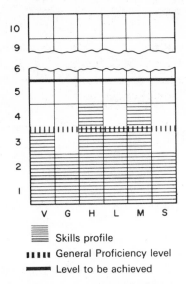

▦ Skills profile

▮▮▮▮▮ General Proficiency level

▬▬ Level to be achieved

Fig. 3. *The outcome of the self-assessment presented in Fig. 2*

As is apparent, the diagnostic information is given in the form of a skills profile; that is, in terms of the relative status of the student's various skills. Therefore, our test probably does not conform to conventional diagnostic tests: instruments by means of which teachers can find out what sorts of errors their students make, particularly in the fields of pronunciation, grammar and vocabulary. We believe that such diagnostic instruments can and should be constructed by the teachers themselves in accordance with the relevant syllabus, their knowledge of the class, and other factors. A diagnostic test developed by professionals for the entire target population should, instead, aim at revealing weaknesses in a wider sense; namely, in terms of skills. For this reason it would probably be more adequate to classify our test as a diagnostically oriented proficiency test.

We think that, especially in the teaching of migrants, this type of diagnosis is essential, since teachers of Swedish as a second language seem to agree that different migrant groups demonstrate rather deviant profiles depending on such variables as educational and cultural background, time spent in Sweden, sex (for certain groups), etc. It is desirable that both the student and the teacher should be made aware of the student's specific profile at an early stage of the course, so that adequate measures can be taken for an individualized remedial study program. It should be pointed out that not only the student's proficiency but also the "goal-line" can be expressed in the form of a specific profile, especially for careers where certain language skills are of particular importance and therefore given more emphasis than others.

Our use of a graded self-assessment test is not unlike the procedure employed in checking our eyesight by means of a chart containing letters or texts of decreasing size. The person with a visual defect starts off by reading the largest letters or texts and proceeds to the smaller ones. The level where he gets stuck enables the optician – and to a certain extent the patient himself – to make inferences about his eyesight. Once the patient's eyesight ("student's proficiency") has been diagnosed, the optician ("teacher") prescribes adequate glasses ("remedial measures"). In doing so he takes into consideration the patient's visual deficiency for both eyes ("profile") on the one hand, and the purpose for which he needs the glasses, e.g. reading, driving a car, etc. ("goal-line"), on the other.

The question has sometimes been raised why we offer the students three alternative answers to choose from if there is only one that counts. Our motive for giving three options is psychological rather than technical. We believe that students would be reluctant to check the "No" alternative in cases when they are almost certain they know the correct answer, and would find it more satisfactory to be able to answer "I think so" even though this does not affect the outcome of their self-assessment. Furthermore, eliminating this option would invite some students to check the "Yes" box even when they are not absolutely sure of the correct answer, and this would lower the reliability of the test.

Another question we are frequently asked is whether we can rely on the students' frankness in checking the proper alternative and/or their capability of doing so. We have to admit, partly on the basis of experience gained so far, that this self-diagnostic procedure does not suit all individuals equally and that during the try-out period several students were found to have made misleading self-assessments. Still, we firmly believe that most students will give honest answers as long as they know they will neither be rewarded nor penalized for the outcome of their "confession", and as long as they know that they will deceive no one but themselves by intentionally over-estimating or underrating their capacity, and that in the long run they will benefit from a remedial program designed on the bases of realistic self-assessment results. Likewise, nobody would wish to "deceive" the optician even if this were possible. We are convinced that, in the majority of cases, unrealistic self-assessments are due to insufficient information about the real purpose of the test, and perhaps to the student's deep-rooted ambition to achieve, on any test, as high a score as he possibly can.

To the question whether we can expect students to be capable of making reliable judgements about their mastery of the test-content we reply with another question: Who should know better than the student himself whether he understands a word or sentence, whether he would be able to express himself adequately in a given situation, etc? We wish to point to the fact that by self-assessment we do not mean sophisticated descriptions of the student's own proficiency or profile. We do not even ask the student to choose among several descriptions of proficiency levels the one that would best correspond to his own level, a task that may be quite demanding for people with modest educational or linguistic backgrounds. The only thing the student is supposed to do is to state honestly the degree of his knowledge of specific items according to the above-mentioned alternative answers. Thanks to thorough developmental work, the interpretation of his accumulated "Yes" answers is built into the instrument and will be a mere routine procedure both for the student himself and for the teacher. It is true that some items are easier to make judgements about than others and in some instances, owing to misunderstanding, the student may unintentionally give false information, but we believe that these are exceptions rather than the rule.

Another question that may be justified is this one: How are we to know where to draw the proper "goal line" for different purposes? The answer is: at this stage we do not have an exact knowledge of what our difficulty levels mean in explicit terms, which also explains why we have limited ourselves to merely assigning numbers to our levels. However, once the final version of the test has been developed and used for a certain time, it will be quite possible through experience and by means of correlation studies to determine the "goal lines" or "goal profiles", at least for the most frequent and important purposes. For the time being our "goal lines" are hypothetical and we merely use them as a demonstration of how the test is meant to be used.

Content and Levels of Difficulty

So far very little has been said about test content. One of the advantages of this type of test is that, as far as choice of subject matter is concerned, it is free from the limitations of conventional, especially multiple-choice tests. This means that practically any linguistic material can be included, which of course is of great importance for test validity. Our guiding principle in constructing items has been to use as much authentic material as possible. We have also been anxious to distribute the language samples to sub-tests in which they would fit in naturally. Thus the items that ended up in the listening comprehension units consist of samples of everyday spoken language: at lower levels simple questions, statements and instructions, more than once containing commonly used slang expressions, and at the higher levels excerpts from broadcast material, messages through loudspeakers, etc. Similarly, the reading comprehension units contain the kind of language samples that are likely to reach the migrants in written form: signs, messages, headlines, excerpts from brochures and the press, etc. The oral and written parts were constructed according to similar criteria. In the vocabulary and grammar parts we could not follow the same principles. We selected words and grammar structures that experienced teachers regarded as relevant and important. We believe that, although the test content was not compiled on the basis of a systematic needs analysis, the substantial material comprised in 1,500 items constitutes a representative random sample of the Swedish language.

Another important task besides selecting subject matter has been the distribution of items to various difficulty levels. It is not enough to grade items so that the units with higher numbers should be increasingly difficult. It is just as important to achieve a balance horizontally; that is, to make the various sub-tests of the same level equally difficult. In the first version of our test this had to be done by means of the subjective judgements of a number of highly qualified and experienced teachers. In the second version, however, we could use the statistical data gained from the first try-out.

The Try-out Run

The first experimental version of the self-assessment test battery was tried out during the academic year of 1981/82. It was given to roughly 300 adult migrants enrolled in various courses of Swedish. They represented a wide range of proficiency levels from beginners to near-native speakers.

The teachers who engaged themselves in the project had a very important part to play in the try-out. They were to select subjects from their classes, distribute and collect test material, assist students with instructions, complete answer sheets with data on background variables, etc. Their most important contribution, however, was what we called the follow-up procedure, which enabled us to study the reliability of the self-assessment.

The purpose of the "follow-up" was to find out how reliable the student's answers were. This meant that the part of the test the student had done was gone through once more, but this time with the assistance of the teacher, whose task was to test the student on each item he claimed, or thought, he knew. Now it was the teacher who did the marking on the student's answer sheet according to the results of this testing procedure.

Figure 4 demonstrates the principle of the teacher's task and the possible relationships

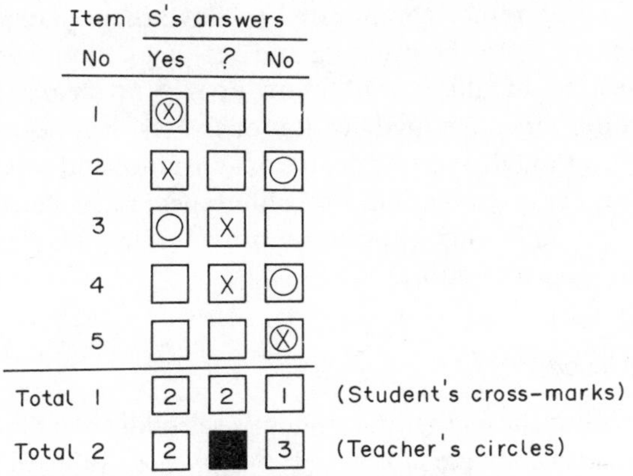

Fig. 4. *Excerpt from answer sheet showing self-assessment and follow-up results*

between the student's and the teacher's markings or, in other words, between self-assessment and "real" knowledge.

If the student marks the first box, thereby stating that he is absolutely certain he knows the item, and can then verify it in the follow-up, the teacher puts a circle around the cross-mark (as in Item 1). If, however, it turns out that the student does not know the answer in spite of having checked the Yes-box, the teacher puts the circle in the "No" alternative (Item 2). In cases when the student marks the second option – if he is not quite sure about the correct answer – there are two possibilities for the teacher: either he puts the circle in the first box (as in Item 3), which means that the student knows the item, or in the third box (Item 4), which means he does not. Thus the second alternative is eliminated from the teacher's marking, which is logical since in reality there are only two alternatives, at least according to our criteria: either the student knows the *exact* answer or he does not. Finally, if the student has given a straightforward "No" by marking the third box, the teacher *always* puts the circle round the student's cross-mark, which means that there is no need to test the student on these items. The reason for this is that, even if it turns out that the student has a command of such an item, it would be most probable that he has learnt it after – and perhaps because of – having been confronted with the problem during the self-assessment. Otherwise he would not have checked the third option.

Thanks to the different markings used by the student and the teacher on the answer sheets it was very simple to feed the results into the computer and to study the relation between self-assessment and real knowledge (as measured by the teacher), both on individual items and in more global terms.

These follow-ups were both demanding and time-consuming since they involved a kind of oral testing comprising hundreds of items per student. In cases where the teacher could speak the student's native tongue, or where they had some other common language to communicate in, the procedure was fairly smooth. In the majority of cases, however, the follow-up had to be carried out by whatever other methods were available; for example, by non-verbal means. In most cases the students managed to demonstrate their knowledge by using their limited Swedish proficiency, aided by gestures, paper and pencil, etc. On the whole, the teachers had no serious problems in carrying out the follow-ups, but it was obvious that some types of items were more complicated or time-consuming to test than others. Thus, whereas it was relatively easy to test the student's knowledge of individual words, it was rather complicated to have them explain or paraphrase the meaning of long sentences in the listening and reading comprehension sub-tests.

It must be emphasized that this type of follow-up is by no means meant to be part of the self-assessment process once the final version of the test has been published and made available for use, even though a certain degree of assistance and supervision on the part of the teacher will always be desirable, if not absolutely necessary. During the developmental period, however, the follow-up procedure provides invaluable information and is therefore worth the time and effort.

Results and Experience

Data from the try-out shows that the student's self-judgements were highly reliable as far as their "Yes" answers were concerned. We wish to refer to Fig. 4 which can be regarded as a small-scale example of the relationship between student's and teacher's scores. Although there is considerable discrepancy between them, the totals of "Yes" answers are the same. Similarly, in the overall results the differences between these scores were generally small. It did happen, of course, that the student could not verify the knowledge of some items for which he had checked the "Yes" box. On the other hand, this loss in scores was usually compensated for by those items that the student proved to know in spite of having checked the second alternative. In most cases, however, it turned out that a mark in the second box was in reality equated with lack of knowledge. Consequently the student's and the teacher's total scores in the third column showed considerable differences. These results then seem to support our decision only to consider the "Yes" answers when interpreting self-assessment scores. We also wish to refer to what was said above about our cutting scores: a student is considered to have passed a difficulty level when the number of his "Yes" answers amounts to a minimum of 20 out of 25 items per unit. This means that even though there is normally a difference between the student's and the teacher's total scores in the "Yes" column, it seldom affects the final outcome: the pattern of his skills profile.

It must not be denied, however, that despite the high general agreement between the student's and teacher's total scores in the first column we had quite a few extreme cases of both over-ratings and under-ratings. Both data and teacher's experience indicate that there is a certain correspondence between under-ratings and over-ratings on the one hand and some variables like educational, national, and cultural background, sex, proficiency level, etc. on the other. Nevertheless, we prefer to wait and see whether these preliminary results can be confirmed in a second try-out before we venture conclusions.

Correlations between self-assessment and follow-up scores were computed for all (60) units of the test battery. Owing to the small numbers and/or high scores in some cells these correlations must be interpreted with caution. Correlation coefficients were generally high (between .60 and .97) with the exception of the grammar sub-tests that yielded values between .45 and .65 for seven out of ten units. The teachers confirmed, on the basis of their experience from the follow-ups, that it was in the grammar sub-tests that the students made the largest number of misjudgements. This is not surprising, since it is probably in the area of grammar that language learners are least aware of the errors they make.

Data from the try-out was also used to investigate the difficulty level of both individual items and entire units. It was found that we had succeeded fairly well in constructing units of increasing difficulty for each level (i.e. vertically) in spite of the fact that, not being in the possession of previous data, we had to rely on the subjective judgements of the teachers in the distribution of items to the various levels. On the other hand, we were less successful in achieving similar difficulty levels horizontally: in the various sub-tests belonging to the same level. The listening comprehension, for instance, was considerably easier at levels 1–6 than any other sub-test at the corresponding levels. The usual pattern of skills profile achieved by our subjects, characterized by extremely high listening comprehension, did not therefore reflect the real state of their proficiency, but was due to this deficiency in the test battery. In developing the second version we were anxious to remedy this deficiency by re-distributing a number of items to more appropriate difficulty levels and by substituting new ones for others. In this compilation we, of course, made use of the item-analyses from the try-out.

Whether we have succeeded in our effort cannot be determined until the try-out run of the second version has been carried out. One reason why item analyses may provide insufficient information is that subjects take different sections of the test battery, which results in different samples for all levels.

As was implied above, we did not confine our evaluation to the processing of computable data. We also took stock of the experiences and subjective judgements of the teachers involved in the try-out.

One of the most important findings was that the test was very popular with the students. They generally regarded the test as a teaching aid rather than a test, and the atmosphere while they worked on it was relaxed. They were eager to find out how far they could "climb" the scale and what sort of profile their scores would yield. They were equally anxious to find out the correct answers to all items they were uncertain about or did not know. This can be seen as a beneficial spin-off effect of the test and we think it is extremely important that the curiosity and motivation this self-assessment procedure arouses should be taken advantage of in the learning process. It was also reported that in a few cases the test did not function according to our intentions. Some students would fail to recognize the real purpose of the test, which resulted in skills profiles far above their actual proficiency. In extreme cases they refused to subject themselves to any type of follow-up procedure.

The teachers also reported that the test had met with approval by their colleagues. They particularly appreciated the opportunity of sharing with the student the responsibility for evaluation. They also thought that the diagnostic information provided by the outcome of the self-assessment could be a valuable help in their efforts to design adequate syllabuses and to individualize instruction. It was also regarded as a great advantage that, contrary to some other evaluation instruments, the content of this test could be discussed with the student, which must have a beneficial effect on learning.

Some Problems and Future Plans

One of the major problems of the test is that, if taken and followed up in class, it interferes with other classroom activities. Therefore, it is important that in the planning of a course sufficient time should be assigned to the use of the test. One possibility for avoiding clashes between self-assessment and other classroom activities would be to allow students to do the job at home, which, of course, presupposes appropriate instructions about the test, its purpose and use. Another suggestion was that, in order to make the follow-up less time-consuming for the teacher, a complete key to test items should be made available for the students. Although this would be desirable, and also possible with several types of items, it would hardly be viable with others, especially where the only proper key would be translation. Since we are dealing with a multilingual target group with more than a hundred different native languages this is practically impossible and should be limited to the vernaculars of some of the largest national groups.

Among the problems to be solved we can mention the need for a better computer program, tailored to the assessment of the difficulty levels of our test items. This is important if we are to succeed in improving the battery with regard to the difficulty levels of the various sub-tests.

As for the use of the test it is imperative that the results should only be used for diagnostic purposes in order to assist the student in the learning process. Rewarding or penalizing students on the basis of their results would prevent them from giving honest answers and would jeopardize the beneficial effects of the procedure. We also believe that the test should be made part of a continuous diagnostic procedure, which implies that it should be taken at regular intervals during the course. In this way the test could not only provide the student and the teacher with up to-date diagnostic information, but also show the student's advance towards his goal-line. Nevertheless, parts of the test that have been used before cannot be taken repeatedly without a loss of reliability. In the ideal situation there should exist two or more parallel versions, the development of which would require, of course, time and financial resources.

A try-out run of the second version of our test is now in progress. After the computation of new data as well as forthcoming conferences with teachers we shall present a final version of the test by the end of the academic year of 1982–83.

The result of pioneer work, our final test may very well suffer from initial deficiencies. The primary aim of our project, however, is not so much to produce a perfect instrument, but rather to find out whether the promising preliminary findings of our experiments with the test described in this paper can be substantiated. If so, our model will hopefully stimulate colleagues to adopt the idea of diagnostic self-assessment tests and to construct new varieties that will best suit the special needs of their own students.

The English Proficiency Test Used in China: A Report

YANG HUI ZHONG AND GUI SHI CHUN

The English Proficiency Test (EPT) is a nation-wide standardized test, the first of its kind in China. It was developed by a group of test-setters under the Education Ministry of the People's Republic of China. The test is designed to provide valid test scores for English proficiency assessment. It has been widely used since 1980.

Background

With the rapid development of the national economy there has been an upsurge in foreign language (especially English) learning in recent years. Students at the secondary and tertiary levels are required to learn at least one foreign language, and the overwhelming majority of them select English. It is estimated that there are roughly 50 to 60 million learners, or potential learners of English, at these levels. Furthermore, no one could give an exact figure for those attending extra-mural English classes. As a result, the need for an English proficiency test (or a series of English proficiency tests) which can measure and thereby certify the different levels of English learners began to be felt. At colleges and universities an academic degree system is being adopted. The degree system also requires a test to certify the degree candidate's English proficiency.

China is currently sending thousands of scholars of science and technology to study abroad. We need a nation-wide standardized test to help select candidates. It would be extremely uneconomical for them to spend time in English-speaking countries merely learning the language.

An English proficiency test can also solve the problem of assessing the achievement of English learners in a variety of courses which ostensibly have the same subject-matter but actually vary considerably in content and rationale. Both teachers and learners in these extra-mural classes would welcome the introduction of an English proficiency test which would represent some official or semi-official recognition of their achievement.

More important, we are aware of the inadequacies of current English language teaching and learning in China: too much emphasis is laid on the teaching of the forms of English rather than the use of English. The introduction of an English proficiency test will eventually have some beneficial influence on ELT in China. We hope to achieve this reorientation in ELT in China by amalgamating syllabus design and test design.

A special group has been set up under the Education Ministry to design a standardized test which will hopefully meet these needs.

The Purpose and Formats of EPT

EPT consists of two papers with five sections in total. Paper One includes grammatical structure, vocabulary and reading comprehension, and cloze. It is designed to measure the English language ability of university and college graduates who have at least 2 years of service English and some follow-up training in reading ability. It is also appropriate for intermediate-level extra-mural English programmes. The testees are expected to know the rudiments of English grammar and have a vocabulary size of a little more than 5,000 common English words. They are also expected to understand mature reading materials of the kinds designed in general college courses. Paper Two includes listening comprehension and guided writing. It is designed to measure the English language ability of those who intend to pursue further studies abroad as postgraduates in any subjects other than the English language. The testees are expected to comprehend short statements and dialogues (as spoken by native speakers of English). They should also be able to manipulate the grammatical structures occurring in spoken and written English. Those who intend to study abroad will be evaluated according to the results of both Paper One and Paper Two.

At present EPT is mainly used for this purpose.

Format of Paper One

	Sections	No. of Questions	No. of Marks	Time (in m.)
I.	Grammatical Structure			
	Part A	10	10	10
	Part B	10	10	10
II.	Vocabulary and Reading Comprehension			
	Part A	20	20	15
	Part B	40	40	45
III.	Cloze Test	20	20	20
	Total	100	100	100

Format of Paper Two

	Sections	No. of Questions	No. of Marks	Time (in m.)
IV.	Listening Comprehension			
	Part A	20	20	30
	Part B	15	15	
V.	Guided Writing	1 (or 2)	25	30
	Total	36 (or 37)	60	60

Some Major Conclusions

For the development of an English proficiency test in China, it is necessary to lay down some underlying principles as starting points:

(1) EPT is a proficiency test rather than an achievement test. The content of an achievement test is defined by a particular syllabus or course book. Since EPT is a nation-wide standardized test and since the testees may have followed English programmes which vary considerably in content and rationale, it should be a proficiency test in nature. In China, where the educational system is very much a centralized one, there have been some objections to the idea of not setting the test in accordance with a particular syllabus, but the belief has gained ground that EPT should keep to a standard not lower than the current standardized English tests used abroad, so that educationalists at home and abroad have some common ground for the evaluation of Chinese students' English proficiency.

(2) EPT is basically an objective test rather than a subjective one. EPT may involve tens of thousands of testees and a great number of test markers. To ensure the reliability of the test and the uniqueness of the scoring, EPT has got to be an objective one. To compensate for the shortcomings of discrete-point tests, two sections – Cloze and Guided Writing – have been incorporated into EPT. These two test forms are usually classified as subjective. To lessen the degree of dependence on the examiner's subjective judgement, we use Guided Writing instead of free composition, and modified Cloze with M-C items instead of the classic form with mechanical deletions.

(3) EPT is a standardized test that will be administered regularly on scheduled dates every year. It must be tried out on random samples of the population for whom it is intended. Statistics must first show that it is both reliable and valid. Ease of administering and scoring must be taken into consideration because the test will be given simultaneously in various centres throughout China. It is hoped that it will be monitored and recognized by other institutions abroad. The level of the test should not be lowered and no pass-fail distinctions will be made. EPT should be norm-referenced so that it may reflect the normal distribution of English language ability among the population of testees.

Some Statistical Analysis

EPT has been administered two to three times every year since 1980 in different centres throughout China. The testees are mainly scientists and technologists who intend to pursue further studies abroad. Table 1 is the percentile rank of testees from Southern and Central China who took part in one of the three tests administered in 1980 and 1981. Figure 1 is a corresponding histogram showing the normal distribution of test results. This seems to indicate that EPT has a fairly high discrimination power.

The two papers of EPT have an adequate level of difficulty. Table 2 is a comparison, in terms of the percentage of correct answers, between EPT and TOEFL among over 400 testees of 1981 in Beijing, Shanghai and Guangzhou test centres.

A comparison of the difficulty level of the different parts of the test (between EPT and TOEFL) is shown in Table 3.

To investigate the testees' opinion on the level of difficulty of EPT, a questionnaire was prepared and distributed among the testees in December, 1981. 190 answers were collected and analysed as shown in Table 4.

From the mean percentage it can be seen that 43.4% of the testees hold that EPT is appropriate in its difficulty level, while 32% think that EPT is fairly easy. In other words,

Table 1. *EPR Percentile Rank*

Score Range	Frequency	Cumulative Frequency	Percentile Rank
156–160			
151–155			
146–150	1	494	99.9
141–145	i	493	99.7
136–140	1	492	99.4
131–135	16	491	98
126–130	29	475	93
121–125	41	446	86
116–120	64	405	75
111–115	47	341	64
106–110	54	294	54
101–105	52	240	43
96–100	37	188	34
91–95	28	151	28
86–90	25	123	22
81–85	22	98	18
76–80	24	76	13
71–75	17	52	9
66–70	11	35	6
61–65	9	24	4
56–60	6	15	2
51–50	7	9	1
under 50	2	2	0.2

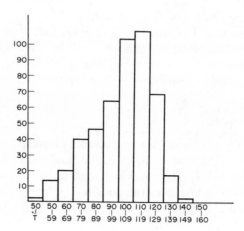

Fig. 1

Table 2

	Percentage of Correct Answers for EPT	Percentage of Correct Answers for TOEFL
Beijing	68	68
Shanghai	71	68
Guangzhou	63	63

Table 3

	Difficulty Level for EPT	Difficulty Level for TOEFL
Listening Comprehension	57.4%	48%
Vocabulary & Reading Comprehension	67.8%	68.3%
Cloze	72 %	—
Guided Writing	38.7%	—
Average	63%	63%

Table 4

	Easy	Fairly Easy	Appropriate	Difficult	Fairly Difficult	No Opinion
Gram. Structure	19%	38%	33%	4%	2%	4%
Vocabulary & Reading Comp.	6%	29%	54%	7%	2%	2%
Cloze	10%	39%	40%	8%	1%	2%
Listening Comp.	6%	25%	46%	20%	2%	1%
Guided Writing	11%	29%	44%	12%	2%	2%

75.4% of the testees regard EPT as appropriate or fairly easy. Only 11.8% of the testees think that EPT is difficult or fairly difficult.

Table 5 is the correlation matrix of the different sections within EPT. The Table shows that Section II (Vocabulary and Reading Comprehension) has the highest correlation coefficient with the total. This indicates that Section II best reflects the testee's English performance and that ELT practice in China is centred on developing the learner's reading ability. Section V (Guided Writing) has the lowest correlation coefficient with the total score. This indicates the marking inconsistencies on the part of the examiners and that, in ESP/EST practice in China, productive skills have traditionally been given little emphasis.

The practice of the last 2 years has shown that EPT correlates fairly highly with TOEFL. Table 6 is the correlation matrix between two EPT and two TOEFL tests.

Table 5

	Gram. Structure (I)	Vocab. and R. Comp. (II)	Cloze (III)	List. Comp. (IV)	Guided Writing (V)	Total (VI)
(I)	—	.70	.62	.55	.08	.77
(II)	.70	—	.66	.67	.25	.92
(III)	.62	.66	—	.64	.21	.81
(IV)	.55	.67	.64	—	.17	.80
(V)	.08	.25	.21	.17	—	.39
(VI)	.77	.92	.81	.80	.39	—

Table 6

	EPT (Sample) (I)	EPT (Ml) (II)	TOEFL (Sample) (III)	TOEFL (December) (IV)
(I)	—	.86	.86	.85
(II)	.86	—	.86	.86
(III)	.86	.86	—	.87
(IV)	.85	.86	.87	—

With such a high correlation coefficient an EPT score may be used to predict a testee's TOEFL score.

A factor analysis was completed recently which seems to reveal that EPT measures more linguistic abilities than TOEFL does, though some of the factors are identical. ETS reports (TOEFL Research Reports, 6, Dec. 1980 – see Table 7) that, for Chinese examinees, items with the highest factor loadings include Grammatical Structure, Written Expression, and Reading Comprehension for the first factor; Listening Comprehension for the second; and Vocabulary for the third. For EPT (see Table 8) the first factor manifests itself on Vocabulary and Reading Comprehension, and Listening; the second on Grammatical Structure, Vocabulary and Reading Comprehension; and the third on Cloze and Guided Writing. This is because, in comparison with TOEFL, EPT has incorporated in it certain elements of productive skills.

Table 7. *Language Goup: Chinese*

	n	I	II		III	IV	
Listening Comprehension	50	8	37		4	1	
Structure	14	8	1		4	1	
Written Expression	25	16	1		6	2	
Vocabulary	30	7	0		23	0	
Reading Comprehension	30	26	0		2	2	
Variance		17.2	13.1		8.6	3.0	
Roots	33.0| 3.9	3.4	1.9	1.6	1.5	1.4	1.3
Trace	48.72						

$\Sigma h^2 = 42.18$

Table 8

	I	Factor II	III
Grammatical Structure	.30	.68	.30
Vocabulary and Reading Comprehension	.67	.53	.18
Cloze	.32	.40	.52
Listening Comprehension	.78	.20	.26
Guided Writing	.36	.30	.56
Contribution of Factor	1.39	1.03	.77
Percentage	27.7%	20.5%	15.3%
Total Percentage		63.5%	

The Future

Until now EPT has mainly been used to help select scholars who aim to study overseas. It has, nevertheless, already produced a positive influence on the teaching of English in China. As the first nation-wide standardized test it is welcomed by most English teachers. They believe that EPT will play a part in the reorientation of teaching outlook, in the design of syllabuses and in the development of materials. To validate the test, however, more research has to be conducted concerning: the right proportion of items on productivity and on receptivity; the right proportion of integrative skills items and discrete-point items; types of Cloze tests and their forms; effects of multiple-choice items on the classroom practice of English teaching, etc. A computer-assisted item analysis system is yet to be developed. We believe that EPT will make its own contribution to ELT practice in China.

Experiments in Large-scale Vocabulary Testing

ARNE ZETTERSTEN

In this paper I am introducing some experiments in vocabulary testing which I carried out in various Scandinavian countries. The purpose of my experiments was to find methods by which large populations could be tested. The main investigation was an experiment to compare the English vocabulary proficiency of first-year students of English at universities in Denmark, Finland, Norway, and Sweden. In addition to the various statistical results reached by means of the computer programme, I paid particular attention to item analysis, with a view to criticizing as much as possible my own choice of test words.

In order to get a varied picture of the means of testing large populations, I also used similar methods with the following techniques:

(1) Self-testing with the aid of Videotex (or Viewdata).
(2) Testing vocabulary on the microcomputer (homecomputer).
(3) Testing for specific purposes (TSP) using teletext in TV-programmes.

The best-known cross-national study of achievement in English connected with Scandinavia is the project organized by the International Association for the Evaluation of Educational Achievement (IEA), which started in 1965 and took the form of intensive research conducted in ten countries over some 7 years. The participating countries were Belgium (French region), Chile, the Federal Republic of Germany, Finland, Hungary, Israel, Italy, the Netherlands, Sweden, and Thailand. This study was part of a comprehensive programme which examined six major subject areas – Science, Reading Comprehension, Literature, Civics Education, French as a Foreign Language, and English as a Foreign Language – in over twenty countries. The aim of this extensive study was to examine the differences in achievement between students, schools, and countries.

One of the results gained by the English study was that "cross-national comparisons of achievement in English are possible provided that great care is taken in the construction of the instruments" (Lewis-Massad, 1975, p. 296). This statement may seem self-evident enough, but it is also necessary to emphasize the fact that not only the test instruments but also the types of data analysed in a cross-national study must be identical or nearly identical.

What I called the main investigation was a multiple-choice test scored by computer. The test consists of 120 English words divided into six different groups corresponding to six different frequency bands of English words. These frequency bands are related to different school levels. For each English word there are five different translations (or choices), one of which is correct. This one, called the key, is definitely correct or more suitable than the others. The choice that the scorer assumes to be the correct one is marked on an answer sheet which is read by an optical scanner.

The computer programme provides the following statistics:

67

(1) A survey of answers given, numbers of correct answers, scores and z-scores. The z-score is a coefficient indicating the student's result in relation to the mean score and standard deviation.
(2) A survey showing the right or wrong answers of the individual students.
(3) The results of six sub-groups.
(4) A survey showing:
   Number of students
   Number of parts or sub-groups
   Number of questions (total and no. for each sub-group)
   Grading of the importance of the individual sub-group
   Mean score
   Standard deviation
   Maximum result
   Minimum result
   $K - R$ (20) = the Kuder-Richardson formula 20, which is a reliability coefficient indicating the precision of the test.
(5) Histogram showing the distribution of the z-scores.
(6) Item analysis indicating percentage of answers for each of the five alternatives under each item. A discrimination coefficient $R(P - BIS)$ for each item is also indicated.

The test was given to various student groups in the various Nordic countries. Some Danish teachers' training colleges and schools were tested in the same period.

The investigation can therefore be divided into two parts, namely:

(I) *Cross-national comparisons*, showing the results of the main study, i.e. the vocabulary proficiency of students of English at universities in Denmark, Finland, Norway, and Sweden.
(II) *National comparisons*, showing the results of certain pilot studies in schools and teachers' training colleges in Denmark, and results from institutes for distance education in Sweden.

The investigation yielded the following results. In other words, the following average raw scores were reached by the groups under study:

(I) *Cross-national comparisons*

University of Copenhagen, Denmark	65.4
University of Jyväskylä, Finland	64.5
Åbo Akademi, Finland	60.0
University of Oslo, Norway	67.8
University of Lund, Sweden	69.7

(II) *National comparisons*
Denmark:

Royal Danish School of Education Studies	80.5
Blågård Teachers' Training College 3 II	63.8
Blågård Teachers' Training College 2 II	65.8
Frederiksberg Teachers' Training College	47.4

Herlev State Grammar School	41.3
Rødovre Statsskole, Language Stream	38.8
Rødovre Statsskole, Mathematics Stream	36.0
Rødovre Statsskole, Higher Preliminary Examination	29.9

Sweden:

Distance Education, Hermods, course A1	77.7
Distance Education, Hermods, course AB1	88.2

The conclusion drawn from the cross-national comparison is that the first-year students of English in Denmark, Finland, Norway, and Sweden have roughly the same knowledge of English vocabulary. In the case of the national comparisons, it is interesting to note that the difference in results seems to reflect fairly well the existing difference in experience and teaching hours between the individual student groups.

Owing to the fact that "translating" a multiple-choice vocabulary test from one language into another creates quite a number of problems, the general recommendation for the use of a vocabulary test in a cross-national examination is that one should apply the test as a part of a *test battery*, not as a discrete-point test used in isolation.

There are, however, other problems connected with the use of a vocabulary test which must be taken into account when comparisons between groups of students are made. The following problems are the most obvious ones:

(a) The populations can sometimes be too small for a statistical study
(b) Differences in the background of students can make all kinds of comparison difficult
(c) The test situations may not be absolutely identical.

In addition to the main conclusion that university students in Scandinavia have roughly the same knowledge of English vocabulary, the following general observations can be made:

(1) Owing to the differences between languages (e.g. in respect of semantic fields) a cross-national comparison is more problematic than a national one. A national comparison between results from various provinces, cities, schools, etc., can be most useful.
(2) Like most multiple-choice tests, this test seems to possess the qualities that according to Lado (1961, pp. 31–32) are desirable in a practical test: scorability, economy, and administrability.
(3) This type of test would be particularly useful for measuring the vocabulary comprehension of large populations, e.g. for entrance exams for universities, for teachers' colleges, for students who are going to study abroad, etc.
(4) It might also be used for testing special vocabulary, for example technical vocabulary in various branches of industry.

One major disadvantage of this type of multiple-choice vocabulary test is the fact that we are not provided with any context whatsoever. It would of course be easy to provide a list of 120 sentences and to add four not quite successful synonyms as distractors to one word in each of these 120 sentences. Some part of the artificial nature of this context-free multiple-choice test would then be eliminated. The same computer programme could be used for the marking.

Another disadvantage is the complexity of the distractors. By looking at the print-out of the *item analysis* we can judge if an item is too easy or too difficult. If we give the same test to various levels of students of English, one and the same item will vary a great deal with regard to discrimination. Sometimes the distractors are not sufficiently well chosen and one begins to wonder how often one is actually testing the students' ability to identify distractors rather than to identify the exact meaning of a certain word.

The multiple-choice test used is based on a word bank with fixed choices kept at the Gothenburg Computing Centre, Sweden. The underlying principle of this type of vocabulary test is that, if the selection of items is related to the frequencies of the words, it is possible to measure the *range* of a person's vocabulary.

The items are chosen randomly within each frequency band. The 120 words represent six categories of words corresponding to parts I–VI in the vocabulary test. The number of words belonging to each level is indicated below:

(1) Below the Swedish "Gymnasium": from grade 7 and up: 2,700 words
(2) Grade 1 of the "Gymnasium" (G 1), which is the tenth school year
(3) Grade 2 of the "Gymnasium" (G 2)
(4) Grade 3 of the "Gymnasium" (G 3). The total no. of compulsory words on the "Gymnasium" level is 2,400.
(5) Extra words for the "Gymnasium" level (marked + in Thoren): 1,700 words
(6) The year after the "Gymnasium", e.g. at a teachers' training college (words marked X in Thoren): 2,800 words.

I referred earlier to the item analysis and I should like to take a close look at some of the statistical results of individual items in order to explain how one can improve on the choice of words or phrases.

If, for example, a word among the first twenty items was answered correctly only by a small minority of the students in category 1, one may suspect that something is the matter with the distractors. One of the distractors may be too close to the correct answer; or, as in the case of item 9 *pitch*, the correct answer (B) is a verb forming part of a phrase *to pitch a tent*, which makes the item unusually complicated. The table below shows the poor result of this item (in percentages).

Table 1

Item	Copenhagen	Jyväskylä	Åbo	Oslo	Lund
Pitch	5.3	13.4	14.3	15.9	10.5

In a case like this the correct answer should have been expressed differently or the item should have been exchanged.

By looking at the words answered correctly by 0–20% of the students, we realize what words caused real problems among the five student groups.

Table 2(a)

University of Copenhagen

Part I	Part II	Part III	Part IV	Part V	Part VI
pitch (5.3)	bound (4.6)		exploit (12.5) précis (17.8)	bask (11.8) dingy (19.1) venerable (15.4)	accost (11.2) brimstone (19.1) common room (2.0) debauch (7.9) jolt (15.1) locket (13.2) plod (7.2) plummet (17.8) squall (19.1) treacle (17.8)

Table 2(b)

University of Jyväskylä

Part I	Part II	Part III	Part IV	Part V	Part VI
pitch (13.4)	bound (3.0)	dispatch (11.9) diversion (3.0) hearth (17.9)	inasmuch as (1.5) précis (13.4) premier (10.4) thrush (16.4)	cue (14.9) decorous (6.0) flaw (7.5) sever (13.4) verdant (17.9)	accost (15.4) brimstone (6.0) common room (11.9) debauch (14.9) filibuster (6.0) jolt (16.4) locket (10.4) plod (7.5) seemly (3.0) squall (6.0) swathe (13.4) treacle (17.9)

Table 2(c)

Åbo Akademi

Part I	Part II	Part III	Part IV	Part V	Part VI
pitch (14.3)	bound (0.0)	accumulate (14.3) dispatch (0.0) diversion (0.0)	inasmuch as (7.1) précis (14.3) premier (0.0) repeal (7.1) valve (14.3)	decorous (0.0) dingy (7.1) sever (7.1) venerable (7.1)	accost (7.1) brimstone (7.1) common room (0.0) filibuster (7.1) jolt (7.1) lime (7.1) loot (7.1) marital (14.3) plod (14.3) seemly (0.0) squall (7.1) swathe (14.3) treacle (0.0)

Table 2(d)

University of Oslo

Part I	Part II	Part III	Part IV	Part V	Part VI
pitch (16.9)	bound (6.8)	diversion (13.6)	rogue (13.6)	bask (1.7)	accost (5.1)
				decorous (11.9)	brimstone (1.7)
				sever (15.3)	common room (5.1)
					debauch (16.9)
					filibuster (10.2)
					jolt (18.6)
					lime (16.9)
					locket (11.9)
					treacle (15.3)

Table 2(e)

University of Lund

Part I	Part II	Part III	Part IV	Part V	Part VI
pitch (10.5)	bound (7.0)		exploit (19.3)	bask (14.0)	brimstone (15.8)
			inasmuch as (10.5)	venerable (15.8)	debauch (8.8)
			précis (12.3)		plod (5.3)
			premier (12.3)		seemly (19.3)

Besides *pitch* (in Part I) and *brimstone* (Part VI), *bound* (Part II) is the only item where less than 20% had a correct answer in all the five student groups. The reason for the low scores here is the fact that the phrase *is bound to* has led the students to associate the verb *bound* (= "jump, leap, bounce") with choice E instead of the correct choice C. Choice E is a verb meaning "force", which is obviously misleading in this particular case.

It is obvious that you can improve the selection of test items by analysing the results in this manner. I have chosen these examples in order to illustrate the possibilities if you use a similar computer programme.

The same type of vocabulary test can of course be applied, even if you don't use computer scoring, the difference being that you wouldn't have any statistics or item analysis at your disposal in such a case.

In order to open up new possibilities for large-scale vocabulary testing, some experiments were also made with different media. The following techniques were used in these experiments:

(1) *Videotex* (or *Viewdata*) by which the viewer is connected with a data-base through the telephone system using a TV-monitor, a modem, and a terminal or key-board. This is the system known as Prestel in Britain.

(2) A *microcomputer*, in this case the Swedish ABC 80 and ABC 800.

(3) *Teletext*, run by TV-companies, is a system of using the extra lines on the TV-screen which are not needed to transmit the TV-programmes.

The following experiments were carried out and the following conclusions as to the applicability of the systems were drawn:

(i) On the *Videotex* system a series of pictures showing 20 words were shown. The words were taken from a corpus of 10,000 words. One progresses in the test system according to one's ability to identify the words indicated on the screen. It was obvious that the system was suitable for self-testing. The result for each individual was a statement indicating the range of his vocabulary. The number of pages one can send with Videotex is nearly unlimited, but the users of Videotex or Viewdata are so far mainly business companies and organizations.

(ii) Similar tests of English grammar and vocabulary were applied to the *microcomputer* for use in schools. Such tests can be used for self-testing or in a classroom situation under the guidance of a teacher. If a printer is applied to the microcomputer, the print-out can be kept and used as the result of a diagnostic self-test or even as an exam result.

(iii) In the *Teletext* system there are only a few pages at one's disposal for a language test. The advantage is that you can reach a great many users at one time. In a distance education programme a diagnostic test can be announced at a given moment. There is also the possibility of combining two media. If you receive your test by Teletext, the results could be sent in by Videotex to an institute for distance education.

To sum up then, I have drawn attention to five ways of carrying out large-scale vocabulary testing, namely:

(1) A multiple-choice system using computer-scoring and a detailed item analysis.
(2) The same test using manual scoring and no item analysis.
(3) Videotex testing.
(4) Microcomputer testing.
(5) Teletext testing.

My views on the applicability of the five methods can be summed up as follows:

(1) The first system is usable when the aim is to test the vocabulary proficiency of large populations and when comparisons between schools, communities, provinces, or even entire countries are desired.
(2) If computers are not available, manual scoring can still be applied, but the results will be quite limited in scope and the statistics almost non-existent.
(3) Videotex (or Viewdata) testing is suitable for self-testing, the great advantage being the large number of pages at one's disposal.
(4) Microcomputer testing is suitable for self-testing but it can also be used in an examination situation in schools.
(5) Teletext is suitable for self-testing as well, or as information or instruction for users who combine teletext with a test based on a different technique, e.g. microcomputers (home-computers). Teletext testing is ideal in combination with specialized TV programmes for language instruction. In this case Teletext testing becomes an efficient method of TSP (Testing for Special Purposes).

Naturally, there are several different ways of testing large populations in the case of vocabulary proficiency. There are, for example, various types of tele-software: combinations of media which will become quite attractive within the near future.

3
Testing Oral Proficiency

Some Basic Considerations in Testing Oral Proficiency

RANDALL L. JONES

During the past two decades the language teaching profession has witnessed a remarkable change in attitude towards the testing of oral language proficiency. In Robert Lado's book *Language Testing*, which appeared in 1961, we were admonished *not* to measure a person's speaking ability directly through a face-to-face test. Such a procedure, he claimed, was not only inaccurate, but also unnecessary. Lado offered as a substitute less direct but more controllable means for assessing oral proficiency; for example, multiple-choice tests of phoneme discrimination, vocabulary, grammar and morphology (1961, pp. 239–47). But Lado was by no means a lone voice crying in the wilderness. He was a pioneer, to be sure, but he was essentially reflecting what was the accepted theory in language testing at that time.

By comparison, direct testing today is becoming very commonplace. This fact was made very clear to me about 3 years ago when my colleague, Harold Madsen, and I made a survey of existing oral tests. Expecting to find just a few, we were astonished to find information about more than a hundred (Madsen and Jones, p. 16). I am certain that the quantity would be even more impressive today. Recently there have been numerous papers, articles, books and even entire conferences dedicated to oral testing. Was Lado wrong? Perhaps. Or maybe he was right and a number of us insist on experimenting just a bit more before we finally admit that we should have listened to him more carefully in the first place.

I would like to suggest that Lado was neither right nor wrong. Or perhaps he was both right *and* wrong: right for his day and purpose, but wrong for today. A great deal has changed in the language teaching profession during the past 20 years. Lado was writing primarily to an audience who were for the most part engaged in what could be called "academic" language teaching and testing. Testing existed primarily to serve the needs of teaching. Its function was to assist with student placement, grading and program evaluation. Language testing as a means of predicting success in real-life situations was simply not as important.

Since then, however, more attention has been paid to problems of language performance, for example: the English language proficiency possessed by international graduate student teaching assistants at universities in the United States (Jones, 1979a, p. 55); the deficiency in English of many foreign medical specialists practising in the United States, Canada and Great Britain (van Naerssen, 1978); the language work of the Council of Europe and the resulting concept of a functional/notional language teaching syllabus (van Ek and Alexander, 1977, pp. 5–14); the decision on the part of several examining boards in Great Britain to include an oral component in their tests (ARELS); the realization on the part of the government in the Federal Republic of Germany that the language needs of "guest workers" and their families would have to be addressed; the increasing use of English as an official language – especially in Education – in countries such as Singapore; the trend towards teaching for communicative competence (Jones,

77

1981, pp. 109–10); the increased popularity of Language for Special Purposes; and numerous other current practices in the language teaching profession.

But as the point of departure for my discussion on oral testing I do not wish to begin with recent trends, nor do I intend to dwell on Robert Lado and his admonition concerning oral testing. Rather, I would like to go back to 1956, the year the Foreign Service Institute (FSI) of the U.S. Department of State began experimenting with a more direct means of measuring the oral proficiency of its Foreign Service Officers (Jones, 1979b). This procedure has come to be known as the FSI Oral Interview. I emphasize here that I am *not* suggesting that this was the beginning of oral testing in the history of the world. The evaluation of second language proficiency through simulated conversation is a very obvious thing, and has probably been practised in some form for many centuries. I use the FSI example for three reasons: (1) it has served as the model or at least the point of departure for numerous other attempts at oral language testing; (2) it is the most documented of any oral testing procedure that I am aware of; and (3) in my estimation the FSI Oral Interview comes closer to meeting its defined purpose than any other procedure of its kind. Let me elaborate on number (3) for a few moments. All considerations of cost aside, the FSI Oral Interview has served the United States Foreign Service very well over the past 25 years. In my estimation it has, to a very high degree of accuracy, done precisely what it was designed to do. It has changed very little over the past two decades. I suggest that this fortunate state of affairs is only *partly* by design, but to a large degree the result of fortuitous circumstances. The measurement instrument is working well almost in spite of itself.

I mentioned earlier that the FSI Oral Interview has been imitated more than just a few times. Unfortunately, it has not always been as kind to its borrowers as it has to the original owner. In most cases the results have not been impressive and in some instances they have been nothing short of disastrous. There are, I feel, several important reasons for this unfortunate problem. Some very basic considerations are often ignored when a decision is made to develop or adopt an oral testing procedure. If we examine the published information about oral testing during the past 10 years, we find that the majority of articles deal with the question of validity and reliability. These are important areas to be sure, but we should not overlook what it is that contributes to these two factors.

Purpose

The first and perhaps most important consideration is that of purpose. It may be dwelling on the obvious to even mention it, but I fear that it is often overlooked. The purpose of developing the FSI interview was very clear, and the work was done with this purpose in mind. But the needs of the U.S. Foreign Service are not the same as the needs of, say, the average American high school or college language program. Nonetheless, there have been attempts to use the FSI Oral Interview – basically just as it is used by the State Department – in high school and college language programs. The test obviously has high face validity, and thus it appears to many to be a good choice for any oral testing situation. Unfortunately it has not worked very well and, as a result, some language teachers have become critical of the FSI Oral Interview in general, without realizing that it was the *application* of the instrument and *not* the instrument itself that is at fault. Using an analogy of John Oller, it is a bit like trying to use a toothbrush to paint a house, then criticizing the toothbrush because it does not work very well.

Before any test or testing instrument is used or developed, the purpose for which it is to be used must be clearly established. The instrument must fit the need. In the case of improper applications in the use of the FSI Oral Interview in non-government programs, the implicit need is probably the conviction on the part of the teachers that some kind of oral testing instrument is needed if oral production is one of the objectives of the course. In my own personal opinion the FSI Oral Interview in its conventional form is *not* a good choice for most academic language programs. In recent literature we are seeing more and more reference made to "modified" FSI tests, or "FSI-type" tests. This says a lot. How much modification is allowed before the result is no longer even a close relative of the original? Is there really a need to begin with the FSI format at all? Many of the tests that Harold Madsen and I examined obviously did not use the FSI as a starting point. Many of the oral tests that have been described in recent literature have been developed on the basis of a needs assessment. In my opinion this is the unavoidable first step.

Before leaving the topic of test purpose, I would like to point out that in some cases a needs assessment might reveal that an oral test is really not desirable. Perhaps the purpose could be accomplished by using a less costly instrument. Or perhaps only a certain subgroup of students need to be evaluated for oral proficiency.

Resources

The next important consideration is that of available resources. The FSI Oral Interview is, quite frankly, a very expensive instrument, more expensive than most schools or universities can afford. The associated expense is one of the reasons for the modifications mentioned earlier. Instead of two examiners for 30 minutes with a concealed tape recorder, it will have to be one examiner for 5 minutes with no tape recorder. I am not suggesting that a reduction in cost will necessarily mean a corresponding reduction in quality and effectiveness. It is convenient to have two examiners, especially if one of them is mainly involved with elicitation and the other with scoring. But that is, of course, the Rolls Royce model, which most of us cannot afford. I also feel, however, that we cannot afford to ignore oral testing, if for no other reason than the backwash effect. Oral tests can be shorter, administered less frequently, and even be group oral tests. In our German Program at Brigham Young University (BYU) we administer oral tests to all students in each of three levels four times per semester. With an average enrolment of approximately 400 students per semester, this adds up to about 1,600 individual oral German tests each semester. The tests are for the most part administered by the instructors and last for 3–5 minutes, depending on the level. The attitude of language programs with regard to oral testing should not be, can I afford to measure oral proficiency?, but rather, what kind of oral testing program can I afford?

The Essence of an Oral Test

It is important to distinguish between a structured oral test, such as the one contained in the ARELS Examination, and an interview procedure, such as the FSI. Each has its own advantages and disadvantages. A structured test consists of a standard set of stimuli and explicit instructions to the examinee as to how to respond to them. There is generally little if any interaction with an examiner. The structured oral test is generally used for two reasons. First, it is easily adapted for administration in a language laboratory. All instructions can be printed or recorded. The examinee simply has to read (or listen to) the items and respond to them. (This type of oral test is sometimes referred to as a semi-direct oral test.) The second reason for using a structured oral test is because it is more standardized. All examinees respond to an identical set of questions, and the responses are quite easy to compare against a set of accepted answers.

The interview procedure is always a live test and has the advantage of more closely approximating real language behaviour. I purposely avoid the use of "unstructured" oral test, because there must be a certain amount of structure in it. The important fact to keep in mind here is that an oral interview is in a strict sense of the word *not* a test but a *testing procedure*. A structured oral test is generally robust and does not require a trained examiner. It can be sent to remote testing sites to be administered. An interview procedure requires extensive training. It is fragile and it is in constant need of fine tuning. One might say that it is similar to a rumour in that, as it is passed on from one point to the next, it can assume a slightly different form. Group A trains Group B, which in turn trains Group C, etc. But Group A does not recognize what Group F is doing.

One need not be discouraged. In my opinion the interview test is the highest form of oral testing, and the only one into which performance can be structured.

Examiner/Examinee Relation

In 1972 and 1973 I spent several months observing oral interviews at the FSI and CIA in Washington. During this time I witnessed more than 100 tests in about fifteen languages. I was struck by the fact that there was seldom any apparent anxiety on the part of the examinees. One of the criticisms of direct oral testing that I have frequently heard is that it is anxiety inducing. I came to the conclusion after observing these many oral tests that this claim was an unfounded assumption. This observation was further substantiated by oral testing research done at BYU and elsewhere.

In a talk I gave at an IUS (Interuniversitäre Sprachtestgruppe) language testing symposium in Darmstadt in 1980, I boldly made the claim that an oral testing situation was rarely anxiety inducing. During the discussion a young woman took strong issue with this claim, and reported that when her pupils – all teenagers – had to take an oral language test they became extremely disturbed, and their performance was obviously affected by this anxiety. So much for my bold claim! In thinking about this after the IUS Symposium an important realization came to mind that I had previously overlooked. At the FSI and CIA and to a lesser extent at BYU, the examiners *and* the examinees were in almost all cases upper middle-class educated adults. There was a close social fit. These were people who could easily strike up a conversation as strangers on an airplane or waiting in a line. The affective barrier was very low, as Krashen might say. I was reminded of a statement William Labov made about the difficulty he and his research team first encountered in getting some of their informants to speak. Upper middle-class educated white adults were encountering problems communicating with young blacks from the ghetto. I was also reminded of the experiences I once had in driving baby sitters home – young girls of about 13–15 years old. "Well how are things going at school?" "Oh fine, I guess." "What's your favorite class?" "Oh, I dunno." (pause) "How are your mom and dad doing?" "O.K." It was always the longest two-mile drive I could remember.

All of this points to the fact that ease of elicitation in an oral interview is often affected by the social relationship between the examiner and the examinee. The factors can include age, race, social class, education and professicn. These problems are sometimes to be accepted as one of the hazards of the profession, but they can, to a certain degree, be overcome. For example, peers can be used when testing teenagers. An adult can be present to observe the performance, but the verbal interaction would be between the examiner and an examinee of the same age. Another possible solution is to use group oral testing, in which a native or high-level "instigator" promotes a discussion among several examinees. Inhibitions which are manifested in a one-to-one situation sometimes dissipate in a group.

Degree of Directness

Just like equality among George Orwell's animals, some direct oral tests are more – or less – direct than others. Every test is to some degree contrived. When I am speaking to one of my students in an oral test and I ask about hobbies or music or what he or she had for breakfast, that student probably knows that I am not terribly interested in learning all this; I merely have a job to perform. A real direct test of a person's oral performance would require surreptitious observation over a period of several days or even weeks. But even the FSI cannot afford that!

So we are reduced to a structured interview in which we try to be as efficient as possible in eliciting the necessary samples. But the interview procedure has a major built-in weakness: it does not easily allow for examinees to use certain structures such as questions and commands, and it does not easily allow for special situations such as are necessary for performance situations. This means that it is sometimes necessary to come down one or two levels in directness. Some testers feel that such techniques are too far removed from what one might find in real language use. From a practical point of view, however, it seems only sensible that the test be moulded to fit the need and not the other way around.

Examinee's Language Learning History

Krashen claims that there is a definite difference between second language learning and second language acquisition, and that this difference is often manifested in the act of using the second language. Even Krashen would agree that few second language learners are the product of *only* learning or acquisition, but most of us are aware of a marked difference between students who have learned virtually all of their language in the classroom and those who have learned it among the people.

This difference has some real implications for testing. A few years ago I was asked to test several students who wanted to "challenge" our introductory German courses. I gave them the same written exams that are used as final exams in our program, and then I gave them each a face-to-face oral test. All of these students had learned German in Germany as dependent children of military or embassy personnel. They had attended German schools and had associated with Germans their age. Not surprisingly, they sounded more like German speakers than did any of the classroom-bred students. Yet they made errors, in some cases more than our classroom products. The obvious problem: How was I to score their performance?

Another problem relating to learning history is the phenomenon sometimes referred to as "terminal" cases. These are people who are turned loose among the natives, so to speak, and come away using the language with a high degree of fluency and a low degree of accuracy. They possess, at least according to some definitions, a great amount of communicative competence. Yet, as they speak, one can notice the real native speakers grimacing with every syllable. It is often difficult to place these hopeless cases on any kind of scale. In most cases they feel that they are really better than a test might judge them to be. After all, "dozens of people in Munich told me that I sound just like a German." All I can say is that we need to return to the first consideration, viz. that of purpose. If there is a high likelihood that the testing program will encounter a large number of such speakers, the scale used will have to be devised in such a way as to accommodate them.

Levels of Proficiency

One of the complaints voiced by high school and university teachers who have used the FSI Oral Interview has been that all of the students seem to get the same score. This is due primarily to the scoring procedure used. The FSI uses an 11-point scale: 0–5 with pluses possible for levels 0–4. After 2 years of a college language program most students do not get beyond 1 +. There is currently a project under way in the United States sponsored by The American Council for the Teaching of Foreign Languages (ACTFL) to refine the FSI levels 0–2 +, or the bottom half of the scale. It would then be more useful for testing graduates of university language programs.

A problem that I have observed among FSI testers concerns the upper levels of the scale: 3 + –5. Possibly because there are so few candidates that are tested at this level, the examinees are often unable to remain sensitive to the differences. I feel that the techniques used for elicitation are also part of the problem. In 1977 I experimented with four techniques that I felt would discriminate well among high-level speakers of a second language (Jones, 1978, pp. 93–96). The performance criterion for FSI level 5 is that of an educated native speaker. I therefore compared five educated native speakers with five high-level non-native speakers. The interview as such did discriminate, but not as precisely as one would have wanted. Three of the four techniques that I used – specialized vocabulary elicited through pictures, elicited imitation, and anecdote retelling – discriminated well between the native and non-native groups, as well as among the individual non-native speakers.

It is doubtful that many testing programs will have need to test across such a wide range of proficiencies as does the FSI. The levels that might be represented, however, need to be considered.

Proficiency and Achievement Tests

One of the problems that caused the "borrowers" of the FSI Oral Interview a good amount of grief is the fact that it is a proficiency test, whereas they are usually interested in measuring achievement. Even though the FSI Oral Interview is used as part of a teaching program, the examiners do not pose their questions in relation to an established syllabus. Instead they are seeking to evaluate general functional ability in the language.

An oral achievement test cannot be an open-ended general conversation. It is necessary to formulate questions in such a way that discrete units of the language are tested. This, of course, affects the naturalness and the direct nature of the test. In an oral proficiency test the examiners can use the response of one question to lead to another. Only occasionally is it necessary to break the flow and move on to a different topic or level. An achievement test, on the other hand, often comes out sounding like an interrogation: What is this? What colour is my shirt? With whom do you often speak on the telephone? What do you plan to do this week-end? Each question is trying to get at a particular feature of the language, and there is usually little time to chat about things in general. Because an achievement test focuses on such a narrow range of language structures, it is possible for a student to prepare for the test, something which is quite difficult in the case of an oral proficiency test. In fact, a teacher might do well to pass out to students preparing for an oral achievement test a list of questions in advance from which the actual test questions are selected. One major drawback about a narrowly focused oral achievement test is that information about what the specific questions are can easily become known to those students who have yet to take the test.

The Evaluation Criterion

The criterion on which the test is to be evaluated relates directly to the first consideration: that of purpose. Unfortunately, this criterion is sometimes lost in the process of administering and scoring the test. Traditionally language tests have focused on language factors: pronunciation, vocabulary, grammar, etc. With a new emphasis on communicative competence and functional ability we have begun to realize that it is possible to communicate effectively and still make a limited number of errors. But this is where the waters begin to become muddied. How does one measure functional communication and how many of which kinds of errors are allowed? Another dimension, that of sociolinguistic competence, makes the situation even more complicated. It is not sufficient to say it *correctly*, but it also has to be *appropriate*!

A very interesting situation with regard to test criterion is the set of level definitions for the FSI Oral Interview. The definitions are phrased in terms of functional ability, but the rating sheet that is used by the examiners is based entirely on language factors: pronunciation, grammar, vocabulary, fluency and comprehension. In fact experienced examiners use neither the definitions nor the rating sheet, and score according to their experience. They simply know what a 1 + or a 3 is.

Global and Discrete Scoring

Depending on the purpose and the defined criteria of the test, the scoring procedure may range from global on the one hand to very discrete on the other. Two processes are implied here: one is the determination of the score, the other the reporting of it. At the one extreme a tester may simply look for an overall impression, then determine that the examinee has either passed or failed. Or the same kind of final score – pass or fail – could be determined by a very complex set of criteria.

Some testing programs choose to assign points to individual items throughout the test. The final score is then the total sum of the points. Others assign points to specific categories, such as pronunciation, grammar, etc. and then total these points to determine the final score. Some tests report a single overall score; others choose to break down the score into various areas.

It is important to keep in mind that totalling points to determine a final score can be very misleading. It is possible that the same score could be arrived at by means of a number of different combinations. Furthermore, important information about individual sub-skills may be lost. Picture, if you will, five glass measuring cups, each containing a quantity of coloured liquid. Each measuring cup represents one of five factors measured by the test, and the quantity of coloured liquid reflects the degree to which the examinee has developed proficiency in that factor. We have a very clear visual image of the examinee's ability in each of the areas. However, if we pour the contents of each cup into a larger glass container in order to determine the composite score, we have a murky substance whose volume can be measured but whose individual characteristics are no longer discernible (Robinson, 1976).

It has been my intention in this presentation to bring out ten important considerations regarding oral testing. I am convinced that the measurement of oral proficiency is not only desirable, but that it is essential. It also becomes very possible if certain carefully outlined procedures are carefully followed.

Simulating an Academic Tutorial: A Test Validation Study

DONALD M. MORRISON AND NANCY LEE

Introduction

The Language Centre of the University of Hong Kong annually administers a battery of tests known collectively as The Language Analysis Sessions (LAS). These are aimed at identifying first-year students in the Arts Faculty whose first language is normally Cantonese and who may be in need of special assistance in English Language Skills. The present paper is concerned with an attempt to validate the oral component of this battery, which in recent years has taken the form of a simulated academic tutorial.[1]

Recent literature on oral proficiency testing (e.g. Morrow, 1978, Carroll, 1980) notes the need for instruments aimed at testing features of authentic communicative activities with direct functional relevance to the context of target language use, rather than features of language restricted primarily to the testing situation itself. This point is particularly meaningful in our context. Formerly, the oral test given by the Language Centre was a traditional face-to-face interview where the candidate's oral ability to communicate within an academic context was checked by only one examiner on the basis of a discussion of a general nature. But, since students were required to use English in tutorials and seminars, where they had to expound ideas and had to be able to argue various points in interaction with each other as well as with teachers, it was suspected that the one-to-one oral interview did not have direct relevance to the context of students' language needs at the University. It was therefore decided to develop a new type of testing instrument which would simulate, as directly as possible, the conditions of an academic tutorial: a teacher-led discussion of an academic topic based on one or more prior reading assignments. To this end we put together sets of short reading passages related to different topics selected for their general interest for different segments of the student population. (This meant that different topics could be used in different testing sessions, thus diminishing the possibility that students would be able to undertake special preparation.)

The three topics chosen for discussion were:

(1) Bilingualism and education
(2) Population density
(3) Motivation in language learning

To simulate the atmosphere of teacher-led group interaction, it was decided to test students in groups of four or five, with one ESL staff member playing the role of "tutor", and two others serving as non-participant evaluators. To encourage interaction and active listening, the reading materials were presented to the students on notecards in jigsaw form, such that each participant had different but overlapping information relevant to the topic.

At the beginning of a test session, the students were given 5 minutes to read, take notes and absorb their portion of the information provided. The tutor conducting the simulated tutorial instructed the candidates that they would have to discuss the information they had read in relation to information that the other testees might have, such as happens in a tutorial, and that they should also be able to offer their own opinions on the subject in the latter part of the session. The cards were then taken back and the students had to rely on their notes to discuss the topic at hand. Whilst one tutor initiated the discussion, two other silent markers as well as the participant tutor began to assess the students' abilities based on the agreed marking scheme (see Fig. 1).

Validation

The resulting test format seemed to provide us with a good sample of the type of language behaviour required in an actual tutorial, and thus allowed us to make better predictions about future performance than appeared to have been possible with the previous, one-to-one interview format.

The validity of a test cannot be satisfactorily established by appearances alone, and a number of potential problems needed to be examined. The present paper focuses on two in particular. Firstly, if the ESL evaluators were basing their judgements of student ability on a sample of language behaviour that was fundamentally different from the type of behaviour required in the target context, it is hard to see how one could be sure that these judgements would be relevant to the expectations of the academic subject teachers.

The second problem is whether the subject teachers themselves would tend to make similar predictions, given the same sample of interactive behaviour. In fact, there was reason to believe that there would be a difference in perspective among the different evaluators, with resulting disagreements about what would constitute an acceptable level of English proficiency. For example, one might expect that ESL teachers would have stricter standards for English "proficiency", grammatical accuracy and pronunciation, whereas the subject teachers would be less concerned with these factors and more concerned with basic communicative ability. We also wondered if there would be any differences between male and female raters and, as both groups included native and non-native speakers of English, we were curious as to whether language background might be a confounding factor. It seemed possible that native speakers of English would have stricter standards. Finally, we were interested in the confidence that the different raters might attach to their ratings of the students being tested. We suspected, for example, that the ESL staff might have more confidence in their ratings of English proficiency, but less in their ability to rate a student's ability to function in an academic environment.

For the purposes of validation, videotapes were made of actual test sessions. From these an approximate stratified sample of three test sessions was selected, representing what was felt to be a cross-section of good, average, and mediocre performances on the part of the students involved.

With these samples in hand, we invited Language Centre (ESL) staff to view the videotapes and record impressions of individual student performance using the marking scheme shown in Fig. 1.

English "proficiency" was defined as referring to the subject's apparent mastery of the English language system, with special attention to grammar, pronunciation and general fluency. The "ability to communicate" category was explained as a means of evaluating the subject's apparent ability to play an active and meaningful role in the exchange and critical analysis of complex ideas and meanings, such as might be expected in an academic discussion. Finally, following Edwards (1979), the evaluators were asked to make a guess

	ASSESSMENT				CERTAINTY				
SCALE	Unsatisfactory	Satisfactory		very good	low		medium		high
ENGLISH PROFICIENCY	1 2	3	4	5	1	2	3	4	5
ABILITY TO COMMUNICATE	1 2	3	4	5	1	2	3	4	5
ACADEMIC POTENTIAL	1 2	3	4	5	1	2	3	4	5

Fig. 1. *Marking Scheme*

at the subject's "academic potential", here defined in terms of the British university marking system, with a "5" indicating potential 1st Class Honours, a score of "4" or "3" for Upper and Lower Second Class Honours, and scores of "2" and "1" for 3rd Class Honours, Pass or Fail. Also following Edwards (1979), the markers were requested to indicate the degree of certainty they attached to their scores on each category.

After data had been collected from nine Language Centre evaluators, letters were sent out to the academic departments in the Arts Faculty where English is used for tutorials, inviting teachers of first-year students to come to the Language Centre, view the videotapes, and record their impressions of student performance, using the same scales as had been used by the ESL teachers. A total of 28 subject teachers eventually viewed the tapes, four each from the Departments of English Studies and Comparative Literature, Geography and Geology, History, Philosophy, Political Science, and Psychology together with Sociology. Two of the teachers from each department were native speakers of English, and two were non-native speakers. Taken together with the ESL teachers, this gave us a total population of 37 markers. Of these, there were 19 native speakers of English and 18 non-native speakers: 26 males and 11 females.

Results

In a search for significant differences in the scores assigned to the twelve students on the sample by the three relevant subcategories of judges, mean scores awarded to the individual students were computed for each group: (1) ESL staff vs. subject teacher; (2) native speaker of English vs. non-native speaker; and (3) male vs. female. The ranked means are presented in Tables 1 to 3.

As can be seen from Table 1, the academic subject teachers tended to award higher scores than the ESL teachers on all three of the parameters: "overall proficiency", "communicative ability" and "academic potential". T-tests for paired observations (Morrison, 1982) confirm that these differences are significant at the .05 level. This does not seem surprising – ESL teachers are paid to be critical of student L2 performance – nor does it in itself constitute a threat to the reliability of the testing instrument, so long as the two groups of markers assign the same *relative* values to the same students. That ESL teachers and subject teachers do in fact tend to agree in their reactions to the performances of the twelve students (as recorded on the videotapes) may be seen by comparing the

Table 1. *Ranked mean scores broken down by departmental affiliation of judges*

Subject	English Proficiency		Communicative Ability		Academic Potential	
	Subject teachers	ESL teachers	Subject teachers	ESL teachers	Subject teachers	ESL teachers
9	4.46 (12)	4.00 (11)	4.61 (12)	4.67 (12)	4.43 (12)	4.22 (12)
1	3.89 (11)	4.22 (12)	3.79 (9)	3.89 (11)	3.64 (11)	3.44 (11)
3	3.79 (10)	3.67 (10)	3.61 (8)	3.44 (10)	3.56 (8)	3.33 (9.5)
7	3.61 (9)	2.89 (8.5)	3.86 (10.5)	3.22 (7)	3.54 (7)	3.22 (8)
2	3.32 (8)	2.78 (6.5)	3.86 (10.5)	3.33 (8.5)	3.57 (9)	3.11 (6)
11	2.96 (7)	2.56 (3.5)	3.46 (6.5)	3.0 (5.5)	3.18 (4)	3.11 (6)
12	2.89 (6)	2.67 (5)	3.0 (2.5)	3.0 (5.5)	2.86 (2)	2.78 (1.5)
6	2.86 (5)	2.89 (8.5)	2.0 (1)	2.11 (1)	2.57 (1)	2.89 (3.5)
10	2.75 (4)	2.56 (3.5)	3.11 (4)	2.67 (2)	3.18 (4)	3.11 (6)
4	2.61 (3)	2.78 (6.5)	3.46 (6.5)	3.33 (8.5)	3.61 (10)	3.33 (9.5)
8	2.43 (2)	2.11 (2)	3.0 (2.5)	2.78 (3)	3.18 (4)	2.89 (3.5)
5	2.42 (1)	1.78 (1)	3.43 (5)	2.89 (4)	3.29 (6)	3.78 (1.5)
Mean	3.17	2.91	3.43	3.19	3.38	3.18
S.D.	.65	.72	.64	.64	.46	.39
T value	2.78	$P = -.018$	3.01	$P = .012$	3.21	$P = .008$
Spearman rank-order correlation	.85	$P > .001$	.85	$P > .001$	.84	$P > .001$

Table 2. *Ranked mean scores awarded by native vs. non-native speakers of English*

	English Proficiency		Communicative Ability		Academic Potential	
Subject	Native speaker	Non-native speaker	Native speaker	Non-native speaker	Native speaker	Non-native speaker
9	4.16 (11.5)	4.56 (12)	4.53 (12)	4.72 (12)	4.26 (12)	4.50 (12)
1	4.16 (11.5)	3.78 (11)	3.95 (11)	3.67 (9)	3.84 (11)	3.33 (8)
3	3.90 (10)	3.61 (10)	3.58 (8.5)	3.57 (8)	3.39 (9)	3.61 (11)
7	3.32 (9)	3.56 (9)	3.58 (8.5)	3.83 (10.5)	3.37 (7)	3.56 (9.5)
2	3.11 (8)	3.28 (8)	3.63 (10)	3.83 (10.5)	3.37 (7)	3.56 (9.5)
12	2.84 (6.5)	2.83 (5)	3.11 (3)	2.89 (3)	2.95 (2)	2.72 (2)
10	2.84 (6.5)	2.56 (4)	3.05 (2)	2.94 (4)	3.37 (7)	2.94 (4)
11	2.74 (5)	3.0 (6)	3.42 (6)	3.28 (5)	3.16 (4)	3.17 (5)
6	2.68 (4)	3.06 (7)	1.95 (1)	2.11 (1)	2.63 (1)	2.67 (1)
4	2.63 (3)	2.67 (3)	3.47 (7)	3.39 (7)	3.79 (10)	3.28 (7)
8	2.47 (2)	2.22 (1)	3.16 (4)	2.72 (2)	3.32 (5)	2.89 (3)
5	2.26 (1)	2.28 (2)	3.26 (5)	3.33 (6)	3.11 (3)	3.22 (6)
Mean	3.09	3.12	3.39	3.56	3.38	3.29
S.D.	.65	.68	.61	.66	.43	.50
T value	$-.32$ (non-significant)		.55 (non-significant)		1.05 (non-significant)	
Correlation (Spearman)	.90 ($P > .001$)		.94 ($P > .001$)		.80 ($P > .001$)	

Table 3. *Ranked mean scores awarded by male vs. female judges*

Subject	English Proficiency		Communicative Ability		Academic Potential	
	Male judge	Female	Male judge	Female	Male judge	Female
9	4.42 (12)	4.18 (11)	4.65 (12)	4.55 (12)	4.54 (12)	4.00 (12)
1	3.85 (11)	4.27 (12)	3.70 (10)	4.09 (11)	3.46 (7.5)	3.91 (11)
3	3.81 (10)	3.64 (10)	3.62 (8)	3.46 (7.5)	3.48 (9)	3.55 (9)
7	3.54 (9)	3.18 (9)	3.73 (11)	3.64 (9)	3.46 (7.5)	3.46 (7)
2	3.23 (8)	3.09 (8)	3.69 (9)	3.82 (10)	3.50 (10)	3.55 (9)
12	2.92 (7)	2.64 (4.5)	3.00 (3)	3.00 (2.5)	2.85 (2)	2.87 (1)
11	2.86 (6)	2.82 (6)	3.35 (6)	3.36 (5.5)	3.12 (3.5)	3.27 (6)
6	2.85 (5)	2.91 (7)	2.04 (1)	2.00 (1)	2.50 (1)	3.00 (2.5)
4	2.81 (4)	2.27 (3)	3.42 (7)	3.46 (7.5)	3.54 (11)	3.55 (9)
10	2.73 (3)	2.64 (4.5)	3.15 (4)	2.64 (4)	3.23 (6)	3.00 (2.5)
8	2.46 (2)	2.09 (2)	2.92 (2)	3.00 (2.5)	3.12 (3.5)	3.09 (4)
5	2.39 (1)	2.00 (1)	3.27 (5)	3.36 (5.5)	3.15 (5)	3.18 (5)
Mean	3.16	2.98	3.38	3.37	3.33	3.35
S.D.	.62	.75	.62	.67	.49	.36
T value	2.44 (*P* = .03)		.22 (non-significant)		− .25 (non-significant)	
Correlation (Spearman)	.95 (*P* > .001)		.95 (*P* > .001)		.84 (*P* > .001)	

rankings across groups. Spearman rank-order correlation coefficients computed on the ranked means for "English proficiency", "communicative ability" and "academic potential" came out at .85, .85 and .84 respectively, all being significant at the .001 level. In other words, there is a fairly strong association between scores assigned by the ESL teachers and those assigned by academic subject teachers.

Turning to the distinction between judges who viewed themselves to be native speakers of English and those who did not, it may be seen from Table 2 that these two groups gave very similar scores for the twelve students in the study, and in fact T-tests computed on the mean differences across the three paired rankings reveal that these differences are not significant at the .05 level. It may be noted also that the correlation coefficients show an even stronger relationship between the three sets of paired rankings than was apparent when the scores were broken down on the basis of departmental affiliation.

Finally, Table 3 shows the breakdowns on the basis of the marker's sex. Again, the differences between the three sets of paired means are non-significant, and there are very strong positive correlations between the rankings on all three parameters.

Having established that we were dealing with an essentially homogenous marker population, it was decided to look at the relationships among the six different variables on the marking scheme, with the markers treated as a single group. Mean scores were computed for each student on each of the six categories, and Pearson product-moment coefficients were prepared. The results are presented in Table 4. Relatively strong positive relationships may be seen to exist between most categories, suggesting that the judges tended to mark along a single dimension. In other words, students who were viewed as having a better command of the language as a linguistic system (i.e. in terms of grammatical accuracy and pronunciation) were also judged to be more capable of communicating effectively in an academic setting, and to have better academic potential as well. It may be noted, however, that the relationship between perceived English proficiency and the other two major categories (communicative ability and academic potential) was considerably weaker than the coefficient of .94 that was computed for the relationship between communicative ability and academic potential. Furthermore, the judges as a whole tended to attach a greater degree of confidence to higher ratings than to lower ones. This might be interpreted as meaning that the judges felt less comfortable assigning lower scores, and expressed this discomfort by indicating a lesser degree of certainty.

Looking at the findings overall, we may note an impressive degree of agreement among the judges in their reactions to the samples of interactive language behaviour recorded on the videotapes. The fact that the ESL teachers appear to have somewhat stricter standards than the academic subject teachers is less important than the fact that they tend to agree on

Table 4. *Correlations between "English proficiency", "communicative ability" and perceived "academic potential"*

	1.	2.	3.	4.	5.	6.
1. English proficiency rating	1.00	.75	.70	.66	.74	.62
2. Certainty of English proficiency rating		1.00	.92	.92	.90	.89
3. Communicative ability rating			1.00	.85	.94	.96
4. Certainty of communicative ability rating				1.00	.90	.86
5. Academic potential rating					1.00	.93
6. Certainty of academic potential rating						1.00

Note: All coefficients significant at .01.

their overall rankings. However, it should be stressed that the degree of association between the ESL and subject-teacher rankings is somewhat weaker than that between native and non-native speakers, or between male and female judges, which is strongest of all. This relative discrepancy is perhaps worth further investigation.

Conclusions

An important type of validity in ESL testing is related to the degree of fit achieved between the language behaviour produced by the test and language behaviour that is relevant to the target context. In our circumstances, the target context is that of an academic tutorial, where the emphasis is on the ability to play an active and meaningful role in the exchange and critical evaluation of relatively complex ideas and meanings with other students, under the leadership of a tutor. Because this is primarily a group interaction context, a traditional oral proficiency test based on one-to-one interviews will probably tend not to produce the relevant behaviour, and predictions derived from student performance on such a test would seem to have relatively poor predictive value in respect to future performance in actual tutorials. For the same reason, a testing instrument that is capable of simulating, to some degree, the conditions of an academic tutorial would appear to have better predictive value in that it would be more likely to generate relevant behaviour.

Because our attempt to develop a test of this type is still on-going, we are not yet in a position to be able to report on the predictive reliability of judgements derived from our simulated tutorial format. However, the current version of the test has been shown to generate student language behaviour that is judged similarly by both ESL and subject-teacher evaluators. Although it remains to be seen whether students judged to perform well on the test are also found to perform well in the actual target context, our current findings give us no reason to think otherwise.

Testing Oral Proficiency: A New Approach

NELSON A. BERKOFF

Background

It is no secret that the testing of oral proficiency is one of the weakest items in our testing battery. Today both validity and reliability are suspect, with the result that the Oral Test is usually relegated to the bottom of the scale in most school leaving examinations.

For example, "O" Level examinations in Great Britain (see Table 1) tend to allocate between 15–20% of their total marks to Oral Proficiency and even less to Listening Comprehension, whilst allocating 25–40% for Reading and 15–45% to Writing. (The Scottish Alternative syllabus is an outstanding exception, but it is worth noting that, although 47% is given to Oral Proficiency, it receives only 10% of the time – 15 minutes out of $2\frac{1}{2}$ hours – and part of the so-called Oral Proficiency consists in "reading aloud"). This in spite of the fact that most British school leavers when they use a foreign language – if they use it at all – are most likely to use it for listening and speaking rather than for writing. The situation in Israel, as we will see, is no better.

What are the reasons for this neglect of the testing and – with the inevitable feed-back – the teaching of this important skill? I can discern at least three:

(1) The strong "cultural" tradition which considers that a foreign language is learned in order to enable one to read the literature and thus understand the culture of the society using that language. Today that tradition has given way to a more realistic attitude which looks on the foreign language as a means of communication. But traditions die hard, and to be able to write an essay in the foreign language is still looked on as the *sine qua non* of language courses in many countries, whereas the ability to speak that language is, consciously or unconsciously, rated much lower.

(2) *Unreliability of marking.* This is a serious defect, although it has not hampered the testing of written composition for the past few thousand years. Unless the Oral Test (or any non-objective test, for that matter) is fairly tightly structured, and marked by at least two trained examiners, it will always tend to be unreliable. But this can be overcome, as I will later show.

(3) *Lack of validity.* The oral examination should be a test of communication, but to include "reading aloud" (see Table 1) as part of an oral test makes the test invalid to the point of absurdity. Even without reading aloud, asking the examinee to describe a picture or to answer questions which have been presented beforehand are hardly tests of "real" communication. However, tests can be made more valid by replicating a real-life situation.

Some teachers and other groups have tried to advance beyond this. The United States' Foreign Service Institute has developed a valuable Oral Test, and I have been particularly impressed and influenced by what has been written about this test by Claudia Wilds (1975) and Randall Jones (1975, 1979b). In his 1979 article Jones maintains that the tasks involved in making a test include:

(i)   Developing appropriate interview techniques,
(ii)   Defining points on the rating scale,
(iii) Establishing the criterion for making ratings,
(iv)   Training testers to administer the test and make accurate and consistent judgements. (Jones, 1979b, p. 105)

I will deal with these points later, but before I do so I would like to give a brief picture of what happens in Israel.

The Situation in Israel

(1) *Oral testing in the school leaving examination*

In Israel pupils learn English for 8 years, from Grades 5 to 12, and then take a school leaving examination which is about the same level as the British "A" Level. English is the

Table 1. *Allocation of marks according to skills by four different examining boards in Great Britain – GCE "O" Level in French for 1979*

	Oxf. & Camb.	U. of London	Scottish Traditional	Scottish Alternative
1. Oral	18 % 12 mins.	15 % 10 mins.	20 % 12 mins.	47 % 15 mins.
2. Aural	18 % 2 hrs.	15 % 30 mins.	12 % 30 mins.	13 % 30 mins.
Total:				
Oral & Aural	36 % 2 hrs, 12 mins.	30 % 40 mins.	32 % 42 mins.	60 % 45 mins.
3. Reading	38 % 1.45 hrs.	25 % 1.30 hrs.	32 % 1.30 hrs.	27 % 1 hr.
4. Writing	26 % 2.30 hrs.	45 % 1.30 hrs.	36 % 1.30 hrs.	13 % 45 mins.
Total:				
Reading & Writing	64 % 4 hrs, 15 mins.	70 % 3 hrs.	68 % 3 hrs.	40 % 1 hr, 45 mins.
Total Time	6 hrs, 30 mins.	3 hrs, 40 mins.	3 hrs, 42 mins.	2 hrs, 30 mins.

Notes

1. *Oral*
   Testing techniques might include:
   (i) reading aloud – this given by *all* four Boards
   (ii) set questions
   (iii) conversation based on pictures or prepared questions
   (iv) role playing – intended to simulate real-life situations
2. *Aural*
   Answers to be written in English, except for one Board which has multiple-choice questions in English.
3. *Reading*
   Two Boards give questions in English to be answered in English: one Board gives questions in French to be answered in French; one Board has multiple-choice questions in French. Three Boards ask for a passage to be translated from French to English.
4. *Writing*
   Two Boards include dictation. All ask for a composition, which may be based on pictures. One Board has an alternative question involving translation from French to English.

(Data taken from A. Moys, A. Harding, B. Page and V. J. Printon, 1980).

first foreign language in Israel and the examination is quite a demanding one – an unseen passage with multiple-choice and open-ended questions, language exercises, a composition, literature, listening comprehension, and oral proficiency, which only gets 10 %.

When I first started teaching English in Israel there was no test of either listening comprehension or oral proficiency, and it took many years to persuade the authorities to introduce such tests. But the oral examination is still the orphan – looked on by pupils, teachers and parents alike as the only piece of light relaxation in a difficult examination. It is conducted as an interview-type examination; the questions are asked and evaluated by one examiner, who is usually a classroom teacher from another school, and who has received no special instructions in the evaluation of speech production other than the Guidelines issued to examiners. These Guidelines are a step in the right direction, but the criteria for evaluation are much too vague, and severe restrictions on topics tend to reduce the conversation to meaningless exchanges of views about the weather, family and sport.

(2) *The group type examination*

A big step towards improving both reliability and validity has been the experimental introduction of the Group Type Examination by Thea Reves (1980). The rationale behind this is that instead of an artificial conversation between a distant and unknown examiner and a nervous examinee, a discussion amongst the examinees themselves would stimulate a "free, real-life conversation" (1980, p. 19).

The procedure is as follows: During the course of the year the teacher and pupils choose some 20 topics or themes about which the pupils would be expected to have definite views: Marriage; The Generation Gap; Religious Coercion; Traffic Accidents; Cheating in Examinations; and so on. These topics are discussed in class during the year, sometimes as debates and sometimes as group discussions. On the morning of the examination one of the examiners (there are two examiners) is given the names of the examinees and he divides them at random into groups of four and the lists of these groups are immediately posted. Thus each examinee knows only the names of his partners on the day of the examination. A stack of cards with the 20 or so topics, together with 2 or 3 questions on each topic, has already been prepared and is handed to the group as they enter. They sit round a table, choose a card, and are allowed a few minutes to discuss amongst themselves whether or not they want that topic. If not, they can make another choice, but that has to be their final choice. Then one of the group asks the first question written on the card and the discussion begins. The examiners do not interfere unless they feel that one pupil is tending to dominate, or that one pupil is being left out, or that the group is running out of steam and needs a provocative question to refuel them or even that they need a different topic. It was found that, with a group of four, about 15 minutes was sufficient to allow the examiners to form a reasonable evaluation of all four of the examinees.

Marking

(a) *Reliability*

In the examinations carried out by Reves the examiners were given an analytic rating scale – one examiner was required to evaluate Fluency (25 %) and Grammatical Accuracy (20 %) and the other Vocabulary (20 %) and Accuracy of Pronunciation (10 %), and both were required to evaluate Communicative Ability (25 %). All were on a scale from 4 to 10. Thus, each testee got six marks, which were converted to a single grade after consultation between the two examiners and the class teacher. This has the appearance of greater reliability, but I found many of her criteria unsatisfactory and we all found that, after a time, the analytic method becomes tedious and unnecessary. I certainly agree with Jones who says that

> "Many testers, especially after they have gained a good amount of experience, found that they did not need to use this scoring system in order to determine a rating; their intuitive judgment was as accurate as the check list." (1979b, p. 105)

However, with an improved Rating Scale, this type of examination is much more reliable than the interview type, insofar as the examiner can concentrate on his evaluation and does not have to worry about trying to put the examinee at his ease or to be thinking about which of his prepared questions to ask next.

(b) *Validity*

This type of test has high face validity since it creates a situation where genuine, serious – and often heated – discussion takes place among a group of equals, and in which each participant is really trying to persuade the others to accept his point of view.

Incidentally, there is also a saving of man-power. In one school I tested, as a single examiner, 98 testees in the interview type of examination over a period of 4 days, and this took 17 hours, which is less than 6 testees per hour; whereas in another school where two of us conducted a Group Type interview we examined 66 pupils in one day. The latter took about 5 hours, which is about 13 pupils an hour.

Possible Ways of Improving the Oral Examination

I will now take up Randall Jones' 4 points that I mentioned earlier:

(1) *Developing appropriate interviewing techniques*

This can best be achieved by issuing clear instructions about the aims of the examination, both to the testees and to the examiners. Such instructions will also indicate the techniques that will be used. This will add greatly to the validity of the examination.

These instructions will have the effect of controlling the methods that the examiner uses. They will also make both the examinee and the examiner realize that the mark will be based on achievement and not on penalization for mistakes.

In addition to knowing the aims of the examination and how it will be conducted, the examinee also needs to know how he is going to be evaluated. This brings me to:

(2) *Defining points on the rating scale* and (3) *Establishing criteria for rating*

Here I find the general criteria suggested by Wilds and Jones satisfactory, and I have used them as a model for my *Rating scale for the oral examination in English*.

These criteria still need to be refined, but I would like to emphasize two points:

(i) Nothing is said about accent or pronunciation. As stated in the *Aims* we expect foreign students to have a foreign accent and, consequently, accuracy of pronunciation is not one of my criteria.

(ii) Nothing is said about comparing the examinee with a native speaker. We all know people who have difficulty expressing themselves in their own language, so that "speaking proficiency equivalent to that of an educated native speaker" is not a criterion by which to judge a school leaver.

(4) *Training the examiners*

In theory this is a good thing, but in practice it is extremely difficult. So far I have relied on the intuitive judgement of experienced teachers who have read and studied the *Aims* and the *Rating Scale*.

An Experiment

So far a number of experiments have been carried out by Reves, but apart from her 1980 article no detailed results have been provided. Recently I carried out an experiment using the *Rating scale for the oral examination in English*.

(1) *Method*

A Grade 11 class was given the *Aims of the oral test in English* and the *Rating scale for the oral examination in English* a few days before the test. On the day of the test they sat round a central table and were asked to write down a self-evaluation rating. Then a group of four students was called to the central table, told to choose a card and the discussion began. When each group finished, the students were asked to rate those who had participated and also to re-rate themselves. The class teacher rated them before the test and after, and an external examiner rated them as well. The results are given in Table 2. Both the examinees' self-evaluation and the class teacher's evaluation were slightly lower after the test than before, but since the differences are extremely small the figures given in Table 2 represent the mean of the two sets of marks, in both cases.

(2) *Results*

(a) *Pupils' self-evaluation*

Most of the pupils gave a self-evaluation lower than that of the Final Mark. This may have been due to modesty or, more likely, to uncertainty. Only three of the 24 gave a self-evaluation higher than that of the Final Mark, as can be seen from Table 2.

(b) *Peer evaluation*

This is naturally an unreliable statistic since personal feelings are so much involved. Nevertheless the peer evaluation and the self-evaluatinon are almost exactly the same, suggesting that the pupils have a fairly stable opinion of themselves and of their peers. It is

Table 2. *Means and standard deviations of the scores of 24 Grade 11 pupils on the group test of oral proficiency*

	Mean	S.D.
Student self-evaluation	4.00	.95
Peer evaluation	4.04	.70
Class teacher's evaluation	4.36	.96
Outside examiner	4.60	.96
Final mark	4.44	1.12

Examinees whose self-evaluation was higher than their final mark

Examinee	Self-evaluation Before	After	Final mark	Peer evaluation
No. 11	5	5	4	3.7
No. 13	4	5	4	3.7
No. 25	4	4	3.5	2.9

Examinees whose peer evaluation was higher than their final mark

Examinee	Self-evaluation Before	After	Final mark	Peer evaluation
No. 21	2	1	2.5	3.0
No. 7	2	2	3	3.7
No. 4	3	3	3.5	3.6

interesting to note (see Table 2) that only three examinees received a peer evaluation higher than that of the Final Mark and these were the three weakest examinees. Perhaps there was some element of "pity" here.

(c) *Class teacher and outside examiner's marks*

The outside examiner was the only person with previous experience of the Group Test and this might explain why his marks were the highest of all: he knew what to expect and was evaluating for general communication skills. The class teacher – like so many teachers – appeared to be marking far too much for grammatical accuracy.

(d) *Examinees' comments*

A few examinees said that they thought it was an excellent method of testing, but many others complained that it was not fair to sit them down and ask them to talk about Traffic Accidents or Marriage since they had not had any practice at that sort of thing in class. This was true – there is need for practice before such tests are given. None of the examinees commented on the marking scale, either adversely or favourably.

(e) *General comments*

One noticeable weakness is the lack of spread in the marks. This may have been due to the fact that the Rating Scale was a 6-point scale, but it must not be forgotten that this was a good class in a good school, and a large spread would not be expected.

Conclusions and Suggestions

(1) No test (and this applies to all tests, not just to oral tests) can be considered valid unless the Aims of the test and the Marking Scale are clearly stated and given to the examinees many months before the examination.

(2) The Group Test, as described here, appears to be a reasonably valid test of Oral Proficiency – it replicates a normal situation of a discussion between equals, and the subjects discussed can be made of interest to 17/18 year olds.

(3) The Group Test saves time and money and makes it possible to have two examiners instead of one – this increases its reliability. In addition, both examiners are freed from all other activities except that of rating the pupils, and this further increases the reliability.

(4) An improved rating scale is needed, but it must not be too analytic since this tends to distract the examiners. The main need is for a valid rating scale which will produce a greater spread of marks.

(5) Training of examiners may result in greater reliability but, under school conditions in which thousands of pupils have to be tested and hundreds of examiners used, this is not feasible. Provided the Aims and the Rating Scales are clearly stated and given to both pupils and teachers, experienced class teachers should be able to give valid ratings.

OLAF N. 73: A Computerized Oral Language Analyser and Feedback System

THOMAS M. PENDERGAST, JR

Some Purposes of Oral Proficiency Evaluation

Oral Proficiency testing is most often used for one of two purposes:

(1) as an exit instrument (from a language course) which acts as a pass/fail criterion
(2) as an entrance instrument (into a company, government organization, school, or special assignment) which acts as a qualifying criterion.

Another use is by the language teaching methodologist and/or materials developer as an instrument for providing an on-going evaluation of his own work. If his teaching/learning system is effective, the results should be measurable, and it is in his professional interest to know whether he is moving in the right direction[1].

Finally, an oral proficiency test may be motivating for the testee if the criteria on which it is based are clear, and if specific feedback on performance is immediately available.

Some Difficulties

As is well known, there are at least three major problems with direct interview measures of oral proficiency:

(1) *Time.* In most cases, a minimum of 15 minutes of face-to-face interviewing is required, with subsequent time for the evaluation. But even this is a compromise, as the extremely thorough testing done in the U.S. Foreign Service Institute's Language Proficiency Interview (FSI/LPI) shows. This version of oral proficiency rating may require up to two man-hours per interview, including multiple (team) interviewers and subsequent reviewing of a recording of the session.

A more reasonable example may be that of the TOEIC (Test of English for International Communication) Oral Interview. At 30 minutes per session, it is considered that one interviewer may comfortably handle as many as 14 interviews per day. An additional day is required for a second rater to evaluate the tapes recorded during the session, i.e. two eight-hour working days for 14 ratings.

In a language program of 250 students, it would take two full-time interviewers working all day every day to ensure that *once a month* the program had this kind of feedback for each student.

(2) *Cost.* The principal cost in oral proficiency rating is in personnel remuneration. In the preceding example the cost would be two professional full-time salaries to provide ratings for each student every month.

(3) *Reliability.* Providing even a semblance of intra-rater (not to mention inter-rater)

reliability requires thorough initial training, with in-service follow-up training and monitoring of the evaluators themselves.

One Solution: N. 73 and OLAF[2]

When the testing program N. 73 is used in conjunction with the OLAF computer it is possible to achieve inter-rater reliability of 3 % within a time frame of 2 to 3 minutes. It is therefore possible for one tester to reliably evaluate up to 15 interviewees per hour, or approximately 100 per day. The ratings are displayed digitally (numerically) and instantaneously (a revised display every second). To take as example the program with 250 students, *one tester* working for two and a half days per month could do the evaluation, that might otherwise require *two testers* working full-time throughout the month.

It is important to note two things:

(1) The research data show not only that the 2–3 minute session is sufficient for evaluation, but also that results do not vary significantly once a stabilized level has been reached, *no matter how much further time is invested.*
(2) In a language training program centred around self-access learning[3], personnel cost and investment of student time in oral proficiency testing may be effectively zero, since it is possible for the classroom teacher to test individual pairs for approximately 5 minutes each, *while the other students continue to study undisturbed in a Mediatec.* (Pendergast, 1983).

Program N. 73

Program N. 73 was designed, along with OLAF, for continuous evaluation of oral proficiency in order to provide a standard for the development of an overall approach to, as well as materials and techniques for, language learning (See Ferguson, 1978).

Validity

For such a test to be acceptable, it must possess *validity*; that is it must be able to be shown that the test (Program N. 73) measures what it purports to measure: oral proficiency.

One way of "validating" such an instrument is to show that it has *concurrent validity*; that is, that results obtained by it are not significantly different from results obtained with the use of a similar direct measure of oral proficiency. For this, a *criterion* was needed, against which the validity could be established.

The Criterion

Ferguson (1980) says that[4]

"The first step was to *define* a standard measurement of expression. It was defined that, if we take a number of students and each gives a sample of spoken language, and if a group of lay native speakers listens to the samples and then ranks the students according to their ability to speak . . . then this ranking is, by our definition, correct."

There are three things to be noted:

(1) The committee of native-speaker evaluators can only judge the quality of the *sample*. Therefore, a substantial sample, adequate for rating, is necessary. At the same time, the number of samples must be large enough to provide a statistically significant population. Since therefore each sample would ideally be of no great length, while yet providing a dense enough content for rating, it is important to construct an elicitation technique which will, in the least possible time, ensure maximum output from the testee and minimum interference from the interviewer.

(2) The committee of evaluators had to be lay, that is, *not* trained linguists or language teachers. Professionals in the language field are often found to have their judgements clouded by prescriptivism: they are far too conscious of form and too little concerned with communicative competence. The lay native speaker is more likely to avoid this distortion and be more attuned to *communication*.

(3) The aim was to achieve, as nearly as possible, a unanimous ranking from the committee. In other words, all would agree that Sample 24 was to be ranked No. 1, and so on. This goal was not, of course, achieved, but it was striven for.

Ranking

200 subjects were tested and had their elicited speech recorded. Random samples of between 2–3 minutes each were taken for ranking, so that the corpus amounted to 200 samples of 2–3 minutes in length each, or a total of about 500 minutes of recorded speech.

Transcription and Linguistic Analysis

The total corpus of speech was transcribed (with notations indicating various suprasegmental phenomena, such as hesitation, intonation, etc.) and then analysed linguistically, according to nine criteria:

(1) Fluency (as a function of time)
(2) Hesitation (number of instances and length of)
(3) Syntactic complexity
(4) Syntactic criteria of correctness
(5) Semantic criteria of word choice
(6) Suprasegmental criteria of word choice and rhythm
(7) Phonemic criteria
(8) Phonetic criteria
(9) Criteria of style

Computerization

The resulting data were fed into a computer, and the computer was instructed to create a mathematical theory of communication based on a correlation of the data from the linguistic analysis and the rank order determined by the committee of native-speaker evaluators.

In other words, the computer was asked to create a formula or program (in fact, the basis for Program N. 73) which would mathematically rank the samples in the same order as that decided upon by the committee of native speakers and, what is more important, which would be able to predict the way such a committee would rank other samples as well.

The Hypothesis

The result led to the formulation of a hypothesis which attempted a correlation between grammaticality (of a rather special sort, to be described shortly) and fluency, to give a *level of expression* which would conform as nearly as possible with the rank ordering of the native speakers. The hypothesis was compared extensively against this criterion and refined, with this formula as result:

$$\text{Expression} = \frac{X^2 + 38.5x}{7 - 6.35y} \quad \text{where} \quad \begin{array}{l} y = \text{correctness} \\ x = \text{fluency} \end{array}$$

$$\text{Fluency was defined as } \frac{\Sigma T}{t}, \quad \text{or} \quad \frac{\text{total tone groups}}{\text{total time in minutes}}$$

$$\text{Correctness}^{(5)} \text{ was defined as } \frac{\Sigma I}{T}, \quad \text{or} \quad \frac{\text{total weighting}}{\text{total tone groups}}$$

Tone Groups (for measuring fluency)

A tone group is a syntactic unit which is used as the basis for measuring fluency. The formula implies that if a subject produces speech at the rate of, say, eight tone groups a minute, then his fluency level is 8.

According to Halliday (1967), a tone group is composed of one stress group with primary stress, together with other less prominent stress groups around it. It gives a basic unit of information.

The following is a passage from Ferguson (1980), showing the division into tone groups:

> "The children get up at 8 o'clock – and their mother prepares breakfast for them. – Their father goes to work after breakfast – and they go to school. – Their mother goes shopping – and then makes lunch at twelve."

Stress Groups (for measuring correctness)

The following examples show how a tone group is analysed into stress groups in two languages:

English: *I go – to the movies – on Thursday.*
Japanese: *Watashi wa – mokuyobi ni – eiga wo – mini ikimasu.*

In Program N. 73, utterances (in this case, tone groups) are rated for correctness (grammaticality) on a scale with four gradations: S_1 (0-point); S_2 ($\frac{1}{4}$-point); S_3 ($\frac{1}{2}$-point); S_c (1-point).

The *S* refers to "syntactic approximation" and the symbols 1-*c* refer to the rank ordering of the *S*.   *S* is a first-order syntactic approximation, which means that a stress group has been encoded *incorrectly*; hence, no points for correctness. But a tone group which contains a stress group rated S_1 receives one point for fluency.

In the tone group *I go to the movies on Thursday*, we could create three S_1 stress groups by incorrectly encoding them as *I goes to a movies in Thursday*. In this example, each stress group is internally defective.

S_2 is a second-order syntactic approximation. That is, each stress group in a given tone group is internally correct, but two adjacent stress groups are incompatible. An example would be *I go in the movies on Thursday*. All of these stress groups are internally correct (e.g., So-and-so is *in the movies*), but the two stress groups *I go* and *in the movies* are incompatible.

S_c (we by-pass S_3 for the moment) is a "conventional" syntactic approximation; that is, a normal "correct" tone group (e.g. *I go to the movies on Thursday*.)

The rating S_3 is given when an otherwise internally correct tone group is incompatible with the tone group which precedes it. An example is *Last week*[6], *I go to the movies on Thursday*.

This evaluation procedure incorporates semantic and, to some extent, pronunciation criteria as well. If a vocabulary item is a neologism (e.g. a freshly coined word), or is incomprehensible, or inappropriate, the tone group is evaluated accordingly, depending on whether the problem is within a stress group, or between stress groups or tone groups.

Graphing

The group[7] shows the correlation between grammaticality, or correctness (on a scale of 0.0 – 1.0, or 0% – 100%) and fluency (as indicated at the top of the graph, in tone groups per minute) with the resulting level of expression (as seen on the bottom and rising up the right side of the graph to a final N, for native equivalence). It can be seen that there is a *normal* curve which occurs when correctness and fluency are well balanced, whether at low or high levels. Furthermore, it should be noted that, at low levels, a small variation in fluency may account for a large jump (or drop) in level of expression, whereas the opposite is true at the highest levels, where small changes in grammaticality make a larger difference. This is because native speakers, after a certain point, vary more in fluency (rapidity of speech) than in correctness.

Finally, it is interesting to note that students with a balanced development are in the best position to make further rapid progress. A student unbalanced in favour of fluency will find it difficult to slow down and *monitor* his correctness. This type of development is typical of those who have "picked up" or "acquired" the language in a natural setting with little formal study.

Conversely, the academic "learned" type of language development will be unbalanced in favour of grammaticality. Such a speaker attends to or "monitors" his speech so carefully that it is difficult for him to "loosen up" and speak more smoothly.

Level of Expression

Level of expression is given numerically, on a scale from 0 – 999. The number refers to an ideal or "normalized" model of language learning and is meant to indicate the number of hours that a learner studying with 100% efficiency would take to reach this level. The model is based on the original rank order correlation study.

Of course, there is no super-learner or course which operates with complete efficiency, but it is possible to approximate a level of efficiency with this instrument. For example, a course length of 1,000 hours (as in Japan's junior and senior high school curriculum, homework included) might yield a level of expression of 30. In this case, efficiency would be established at 3%.

The following table gives a rough correspondence between levels in normalized hours and performance in the spoken language:

885	Native equivalence
600	Ready to prepare for specialization as a simultaneous interpreter
450	Cambridge Proficiency Examination
350	Cambridge First Certificate
	TOEFL (400–500 range)

Evaluation

N. 73 can be given with a stopwatch (to measure tone groups) and pen and paper (for marking correctness), according to the formula. Once the fluency and correctness figures have been obtained, the level can be found on the graph.

It is, however, more convenient and faster (the evaluation is in fact, instantaneous, with a new reading every second) to use a computerized device OLAF (Oral Language Analysis and Feedback system).

OLAF

OLAF is a small digital computer which has been designed to give a simultaneous evaluation of a person's spoken knowledge of a foreign language. It renders in 2 minutes the same information that might take a committee of examiners up to two man-hours.

Training

Given that the evaluator candidate has near-native proficiency in the language to be tested, approximately 6–8 hours is required for training in understanding the program (N. 73) and using the device with confidence.

Once an evaluator has been trained, however, two further advantages accrue to the evaluating organization:

(1) there is almost perfect intra- and inter-rater reliability.
(2) rater bias due to personality variables will be completely eliminated.

Elicitation

Since time is so short, the rating requires a brief but "substantial" indication of what the examinee can do. Elicitation techniques include the use of pictures and/or verbal (written) situations which are presented to the examinee some minutes prior to the session. He is given time to (mentally) compose what he is going to say, to encourage a maximum performance. The evaluator acts as a warm and interested listener.

Oral Proficiency Testing in a Mediatec: Zero-cost Evaluation

In the Mediatec, students study in pairs, totally independent of other pairs in the same "class", with direct access to study materials (books, tapes, cue cards, etc.). The teacher's role is that of coordinator, animator, and monitor. As, however, the group progresses in its ability to function smoothly in self-access learning, the teacher is, more and more, freed to do other things. His presence is minimally desirable for its psychological effect on the security of the group ("He cares what we are doing . . ."), but at this time he may unobtrusively spend 5 minutes or so with each pair to evaluate the pair's oral proficiency. while other pairs continue to work undisturbed. In this way, testing is done by the classroom teacher *during class*, so that

    (1) personnel costs are *zero*, and
    (2) *no special testing schedules* are required

Further Studies

Correlation studies of this program are at present being carried out in Geneva (correlating N. 73 and OLAF scoring with tapes of the FSI Language Proficiency Interview) and in Osaka (correlation with LPI interview tapes made for the Test of English for International Communication, or TOEIC).

Notes

1. The extreme form of the Comprehension Approach to language learning would not, however, allow for oral proficiency evaluation until a very late stage.
2. OLAF stands for Oral Language Analyser and Feedback system. It is a small digital computer developed at the Centre for the Experimentation and Evaluation of Language Learning Techniques (CEEL) in Geneva, Switzerland.
3. An approach in which students work together actively and in pairs 95 % of the class time, while the teacher functions as coordinator, monitor, and animator.
4. Much of the following description is a paraphrase of this work.
5. Ferguson (1980, p. 76): "This system of correctness applies equally well to semantic criteria as to syntactic."
6. Four basic rules for tone groups are given in Ferguson (1980, p. 74).
7. The following graph is taken from Ferguson (1980, p. 35).

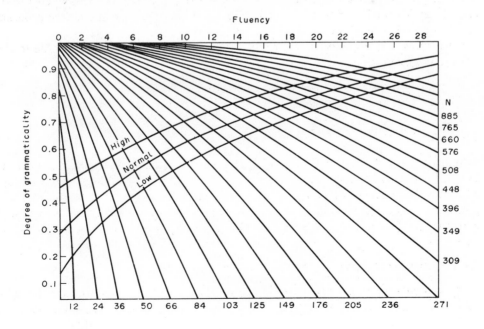

4

Validating Language Tests

Pop Validity and Performance Testing .

DOUGLAS K. STEVENSON

Introduction

Face validity is the mere appearance of validity to the metrically-naïve observer.[1] It provides the psychometrically, unsophisticated self-assurance that allows someone to simply look at a test and, without further technical examination, conclude: "I know a valid test when I see one." Face validity has long donned many seductive guises. One of the most recent of these, for example, is "genuine validity". "Genuine validity", according to Caulfield and Smith (1981, p. 54), is "the ability to communicate in a second language".

In this paper I wish to discuss the resurgence of such popular views of validity. Importantly, these non-technical views seem to have become more common and more active with the renewed vitality of performance tests and testing. Most of us are delighted indeed with the professional work being done to further the quality of performance tests. Yet, at the same time, we must be concerned with the non-professional, popular views of their worth, which seem to be riding along on their well-tailored coat tails. The term "pop validity" is offered (for the sake of discussion only) to allow a separation, a significant one. This separation is between professional views of validity, and "pop", that is, popular, views. The latter are, first, widely held by non-testers, and are extremely common. Secondly, they are popular; they are often approved of, sometimes aggressively so.

A general problem with popular views is that they threaten to overwhelm and negate the traditional validity categories: content, criterion-related, and construct. The specific problem, however, is more closely related to performance tests and testing. Performance tests are those which attempt to *simulate* a criterion-situation to a large degree (Fitzpatrick and Morrison, 1971, p. 268). As such, they are particularly susceptible to naïve, face-valid judgements of what they are measuring. In other words, because they "look so good" they are popularly believed to "be good", "do well", and even "do good", *without further examination considered necessary*. To the metrically naïve observer, then, they seem able to do something *no* language test can do: to directly capture, unharmed and intact, real-life language proficiency.

Validity is a concept, an abstraction, and talking about a concept has its own problems. I would like to proceed, carefully therefore, in the following manner. First, it is necessary to briefly review some widespread, non-professional attitudes towards validity itself. Here is where many of the causative difficulties reside. Secondly, in order to elaborate upon these views, it is helpful to consider various technical definitions of that non-technical "validity" – face validity. It is important to establish why notions of face validity have been kept separate from the technical validities as much as possible. Thirdly, and finally, these various argumentative threads will be drawn together, and areas suggested where popular views are most active, and can do the most damage to the quality of testing in general and performance testing in particular.

Teaching to the Testing

A concern for the demonstrated, construct validity of performance tests such as the well-respected ILR Interview can be seen among the professional testers most closely associated with, and responsible for them (e.g. Palmer, Groot, and Trosper, 1981). I have stressed elsewhere (1983, pp. 172ff.) and will stress again here that the research dealing with such measures is among the most sophisticated and responsible being carried out anywhere. Unfortunately, such validation research and the necessity for it have been of little apparent interest to the language teaching profession in general. But perhaps this lack of interest in what is extremely complex research is not, on second thoughts, so surprising after all.

Surveys and recent studies (see Stevenson and Riewe, 1982) indicate that most practising language teachers simply do not have any coherent background in either language testing or in educational and psychological measurement. Needless to say, this is a more-or-less statement, but it is the less that we as language testers must be concerned with. The Acheson (1977) survey, for example, showed that in two nations often considered to be at the top of the first division in language testing – the United States and Great Britain – few language teachers have more than a cursory knowledge of the area which, we would all agree, should be mandatory. And by comparison, in my own language teaching system in Germany, the situation is even less encouraging. With all good humour and affection, it can even be termed catastrophic. For instance, during two recent semesters (Summer Semester, 1980 and Winter Semester, 1980/81), among the 80 or so colleges and universities in the Federal Republic and in Austria, where one would expect courses in language testing, only three such courses were offered. That Germany was among the foremost pioneers in measurement practice and theory in the 19th century does not do anything to make such facts more palatable. Twenty-one years after the (British) publication of Lado's *Language Testing*, and after all the papers and publications since aimed at the classroom teacher, it is safe to say that we are still far distant from our ideal of the classroom language teacher with a firm knowledge of at least the fundamental principles of language testing and assessment.

Large-scale, professionally designed and controlled testing programs, of course, certainly do a great deal in many systems to maintain educational and psychometric quality, and to direct attention to the questions of validity and validation. Still, the attention we often give such programs should not be allowed to hide the fact that in many systems they provide the measurement exception, rather than the rule. Again, to use the United States as an example, a large-scale survey of some 3,500 foreign language departments indicated that two-thirds of the teachers never used any tests they themselves had not prepared (Stansfield, 1976). And again, for comparison, in my own system there are simply no such standardized, nation-wide language testing programs available.

What we as language testers are faced with, therefore, is that those who are most susceptible to the appeals of face validity because of lack of training, are also those who most need to be warned of its dangers, because they do most of the testing. For several reasons, other than those already mentioned, classroom teachers are also, unfortunately, among the hardest to reach.

Validity: Praise and Practice

The major problem in discussing the concept of validity with anyone other than a specialist can be traced to a paradox. As someone who would discuss face validity must also face this paradox sooner or later, I have chosen the sooner to be the better. The paradox lies with attitudes towards validity. On the one hand, we would all probably agree – students, teachers, and testers alike – that "the central problem of foreign-language testing, as of all testing, is validity", in Spolsky's (1968, p. 94) well-known words. We all tend to nod with acceptance when it is stated that validity is of prime importance. We do this, for instance, when hearing Lado's (1978, p. 117) statement that "without validity all other criteria, including reliability, are worthless". Validity is both idol and ideal, and we all generally adopt expressions of respect in its presence.

On the other hand – in practice the usually dominant one – the topic often causes reactions usually reserved for subjects such as income tax returns, tautological assertions such as "today we will have weather" or, rather commonly indeed, sermons given to red-eyed social workers on how they can best help their fellow men. They have heard it all before. It is dry talk about ideals which are soon lost on the street. They accord it honour, but seldom see any real relevance to what they are doing, and must do. This paradox with discussions of validity has perhaps best been summed up by Ebel (1961, p. 640): validity "is universally praised, but the good works done in its name are remarkably few".

Several reasons can be advanced for why validity and validation are more praised than practised. Johnson and Wong Leung (1981), for example, pointed out at a Singapore language testing seminar that a historical antipathy exists between teachers and testers. Or, one could apply the familiar "two cultures" hypothesis. Most language teachers, as a rough rule, have literary backgounds, but little linguistics, and less, much less, training in the sciences. There is also the anti-numerical tradition, the dislike and distrust of any testing, and what *Time*, with its own pop-vocabulary, has termed "technophobia". A colleague, who once "volunteered" to plead the case of "ed. measurement" to language students, put it this way: "when the sigmas go up, the sighs come out." Or, to take one further example: just a week ago Ulrich Raatz, one of the most respected psychometrists in Europe and, incidently, Testing Consultant to the Interuniversitäre Sprachtestgruppe, was asked by a group of school educators for his opinion of the "goodness", if you will, of the bilingual (Turkish-German) tests they had developed. Having carefully given his opinion, he was rather directly informed that he didn't know what he was talking about. Shocked, if not surprised, he concluded sadly that "Es ist nicht so sehr, daß sie nichts wissen; sie wollen nichts wissen" ("it's not the fact that they don't know, that disturbs me, but rather that they don't want to know").

I would suggest to you that such attitudes towards validity – often strongly held and advanced – should be among our foremost concerns. Despite the innumerable articles on validity, despite all the standards and criteria available, despite all the professional aid and sympathetic advice at hand, most tests and testing approaches continue to be selected on the basis of metrically-naïve notions; most commonly, as measurement specialists continually witness, on the basis of test title or test type. Thus, face validity achieves in practice what it is denied in theory: a popular and prime basis for selecting and judging language measures.

If it is any comfort, we share this major problem with our close relations in educational and psychological measurement. Yet, one receives little comfort when judging the effectiveness of their much more determined and much longer efforts to combat this tendency. Buros has provided the best summary of these efforts – over 45 years' worth – in relation to the well-respected *Mental Measurement Yearbooks*. And the central problem, he has concluded, is the seductive appeal of face validity (1972, pp. xxviiff.):

"Exaggerated, false, or unsubstantiated claims are the rule rather than the exception. Test users are becoming more discriminating, but not nearly fast enough. It is still true, as I said over ten years ago (1961) . . . that 'At present, no matter how poor a test may be, if it is nicely packaged and if it promises to do all sorts of things which no test can do, the test will find many gullible buyers.' "

Now, before moving on to various technical definitions of face validity, please consider this. By common professional agreement – through set standards and ethics – we believe that the best tests are those which specify theoretical bases and assumptions, which report reliability and validity studies and data, which emphasize the "ifs" and "buts", which take care to issue warnings and doubts. In short, the best tests are those which do not push a product through packaging, and do not promise to do what no test can do. As a result, however, popular face-valid judgements will always tend to favour the worst tests – those that tell the gullible that they do what no test can do, and have the looks to "prove" it.

Face Validity, Views of

My intent in this paper is to provoke discussion about a problem in language testing that has received too little attention, rather than to provide definitions for a technical area that has received a great deal. But it is appropriate at this point to attend briefly to some "non-popular" definitions of face validity. This is because measurement specialists have most commonly and carefully placed face-validity considerations in opposition to those of the technical validities (content, criterion-related, and construct). As Buros attests, face validity does affect the quality of testing. And face validity has been of serious interest among validation specialists because it can effectively prevent attention being paid to the technical validities – logical criteria which have been formulated precisely to counter its known and demonstrated failings.

Anastasi (1976, p. 134), for example, has stated that the "validity of a test concerns *what* the test measures and *how well* it does so". Furthermore, what a test measures can "be defined only through an examination of the objective sources of information and empirical operations utilized in establishing its validity". As opposed to such operations and information, face validity refers not to "what the test actually measures, but to what it appears superficially to measure" (p. 139). It is how a test appears to "technically untrained observers". Harris (1969, p. 21) agrees, saying that face validity is "simply the way a test *looks* . . ." He too emphasizes that it "can never be permitted to take the place of empirical validation or of the kind of authoritative analysis" required in content validation. The widely-accepted APA *Standards* (1974, p. 26) are equally hard-nosed, if more abrupt. Face validity, they state, "the mere appearance of validity, is not an acceptable basis for interpretive inferences from test scores". Stanley and Hopkins (1972, p. 105) are also at pains to point out that face validity deals with superficial, naïve views and impressions of what a test measures, and the meaning of this measurement. They add the wry comment that tests with "good content validity will *usually* have face validity; the reverse, however, is much less likely to be true".

Such statements, each with a slightly different emphasis, could be listed "until the perfect test appears", so to speak. Each one, however, emphasizes that face validity is the mere appearance of validity and that face validity judgements are naïve because appearances in testing are treacherous, and well-established deceivers. Rather than list a long column of measurement specialists who have made basically similar conclusions, allow me to offer a statement that sums up, I think, the strength of all similar ones. This professional position, a well-known one, is taken by Cronbach (1970, pp. 183ff.):

> "Adopting a test just because it appears reasonable is bad practice; many a 'good-looking' test has failed as a predictor . . . such evidence as this (reinforced by the whole history of phrenology, graphology, and tests of witchcraft!) is strong warning against adopting a test solely because it is plausible. If one must choose between a test with 'face validity' and no technically verified validity and one with technical validity and no appeal to the layman, he had better choose the latter."

Experience and the Tester/as a Teacher

Several clarifying comments on such technical definitions are called for. First, there is the easily noted vigour with which face validity is condemned as a basis for making inferences. In fact, it can almost be characterized as controlled anger. This can be traced, as Cronbach implies when referring to phrenology and witchcraft, to the fact that face validity accepts *a priori* the validity of a measure. But experience, encapsulated in what are generally called "scientific ways of knowing", has taught that what is obvious today might be considered obscenely wrong tomorrow. As Kerlinger reminds us (1964, p. 7), a scientist cannot accept a proposition as true; he must insist upon *testing* it. In other words, they have learned the hard way that "nothing is so firmly believed as that which is little known". Considering what we still do not know about language learning and language behaviour, this is also fair warning to language testers.

A second point that should be made is that testing experts are aware that because face validity does operate among the metrically-naïve, it can easily be manipulated for more psychometrically acceptable ends. It is known to them as it is to us that unless the medicine fits our tastes, our folk-medicine theories, be they bitter or sweet, the medicine will not be taken, and its proven content will not be allowed to work. And, as we in language testing have recently come to accept, attitudes towards tests and types of tests are important, and must be studied for the same reasons that placebo or halo effects have been.

What is important, nonetheless, is that the two — what appears to be, and what can be demonstrated, — should be kept conceptually separate *as much as possible*, as a fundamental check on our tendency to see what we want to see. For this same reason we require responsible drug manufacturers to demonstrate the total effects of their medications, the dangerous side effects, inappropriate uses, and so on. We do not allow medicines to freely circulate simply because teenagers think cherry is a "yum-yum" flavour, or because many people associate a man in a white coat with a scientist, or because they look good to the man-in-the-street. Even if he doesn't know what, for instance, 5-phenyl-2H-1 is (and I certainly don't), he still might possess common sense. But, for the common good, we do not let him prescribe medicines or, for that matter, swallow whatever "looks good".

The third comment I wish to make on definitions is less apparent at first glance, and has in the past caused some confusion. I have tried thus far to separate, as much as possible, popular opinion from professional theory and theorem. Yet, as I would also argue, there exists no set cline of metrical naïveté any of us would accept. It is also a more-or-less affair, and we are all more or less subject to making face-valid judgements. One could of course develop some "quick and dirty" items. Someone who would confuse a Kuder-Richardson 22 with a Smith & Wesson .38 might be called, for example, either metrically-naïve or extremely sensitive about reliability estimates. Or we might discriminate between those who, when first hearing the name "Lennon", think of R. T., and those who think of John.

Or perhaps even those who think Buros is not "O.K." (his initials) but something quite different. Yet the point is being missed when arguments are advanced as to differences in technical definitions of face validity, or what exactly "metrically-naïve" means. If someone is expert enough in testing theory to argue, for instance, that some facets of face validity might also be subsumed under the rubric of content validity, or thoughtful enough to appreciate the ultimate circularity of all technical validities in that they return, head-to-tail, to theory, then in my eyes at least they are hardly metrically-naïve. And, if they do not know what face validity is, they probably are.

Of course, to some degree we are all subject to jumping to conclusions, to judging books by their covers, medicine by its colour or taste, and tests by their titles. To believe that we are not prone to making face-valid judgements is to make us prey to simple gambits which count on this tendency for their effectiveness.

It is no accident, therefore, that some of the most effective performance tests are those that rely upon the examinee's own self-assurance: "I know a test when I see one." These are the so-called non-overt measures, those which, to the examinee, do not take place. They are often used as checks on more obvious tests. One example is the "simple secretary ploy". The examinee, kept waiting in an outer office for a scheduled interview, is made to feel at ease by a chatty secretary. She ("obviously" a simple and friendly soul, but in reality a tester) is of course eager to learn about the student, his country, interests, and so on. "Would you like some sugar with your coffee?" she might ask. "Yes please, four lumps," and the test goes down, like medicine, sweetly enough.

Pop Validity and Performance Testing

As was noted at the beginning of this paper, the welcomed, renewed vitality of performance testing in professional testing circles has also seen a resurgence of popular notions of validity. These are the ones which testing specialists would assign to face validity. To conclude this discussion, I would like to list some of those areas in which pop validity notions can have unfortunate consequences for language testing. The major problem areas, I feel, are four in number.

First, one of the most persistent and metrically-naïve beliefs is that a performance test — one which *simulates* as much as possible a criterion situation (or situations) — *is* that situation (or situations). In the measurement literature, those discussing direct and indirect measures are usually careful to point out that a so-called direct test is, after all, both sample and simulation. Carroll (1968, p. 51), we will remember, identified as the greatest single problem faced by the tester to be that "he cannot test competence in any direct sense; he can measure it only through manifestations of it in performance". Upshur (1979, p. 79) has also pointed out this fallacy of directness (in the popular sense of the word):

> "*face valid* is often taken to refer to 'what people actually do'. For example, if language learners actually learn L_2 equivalents of L_1 words, a test requiring translation of vocabulary lists may be seen as face valid. But 'what people actually do' is an abstraction which can only be conceived on the basis of some theory — formal or informal, some explanatory or organizing set of principles."

This same point has of course also been made in the literature of validation theory: "judgements about the subject's internal processes state hypotheses, and these require empirical *construct* validation" (Cronbach, 1971, p. 452).

Needless to say, this is also true of work-sample or performance tests. The situations sampled and simulated must be selected upon some theoretical principle. Scoring also requires the same bases in theory if valid *inferences* are to be made. Moreover, as the series of Bachman and Palmer (e.g. 1981) studies have clearly and empirically demonstrated, in all language tests there is always some test method affecting test trait. What pop validity ignores when it sees performance tests as "really valid" and automatically valid, is no less than Labov's (1970) "Observer's Paradox" or, for that matter, Heisenberg's principle that measurement always changes, in some way and to some degree, what would be measured.

A second area in which pop validity can cause problems is already reflected in the language testing literature. An example is the definition (cited earlier) of "genuine validity" given by Caulfield and Smith. There is an unfortunate, marked tendency to see performance tests *as a type* as the only ones able to predict "real-life" language proficiencies. Other approaches are condemned, by fiat, as it were, to being *a priori* invalid. We have all witnessed during the last few years attempts to declare cloze-approaches to testing as inherently valid. Some, in fact, have actively opposed this movement. It is easy to be troubled, therefore, by statements about performance tests such as the following, even if one assumes well-intentioned hyperbole (Jones, 1979a, p. 51)

> "In spite of impressive correlation coefficients, it is impossible for a language test to predict task-oriented proficiency unless it includes or approximates actual samples of the tasks."

If it can be assumed that this statement was intended to mean what it says, then there are problems, one logical and one factual. The logical difficulty is one of circularity. If a test does predict task-oriented proficiency, as evidenced by correlational procedures, then it must include tasks of this nature. Or, we must accept a double-standard in criterion-related validation studies. Tests which appear to have tasks and meet correlational criteria are valid, but tests which do not and yet still meet these criteria are not. The factual disclaimer is not hard to find. As Oskarsson (1980) and his associates have made clear, self-evaluation measures are not bad predictors to tasks in real-life settings. The actual tasks need not be described in the target language, or directly represented. We must be careful not to give the impression that one testing method or approach is the only possibly valid one.

The third problem area is one that has also troubled those who have been most active in the research supporting the FSI (or ILR) Oral Interview. These testing experts (names such as Clark, Clifford, Lowe, and Jones come quickly to mind) are well aware that validation studies done with one specific test, one population, or one set of interpretations, can easily be assumed by the less metrically-aware to apply to any similar approach, regardless of different populations, examiners, conditions, scoring, interpretations, and so on. If one test looks like another test, superficially at least, it is assumed to inherit some "generic" validity. In spite of the commendable efforts of these experts to warn against such popular assumptions, the obvious need for performance tests of proficiency will probably drive such warnings out of the way, if face validity is doing the driving.

Fourth, and finally, there is the problem with pop validity that should concern us most of all, as it goes beyond performance testing. This is that pop validity views are often stated with such assurance that fundamental theorems of measurement are being simply ignored or, in some cases, blatantly disregarded and even derided. There *is* the tendency to see the requirements of reliability and validity as only appropriate for certain tests and types of testing, usually those associated with the psychometric-structuralist (or "modern") trend in language testing; or, to simply toss the entire conceptual network of reliability and validity, and their interrelationships, out the window as so much unwanted baggage from the past.

It would be wrong to see this disturbing tendency as confined to those who are so presumptuous as not to read the Carrolls and Cronbachs of our field, yet still shrug off their considerations as of no account. There is, for instance, the following statement which appears in a widely-praised article (Morrow, 1979, p. 151): one of the characteristics of a test of communicative ability is that "reliability, while clearly important, will be subordinate to face validity". Lest there be any doubt, the definition of "face validity" used was that "the test looks like a good one".

In conclusion, performance tests do show a great deal of promise, and a great amount of psychometric and linguistic sophistication has already been invested in them. However, unless we face the dangers posed by popular notions of validity to which such approaches are so susceptible, much of this promise can easily be lost.

Note

1. I am grateful to the Deutsche Forschungsgemeinschaft, as well as Ulrike Riewe, Richard Brunt, and J. Lee Marklund for their support in the preparation and delivery of this paper.

How Shall a Test be Referenced?

GRAHAM D. LOW AND Y. P. LEE

Introduction

If a test of anything claims to make predictions about a testee's later behaviour, it is clearly essential that the accuracy of those predictions is checked in some way. In this paper the focus is solely on tests of second language proficiency which are intended as university screening tests and which attempt to predict the degree to which the testee would (or will) experience academic problems as a direct result of inadequate second language proficiency. Predictive validity is standardly measured by correlating the set of test scores with a corresponding set of scores which measure whatever later behaviour is being predicted. Now in this case the problem is the fact that *the extent of academic problems resulting specifically from inadequate second language proficiency* is not something which can be easily established or directly measured. Thus, some form of indirect criterion must be used and the question of selecting an appropriate criterion becomes a very important one. It is not uncommon to find that test designers use some variation on grade point average (GPA) or end-of-year exam results as the criterion, without establishing whether or not these are the most suitable figures to use. We may begin by looking briefly at the advantages and disadvantages of a number of possible indicators of actually achieved success which might be used as criteria in a predictive validation exercise.

The most obvious such indicator is the class of first degree awarded. But this will not be available until three or perhaps 4 years after the screening test has been taken, and the likelihood of predicting failure due solely to second language proficiency problems is not very great. A compromise solution would be to take first-year grades in preference to final-year ones. The problem here is that, at least at the University of Hong Kong, most departments appear to try and mark exam scripts for academic content, and consciously play down second-language problems, except in extreme cases. The problem with using first-year grades then, is that the criteria adopted for allocating them are the inverse of the ones adopted for marking a second-language screening test. The implication is clearly that the language test scores could not be expected to account for more than a very small proportion of the variance of the first-year grades, and even if they did, we could not explain the fact.

A second obvious indicator of student success might be the set of marks awarded for assignments done during the academic year. The problem of the criteria adopted for allocating marks remains, however. Assuming that only first-year assignments are used, there is also the question of "rate of adaptation". Students will adapt at varying rates to the demands of university life, which suggests that, from the student point of view, it might be fairer to use only work done later in the year, rather than, for example, averaging the scores for the whole year's assignments.

One way out of this apparent impasse might be to obtain an index of what the markers genuinely thought about the linguistic acceptability of either the examination scripts or the assignments produced during the year. The key word here is *acceptability*. There is

119

little value in knowing the markers' thoughts about the work as literature, but if they were asked to record their reactions about linguistic acceptability at the precise time that the work was being marked, it might be possible to derive a valid and useful criterion against which to correlate the scores from the language test. Unfortunately, people marking exam scripts tend to be under considerable pressure, particularly with regard to time, and the chances of persuading any marker to fill in a comprehensive diagnostic *pro forma* for each script marked are somewhat remote. On the other hand, the pressure to mark assignments is usually rather less, and so this would seem to be a more realistic way of obtaining an "index of linguistic success".

Method

This study[1] focuses on the writing (and to a lesser extent reading) abilities of 83 out of the 89 first-year Arts undergraduates at the University of Hong Kong who were following the *Man and Environment* course taught by the Department of Geography over the academic year 1981–2. All students who enter the Arts Faculty are given a battery of use-of-language screening tests (LAS) by the Language Centre, and we have isolated the results of the September 1981 writing test for consideration here. This test (henceforth *Tutorial Paper Test* or TPT) is intended as a highly direct test of both process and product of writing a tutorial paper (more or less the same as a short assignment essay). There are five sub-tests following a fairly clear line of development. The structure of the TPT is outlined in Fig. 1 and full details of the construction and the theory behind it may be found in Low (1982).

The University of Hong Kong also produces a Use of English Test (henceforth UE)

LABEL	ACTIVITY	SUB-PART OF OUTPUT	TEXT FOCUS
Data	Read	Outline plan	————
Sub-test 1	Proofread (straight text)	Introduction (defining terms + scope of paper)	Syntax (particularly common errors)
Sub-test 2	Write text (from pictures)	Description and recent history of sample village	Describing change over time
Sub-test 3	Write text (from note cards)	Introduction of the two theoretical viewpoints	1 Comparison 2 Referencing (relating ideas to particular researchers)
Sub-test 4	Structure argument (mult. choice)	Application of the two theoretical viewpoints to sample village	Linking terms, connectives in running text
Sub-test 5	Proofread (text with reader's comments)	Conclusion	1 Formality + emotionality level 2 Validity of conclusions

Fig. 1. *Structure of the HKU (Arts) Tutorial Paper Test*

which tests reading and writing skills. For the academic year 1981–2, all students were required to pass it in order to enter the Arts Faculty. The test was taken by these 83 students in June 1981. Although we have used the results in the present study, it must be pointed out that no validity or reliability data are published.

For interest, we also included the results of a third test (henceforth ST) which was given by the authors to all first-year Geography students in early October 1981. It consisted of two parts: (1) the editing for grammatical errors of a fragment of a hypothetical essay about a new town in Hong Kong; and (2) the production of a short paragraph from the middle of a different hypothetical essay concerning the development over time of E. Howard's ideas about town planning. The test was primarily concerned with contextless fragments of text, focusing primarily on their grammatical (or semantico-grammatical) features. Unlike the TPT, this test did not have a coherent line of development through it, since it consisted of two unrelated fragments. The three tests may be seen as decreasing in approximate degree of directness, from the highly direct TPT, through the UE, to the least direct of the three, the ST.

In order to obtain measures of linguistic acceptability, relevant lecturers in the Department of Geography were asked to complete a diagnostic *pro forma* detailing both academic and linguistic reactions immediately after marking each piece of written work for each student over the academic year. Each of the six lecturers concerned was responsible for a tutorial group which he/she took and whose assignments he/she marked. Each student on the course had to complete six written assignments before the end-of-year exams held in June. A facsimile of the *pro forma* is included as Fig. 2. The questions were originally drafted by the authors and then submitted to the relevant lecturers in the Geography Department for their suggestions. As a result, the questions were modified and the revised proforma again submitted to the Department to establish that the lecturers considered the *pro forma* now genuinely reflected their perceived priorities and their ability to distinguish between various categories of information. The *pro forma* was, therefore, considered to have been to a large degree validated by the lecturers responsible for grading the assignments. It was accompanied by discussions and written statements to the effect that Questions 8, 9 and 10 should be answered primarily from a use of language point of view. The marker was asked to circle VG (very good) if he or she had experienced a strong favourable reaction towards the essay and to tick the box if a strong negative feeling had been experienced. In the absence of either reaction, the marker was asked to circle OK. For the purposes of this analysis, only responses which involved a three point scale were used. Scores were summed ('VG' = 1, 'OK' = 2 and 'not OK' = 3) within each of the ten questions, making the assumption that the scale was more or less an equal-interval one.

The first-year exam grades for the students studying Geography are a weighted average of marks for a number of different aspects of their work. In order to make the grades more useful from the point of view of this study, only the unweighted mark for the written exam was used. This exam tested precisely the work that had been covered in the lectures and assignments.

Results

Since the 83 students were divided into different tutorial groups, with different lecturers, it was first necessary to determine whether there was any significant rater effect

Language centre.   Peptest 1981.   Assessment proforma for first-year geography writing

Name [   ]   Univ. No. [   ]   Grade [   ]

Marker [   ]   Date [   ]   Title _____

Emphasis on geography

1	Interpretation of title		VG OK ☐
2	Preliminary reading	Amount	VG OK ☐
		Unclear how much?	■ ■ ☐
		Relevance	VG OK ☐
		Integration of divergent sources	VG OK ☐
3	Interpretation of reading	Personal evaluation amount	■ OK ☐
		Accurate interpretation of sources	VG OK ☐
4	Structuring of ideas	Overall coherence	VG OK ☐
		No logical line?	■ ■ ☐
		Fragmented?	■ ■ ☐
		Repetitious?	■ ■ ☐
5	Use of technical terms		VG OK ☐
6	Referencing	Extent of referencing	VG OK ☐
		Degree of detail given	VG OK ☐

Emphasis on language and language-use

7	Acceptability of grammar + general vocabulary	Grammatical accuracy	VG OK ☐
		Spelling accuracy	VG OK ☐
		Use of non-technical terms	VG OK ☐
8	Conclusion		VG OK ☐
	Should : summary-type conclusion? ☐		
	expansion-type conclusion? ☐		
9	Ability to handle argument / description in English	Linking adverbials	VG OK ☐
		Change over time	VG OK ☐
		Comparison	VG OK ☐
		Conditions if / unless	VG OK ☐
		Cause-effect	VG OK ☐
		Classification	VG OK ☐
10	Copying / quoting	Amount of copying from books	VG OK ☐
		Attribution of quotes	VG OK ☐
		Appropriateness of quotes	VG OK ☐

Fig. 2. *Assignment pro forma*

in the assignment grades and the *pro forma* responses. A series of one-way analyses of variance showed that a rater effect existed in the grades for Assignments 2, 3 and 6; these were accordingly removed from the study. *The pro forma* responses to the remaining three, Assignments 1, 4 and 5, are labelled PR1, PR4 and PR5 in Table 1.

Although it is customary to employ multiple regression to establish predictive validity, in this case there is no clear criterion measure, and so factor analysis is a more appropriate tool, as it can be considered as multiple regression with unknown criteria. The research interest lies in (1) the extent to which academic (ie. exam or assignment) grades are affected by the markers' reactions to the standard of the language used, and (2) the extent

Table 1. *Varimax rotated factor matrix for all 37 variables*

		FAC 1	FAC 2	FAC 3	FAC 4
LANGUAGE TESTS	TPT	—	—	—	.53
	UE	—	—	−.50	.41
	ST	—	—	—	—
ACADEMIC GRADES	YR1. EXAM	—	—	—	—
	ASS. 1	—	−.38	—	—
	ASS. 4	—	−.67	—	—
	ASS. 5	—	—	−.75	—
PRO FORMA RESPONSES	PR1 Q1	.54	—	—	—
	Q2	.87	—	—	—
	Q3	.79	—	—	—
	Q4	.71	—	—	—
	Q5	.66	—	—	—
	Q6	.65	−.50	—	—
	Q7	.77	—	—	—
	Q8	.89	—	—	—
	Q9	.90	—	—	—
	Q10	.84	—	—	—
	PR4 Q1	—	.79	—	—
	Q2	—	.68	—	—
	Q3	—	.63	—	—
	Q4	—	.76	—	—
	Q5	—	.45	—	—
	Q6	—	.55	—	.48
	Q7	—	.69	—	—
	Q8	—	.40	—	.63
	Q9	.57	—	—	.39
	Q10	.44	—	—	.79
	PR5 Q1	—	—	.71	—
	Q2	—	—	.74	—
	Q3	—	—	.71	—
	Q4	—	—	.67	—
	Q5	—	—	.59	—
	Q6	—	—	.67	.48
	Q7	.41	.39	.50	—
	Q8	.61	—	—	.51
	Q9	.66	—	—	.49
	Q10	—	—	.43	.75

to which any of the language tests predict the linguistic acceptability of the academic work.

The variables included in the factor analysis were: the scores for the three language tests (TPT, UE, ST), the first-year grades, the grades for Assignments 1, 4 and 5 and the *pro forma* responses for the three assignments, making a total of 37 variables. These were analysed using Principal Component Analysis, and four factors were isolated for rotation to Varimax criterion. The results are displayed in Table 1. The total percentage of variance accounted for by the four factors taken together was 59 %. Individually, Factor 1 accounted for 25 %, Factor 2, 18 %, Factor 3, 8 % and Factor 4, 8 % of the variance.

Table 1 shows that, with a cut-off point at a loading of 0.35, Factor 1 includes all the *pro forma* responses for Assignment 1, both academic and linguistic, as well as some of the linguistic responses for Assignments 4 and 5. Factor 2 is a bipolar factor, with most of the *pro forma* responses for Assignment 4 and the grades for Assignments 4 and 5 loading negatively. Factor 3 is also bipolar, with most of the *pro forma* ratings for Assignment 5, the UE mark and the grade for Assignment 5 loading negatively. Factor 4 contains, primarily, three of the four linguistic responses from Assignments 4 and 5 (the same three in each case), and the UE and TPT scores.

Discussion

An examination of Table 1 shows that there are three fairly clear assignment factors, based on the *pro forma* responses. By Assignments 4 and 5, the markers seemed able to split their reactions to the academic and linguistic content, whereas in the case of the first assignment they appear to have found this much harder. It is of some interest that even with the two later assignments, the academic reactions (Questions 1 to 6) are never completely divorced from all the linguistic reactions (Questions 7 to 10). It seems reasonable to conclude, therefore, that for both Assignments 4 and 5 the markers' reactions to aspects of the language used are related to their perception of the academic content of the assignment, and that this may affect the overall grade given. Such a conclusion is supported by the finding that certain of the linguistic responses to Assignments 4 and 5 load reasonably highly on Factor 1, with the set *pro forma* responses to Assignment 1.

Factor 4 appears to be a linguistic factor, since it contains the responses to Questions 8, 9 and 10 for Assignments 4 and 5. It is not entirely clear why Question 7 loads with the academic responses to the two assignments rather than with the other linguistic responses. It is possible that this is purely artefactual: markers were asked to rate grammar *and* non-technical vocabulary. They may not have been able to split their reactions to technical and non-technical lexis.

There are two possible interpretations of why Questions 8, 9 and 10 load together. The first is the more optimistic interpretation that the markers became better able to split their linguistic and academic judgements. This is taken to mean that the students' language performance was probably stable and that the markers simply improved their ability to mark in spite of it. The other possible interpretation is that the markers quickly developed stereotyped views of each student's linguistic abilities, which were not modified from Assignment 4 to Assignment 5.

The major interest of the study was to examine the differences between a number of possible criteria as regards the question of validating language, and particularly use-of-language tests. Perhaps the most salient aspect of Table 1 in this respect is that the first-year grades do not load highly on any factor, supporting the original hypothesis that this would be the case. Both the TPT and the UE do however load significantly with the linguistic responses to Assignments 4 and 5, with the more direct of the two tests, the TPT, loading slightly more highly. This would seem to suggest that a useful criterion could be produced by constructing an index of perceived linguistic performance from Questions 8, 9 and 10, as long as assignments coming early in the year are not used. The least direct of the three tests, the ST, does not load significantly with any of the criteria.

Two small problems remain. At first sight it seems odd that the grades for Assignments 4 and 5 load negatively with the markers' reactions to the academic content of the same scripts. It is possible that this is a scoring method effect, in that the assignment grade is a global impression mark whereas the *pro forma* responses represent a series of unintegrated fragmentary reactions. The second problem is the question of why the UE should load so highly with the grades for Assignment 5, but not with the end-of-year exam grades or the grades for Assignments 1 or 4. There would appear to be no clear explanation, and it may perhaps be purely accidental in this particular case.

Conclusion

Establishing the predictive validity of a test of English (or any other language) for Academic Purposes seems often to be envisaged as a straightforward activity, involving no more than the mechanical application of statistical formulae to the set of test scores and a corresponding set of end-of-year academic grades. This paper seriously questions the assumptions made by such a procedure on conceptual grounds, and argues that the choice of criterion is in fact a matter of some importance. It is, however, one thing to point out that there might be difficulties using academic grades as the criterion and actually demonstrating that difficulties do genuinely exist in practice. The second part of the paper therefore looked at the relevance of four possible criteria for validating any one of three test batteries for students following a particular Geography course at the University of Hong Kong. While none of the suggested criteria correlated noticeably with the least direct of the three test batteries, in the case of the two longer and more direct batteries, the only criterion which seemed to have any relevance from a validation point of view seemed to be *the linguistic reactions of the markers to assignments marked towards the end of the academic year*. While markers did appear to make use of linguistic judgements when coming to conclusions about academic content, this was at no point sufficiently clear or important enough to merit the use of the academic grades for any of the three assignments or of the end-of-year exam grades as criteria for establishing the predictive validity of any of the three test batteries considered.

There is, of course, no questioning of the fact that tests which claim to make predictions about future language behaviour must be validated at the very least with respect to whether those predictions can be substantiated. What is being argued is that, where the criterion has to be indirect — in the sense that *academic problems caused specifically by inadequate second language proficiency* are not something which can be directly measured — then the test designer should spend a certain amount of time ascertaining that the most suitable possible criterion from among those potentially available is ultimately selected. The present study suggests that, instead of academic grades, in certain cases an index of perceived linguistic proficiency would be a preferable criterion. How best such an index could be constructed remains, however, for later research to establish.

Note

1. This research was supported by Research Grant 335/086/0003 from the University of Hong Kong. We would like to express our thanks to Ms. Tina Wright who, as research assistant, marked the scripts for test ST, the staff of the Department of Geography and Geology at the University of Hong Kong and to Dr. Douglas Stevenson (Essen), Professor Merrill Swain (O.I.S.E.), Dr. Keith Johnson (HKU) and Dr. Nelson Berkoff (Hebrew University, Jerusalem) for their comments on the data and the first draft of the paper.

Language Proficiency and Related Factors

ANGELA C. Y. Y. FOK

This paper is concerned first with a description of the testing procedures and techniques applied to incoming Arts students at the University of Hong Kong and second, with examining with respect to these students a number of factors which are considered to be closely related to language proficiency.

For many years, the Language Centre of the University of Hong Kong has had the responsibility of teaching English for Academic Purposes to students enrolled in the Arts curriculum. In order to identify the ones in need of supplementary English, pre-course tests are given to all freshmen on entry. These are known as Language Analysis Sessions (LAS). From these sessions language profiles of individual students are obtained, and these profiles are then checked against the perceived language requirements of individual departments in the Arts Faculty. Those students identified as being in need of supplementary language skills are then given relevant assistance in specific language skill areas.

The primary function of these placement/proficiency tests is therefore very specific: to learn whether or not each student can communicate effectively in English in an academic environment so as to benefit from university teaching. Constraints affecting these tests derive, in the main, from three different directions: firstly, from members of teaching staff in the Arts Faculty, insofar as this test is partly a proficiency test and should therefore accurately reflect the language tasks with which the student will be faced; secondly, from members of staff in the Language Centre, insofar as the test is also a placement test and must reflect the content of the remedial courses given; and thirdly, from the students themselves – as it is important that they should be convinced that these tests can successfully sample their own language ability. In order to be answerable to all of the above groups, it is essential that the tests should not only preserve the basic qualities of reliability, which are essential to all tests, but should have, in particular, adequate content and predictive validity. In short, the staff and students concerned would want to be able to tell from looking at the tests themselves whether or not the essential skills have been acceptably sampled and whether the results from the test are genuinely likely to predict the students' future language performance in the Faculty.

Given the above requirements, the type of approach which would satisfy most of the above demands is *performance* testing, with particular reference to the comprehension and production of academic English. Performance testing, by its very nature, tends to involve testing a task holistically; although the task of systematically isolating the specific factors involved in actual communication, and of describing them both in terms of their individual quality and the contribution they make to an overall message is not an easy one. Nevertheless, in designing our tests, special efforts have been made to identify enabling skills which seem to be essential to certain types of academic performance. A number of these have subsequently been validated against the language requirements of client departments (Low and Lee, 1982, Morrison and Lee, 1984). At the scoring stage, performance in individual skills is classified in terms of different communication categories, and teachers have been trained to identify patterns of behaviour conforming to these established categories for placement purposes. Furthermore, the testers have also been concerned with making the nature of tasks to be tested clear to the students, taking care to inform them about the nature of the skills sampled and in some cases how their performance would eventually be scored. The following is a brief description of the tests used:

The Writing Test

This test is designed to test the student's ability to write a tutorial paper. No choice of the kind available in a traditional writing exercise is given. The topic chosen is intended to be reasonably familiar to the students and most of the content provided is in the form of notes, of the type that a student might collect from reference materials. The fact that a test is divided into five parts, each testing different writing sub-skills is explained on the cover of the booklet, where the students are also informed of the specific tasks they will be required to demonstrate. Among the skills tested are proofreading, describing change over time, making comparisons and referencing, producing proper connectives to link up ideas, and producing written language at an appropriate level of formality. Each of these individual tasks is assessed within the total context of an integrated finished product – that of a tutorial paper – and the students are required constantly to relate the individual parts to the whole (v. Low, 1982 for a detailed description and some results of a validation exercise).

The Listening Test

The listening test is divided into two parts, the first part testing the student's ability to understand, recall and make judgements about statements relating to a lecture, and the second part testing ability to identify the different view points that speakers may take in an actual discussion, as well as the ability to pick up certain cues in a conversation. An unscripted lecture is used in the first part and the students are given time to get used to the lecturer's voice before being required to respond. In the second part of the test, students are required to work from a live discussion relayed through a video monitor (v. Fok 1981b for a detailed description and analysis of the test).

The Oral Test

The purpose of this test is to ascertain the extent to which the student is able to cope with certain demands of university study which are dependent on the use of oral English. It is assumed that these demands include the need to participate actively in academic tutorials and seminars, and to a lesser extent the ability to use "social English". The test takes the form of a "simulated tutorial". Four to five students are tested at a time by three markers, with one of the markers acting as a "tutor". The students are given note cards containing various pieces of information relating to the tutorial topic. After a five-minute reading period, the "tutorial" begins with the tutor asking simple questions relating to the information given on the cards. Students are scored according to their ability to respond appropriately to questions both from the tutor and from other students, and on their ability to pick up and develop points in the discussion.

In order to align teacher assessment, detailed marking schemes have been produced, and lengthy rehearsal sessions are conducted prior to the administration of the test. The scores are in the form of composite gradings averaged from the two "observer" markers and the "tutor" (v. Morrison and Lee, 1984 for a detailed description and analysis of the test).

The Reading Test

The reading test is an attempt to test the student's ability to handle academic reading. It has been generally observed that students at university level usually have to plough through a large quantity of printed material in order to locate the information they require and that, very often, the reference material they are asked to read is of quite different levels of difficulty. In order to test reading ability, each student is given a large chunk of text on an unfamiliar topic and is tested on whether or not he/she can follow the main line of argument in the passage as a whole and can reorganize the details in the form of a flowchart. Students are also asked to study a few paragraphs in depth and are then tested on whether or not they can follow closely one particular argument and provide a succinct summary. (This test was developed and validated by Y. P. Lee; the results have not been published).

In addition to the four language skill tests, a cloze test is administered to serve as a control, in case any one of the single skill tests proves to be highly unreliable. A student questionnaire is also given to isolate relevant factors and examine their relationship to academic proficiency.

The battery of tests described above was administered for the first time to 372 students in September 1981. As an aid to validating the battery, the set of grades for the same students from the Use of English University Entrance Examination (referred to henceforward as UE) was obtained. The 1981 version of the UE can be regarded as an achievement test in that it was modelled on a similar format to the 'O' level English paper in the General Certificate Examination (GCE) administered by the University of London; incorporating sub-tests such as speed-reading, reading comprehension, written summary, essay writing and listening. Compared with the tests designed in the Language Centre, the UE was constructed along more formal lines (especially in the listening part), sampling tasks on a more generalized, non-specific basis (e.g. précis writing) than the Language Centre Language Analysis Sessions. Although the LAS presented more limited choices (e.g. in the writing sub-test), a clearer specification of communicative tasks was produced and more emphasis was placed on effectiveness of communication than in the UE. Results from the UE and LAS were collected from the same group of students who took both tests within a period of 5 months during which very little or no formal school teaching had been taking place. Having collected results from two language tests with comparable objectives (to assess students' language ability before they join the university), with each test having a different testing format – performance vs attainment and both tests testing similar language skills (listening, writing, reading, etc.), – it would seem that the results can be usefully employed to explore:

(1) whether or not LAS, which is performance/communicative biased, is tapping the

same general language ability factors as the more traditional (UE) language test,
(2) whether or not higher correlations exist between sub-tests of similar skills than between tests of different types,
(3) whether or not performance tests possess a higher degree of predictive ability with regard to academic language behaviour than "general" attainment tests of English.

In order to explore (1) and (2) above, the scores of the different sub-tests of the UE examination and the LC tests were factor analysed and the results shown in Fig. 1.

	FACTOR		
	1	2	3
UE READING	.09	.45	.83
UE COMPREHENSION	.86	−.31	.01
UE SUMMARY	.84	−.23	−.13
UE ESSAY	.83	−.11	−.03
UE LISTENING	.84	−.14	.23
LC READING	.17	.65	.06
LC WRITING	.35	.71	−.13
LC LISTENING	.22	.66	−.04
LC ESSAY	.21	.61	−.48

Fig. 1. *Factor analysis of sub-tests in UE and LC examinations*

Factor 1 comes out as a UE factor loading high (above .8) on all UE sub-tests except speed reading. Factor 2 stands out as an LAS factor with all the LAS sub-tests loading above the .6 level, and the UE sub-tests all contributing negatively to it. Again, the UE speed reading sub-test performs differently from the rest of its battery of sub-tests, contributing .45 to factor 2. Factor 3 has high positive loading (.8) from the UE speed reading test, and negative loading (− .4) from the LC oral sub-test. Indeed, this factor seems to be a receptive-productive factor, with the two tests representing the two extremes at either end of the scale. These three factors accounted for 34, 24 and 11 % respectively of the total variance. Results from the factor analysis suggest that language behaviour does cluster along the performance axis. For the academic language tasks tested there may perhaps be a general performance factor overlapped by all language skills in the performance of the task. The common variance of this factor would be so great that, once it was extracted, no other meaningful factor attributable to the individual component skills would remain. From the results, it can be seen that the direct LAS test stands out as very different from the UE, and the variance of the sub-tests overlaps according to similarity of test-type rather than similarity of language skill.

Having established that the more direct LAS test indeed lies on a different axis from the more traditional UE, the next step is to examine the predictive power of the two tests in anticipating academic performance. Different subjects in the Arts Faculty are believed to require different levels of English proficiency, with the spectrum extending from almost nil for Chinese Studies, on the one hand, to very great dependency in the case of English Language and Literature on the other. Accordingly, the degree of variance overlap between the subject grades and English would clearly be expected to vary widely from subject to subject. At the same time, it is also assumed that the correlation indices between

English ability and subject grades would not be too high, as many factors other than English come into play in the assignment of subject grades. Figure 2 contains the correlation indices between LAS and UE results and the first-year examination grades. (The subject grades used are from the students' end-of-year examination results. They may be simply written examination grades or an amalgamation of these grades and continuous assessment grades.)

	UE Exam Total		LC test Total
University First-year Results in German	.79	University First-year Results in German	.95
History	.38	History 3	.60
English Literature	.38	Contemporary English	.54
Sociology	.31	Chinese Language	.52
Contemporary English	.22	Psychology	.52
English Literature	.22	Translation	.45
Political Science	.22	History	.44
Translation	.21	Economics	.43
Economics	.16	History 2	.37
Chinese B	.15	English Lit. 1	.37
History 3	.13	Sociology	.36
History 2	.13	English Lit. 2	.33
English Studies	.10	Philosophy	.29
Philosophy	.09	Fine arts	.28
Geography	.04	Political Science	.26
Chinese Language	.01	Geography 3	.25
Geography 2	.00	Chinese B	.22
Geography 3	− .02	Chinese History	.21
Statistics	− .02	Geography	.13
Fine arts	− .03	Geography 2	.06
Mathematics	− .03	English Studies	.01
Chinese History	− .06	Statistics	− .03
Chinese A	− .18	Chinese A	− .13
Psychology	− .31	Mathematics	− .19

Fig. 2. *Correlation indices between LC and UE results and first-year examination grades*

Comparing the two sets of results, there is a general tendency for LAS to have significantly higher correlational indices with the individual Arts subjects than UE. If we use the Arts grades as the criterion behaviour, then the LAS tests have demonstrated that they have more in common with the varying types of target performance than the UE results. This claim would be more satisfying if we could identify the factors contributing to the assignment of subject grades and isolate the proportion of variance attributable to English language within that subject. Such a task, however, is almost impossible as there may be an infinite number of variables involved. The paper by Lee and Low (1982) makes some comments on this problem in the case of one Geography course. At present we have to be content with statistical analysis only.

If we examine the hierarchical order of the correlational indices between first-year subject grades and LAS results, we find that German comes first, showing over 80% variance overlap. English, History, Psychology, Sociology and Philosophy all exhibit a correlation index of above .3, and subjects such as Statistics, Mathematics and Chinese appear to be negatively correlated with LAS. Surprisingly, English Studies, a subject which one would expect to have high correlation with English language proficiency, demonstrated almost no relationship at all with LAS ($r = .01$) whereas the translation grade for the same group of students correlated at a level of .45 with the same language test. This low correlation seems to be consistent across other language tests such as UE. In Fig. 2 the correlation index between end-of-year subject grade and UE for English Studies is also very low ($r = .1$), below that of Chinese B. Without looking into the assessment procedure of the English Studies paper, one can only note that English proficiency has very low predictive power vis-à-vis this subject and that scoring high in this subject has little relationship with the students' academic ability in English. (The English Studies paper is a course which introduces English Language and Literature. Non-academic abilities such as creative writing may have a high rank in the list of abilities assessed).

A clearly noticeable discrepancy between the two columns of correlation indices is Psychology, which correlates -0.31 with UE but .52 with LAS results. The reason for this is hard to explain. It may be that there is an important skill inherent in Psychological Studies which has not been sampled by UE. Detailed investigation has to be made before this incongruity can be precisely explained. From the set of results shown, one can only say that LAS has higher predictive validity with reference to performance in Psychology than UE.

Factors Relating to Language Proficiency

In order to explore factors relating to academic English proficiency, data from the background questionnaire was utilized. A total of three indices were created: (1) the student's knowledge of languages and dialects (referred to as the "language factor"); (2) the student's socio-economic background (the "socio-economic factor"); and (3) the preferred language when reading and listening for pleasure (the "reading habit factor"). These factors were then examined against the English language proficiencies of the group.

The Language Factor

The language factor consisted of a variety of dialects and languages students say they understand. This knowledge is categorized into four degrees of self-perceived proficiency: (1) ability to comprehend but not to speak; (2) lack of fluency; (3) fluent performance; (4) native-like proficiency. Data collected on Chinese dialects was grouped by dialect group and the results were then compared with results from LAS. It was discovered that:
(1) Proficiency in the native dialect, or the national language (Modern Standard

Chinese) does not correlate highly with proficiency in academic English: the correlation indices between these variables were so low as to be almost negligible. In fact, when measured against LAS results, none of the Chinese dialects except Hokkien had any significant positive correlation with English. If we examine other languages like Japanese, French and German, the picture is very different: they demonstrated high correlational indices: .6, .4 and .8 respectively.

One immediate reaction to this outcome is that it appears to conflict with results obtained in a number of bilingual studies, which suggest that proficiency in L1 relates closely to proficiency in L2. On closer examination, it turns out that we do not in fact have a contradiction: for what Cummins (1976) and Swain (1981b) stressed was that the acquisition of L1 and L2 are interrelated, and that it is not advisable to totally submerge a child in L2 without relevant L1 reinforcement. This is true for both majority and minority groups. What these investigations were concerned with is the difference in the degree of longitudinal improvement in L2 between experimental and control groups in different programmes. Large-scale longitudinal correlation between different language proficiencies has not been considered. Results obtained in this study seem to suggest that proficiencies are highly correlated among similar language types and not correlated, or even negatively correlated, among dissimilar language types. Being good at English seems to have little correlation at all with being good at Chinese, but is, on the other hand, highly related with being good at German or French.

Another explanation for this phenomenon may be that, in general, Chinese dialects are not learned in the formal sense; they are acquired in natural situations. That is to say, the student has to communicate with his parents, relatives, friends, servants, etc. in that particular dialect. Knowledge of French and German on the other hand is usually formally acquired in language classes. Therefore we see a stronger relationship between English and classroom acquired languages than English and situationally acquired dialects.

(2) When we take into account all the languages/dialects a student claims to know, we can examine whether or not our data can support the assumption that the more languages one knows the more flexible the mind becomes to different pronunciation, structure, etc. and therefore the better equipped the student will be in learning a new foreign language. From the results obtained, the hypothesis cannot be supported. In fact, the emphasis seems to be on quality rather than quantity – on how well a student knows the language(s) and what language type the language(s) belong to, rather than on the number of languages and dialects he claims to know.

The Socio-economic Factor

The socio-economic index was a composite of the following: the father's educational background, the mother's educational background, the father's occupation, and the type of housing in which the student's family resided. The relationships between this variable and language proficiency in English and Chinese were explored. It was discovered that socio-economic status (as defined) was positively related to English grades at School Certificate level (the English result obtained in the fifth year of secondary/middle school) and first-year university level (.20 and .62 respectively), but negatively related to Chinese grades at the same school level and first-year university level ($-.12$ and $-.05$ respectively). While it is perfectly understandable that socio-economic status should have a strong relationship with the prestige language – English – it is rather puzzling that negative indices actually exist between this socio-economic factor and Chinese. If family background makes a positive contribution to the language development of a child, the first language should be receiving equal if not more attention.

In Hong Kong it is known that socio-economic status is largely determined by education and a large proportion of local schooling is carried out in the medium of English. Hence, educational experience may cause parents to pay extra attention to training the child in the language of "success" and make parents indifferent or even resistant to ensuring a foundation in the native language – Chinese.

The Reading Habit Factor

The Reading Habit Index was a composite index of the preferred language outside the classroom. It included activities like reading for pleasure, reading newspapers, watching television and films; it also included the language students use in talking and writing to their friends. The extent to which English is used in the above situations was collected on a five-point scale, and a general index for every student was compiled. Results obtained showed that this index correlated .38 with LAS and .27 with School Certificate results. Although, for the average student, natural situations involving the use of English outside the classroom were very few, if a student makes a point of using English more frequently, he will achieve higher proficiency. On the other hand, the influence may be in the opposite direction: the better the student is at English, the more likely he is to choose that medium. The tie this "reading habit" has with English has shown up as stronger at university level than at secondary school level.

Conclusion

The purpose of this paper has been to illustrate the use of a direct performance approach to academic language testing and to discuss, by means of comparing actual results from two different approaches (general attainment vs. direct performance), how far the effort of adopting a more direct approach may be worthwhile. It has long been the belief of Language Centre staff that skills tested should closely resemble the task required and that the further the skills are removed from their communicative purpose (e.g. writing a précis of one third the length of an original passage) the less one can be certain of its predictive ability as regards actual performance. The language skills tested in UE and LAS may be considered to be *prima facie* similar, to the extent that they both test reading, writing and listening skills (with the exception of an addition of oral skills in the LAS test battery) yet the factor analysis computed on all the sub-tests of the two examinations has shown that they can be classified into two distinct factors according to test types, rather than grouped in terms of their language skill modalities. Moreover, correlation indices calculated from the two test results (UE and LAS) and end-of-year academic performance confirms the superiority of the performance test in its predictive power (the same trend has now been shown for two consecutive years).

Among factors affecting language performance, the "language" factor demonstrated a positive relationship between languages of similar type and an almost nil to negative relationship between language of dissimilar type. Family background seems to be a very important factor affecting English performance. This influence has been demonstrated by the significant correlation between English and the following two factors: the socio-economic factor and the reading habit factor. This strong relationship in Hong Kong between proficiency in the second language and the type of home was first demonstrated for secondary school students (1980), and again for University undergraduates at Hong Kong University.

Investigating the Validity of the Cloze Score

Y. P. LEE

Introduction

The construct validity of the cloze procedure (Taylor, 1953) has always presented problems to professional language testers and language test administrators alike. Cloze scores often are very unpredictable, and different studies on the cloze procedure have made different claims about what the cloze procedure measures. Oller (1973, 1979) maintains that the cloze procedure measures some sort of general language proficiency, possibly of the type that he has called "grammar based expectancies" (Oller, 1975 and 1979). On the other hand, Anderson (1976) suggests that the cloze procedure may amount to no more than a reading comprehension test. More recently, Chihara *et al.* (1977) have concluded that the cloze procedure may tap discourse constraints across sentences. Alderson (1979), through extensive studies on passage difficulty, scoring criteria and deletion ratio, has arrived at the conclusion that the cloze procedure probably measures only lower-order language skills. More recently, Klein-Braley (1983) also has posed serious questions concerning some widely held assumptions about the cloze procedure.

Such a confused state of research has led some researchers to regard the method of *n*th word deletion itself as the possible cause of the erratic behaviour of the cloze score and to propose the use of rational deletion. Weaver and Kingston (1963) identify a so-called "redundancy utilization" factor among cloze passages with both *n*th and "only main verb and noun" deletion. Ohnmacht, Weaver and Kohler (1970), after an extensive study of several cloze passages and other closure tests, conclude that rational deletion will yield similar, or even better, results as compared with *n*th word deletion. A similar suggestion is made by Bachman (1982) who demonstrates that rational deletion can reveal specific aspects of students' language ability.

It should be pointed out that, among the many conflicting conclusions concerning the cloze procedure, one question has rarely been raised: the validity of the way a cloze score is derived. The standard way of deriving the total score for a cloze passage is to calculate the unweighted sum of the scores of the items. In all the studies mentioned above, the scores are of the unweighted sum type. The only exception is Bachman (1982), who used sub-totals of various groups of items. However, to derive a total score for a cloze passage by obtaining the unweighted sum of the scores of the items assumes that the blanks measure a single, more or less homogeneous dimension. This has never been demonstrated (Klein-Braley, 1983 makes a similar point). It follows, therefore, that if the items do not always measure the same homogeneous dimension the total score would not always yield consistent results. This may be the reason why studies on the cloze procedure have to date yielded conflicting results. Indeed, each item, from which a total score is derived, should be considered as a sub-test (*v.* Guilford and Fruchter, 1978, p. 421); and the validity (and also the reliability) of the total score is therefore only as good as the validity (or reliability) of the individual items concerned.

The present paper is an attempt to study the construct validity of the cloze score by an examination of the construct validity of the items. It tried to find out whether the items in a cloze passage all measure a single underlying dimension, or whether there is more than one dimension (or construct) being measured. As the study reported here forms part of a project on the cloze procedure which the author has been undertaking over the last 2 years, the results should be taken as an initial report only.

The Experiment

(1) *Materials.* Three passages of prose were selected: the first on a neutral subject, the second a philosophy text, and the third an engineering text. The neutral passage was taken from an article, entitled *The Road to Happiness* published in *The Listener* and reprinted in the *English Studies Series* (Vol. 2, Selection 29, London: OUP). The philosophy passage was taken from Whiteley (1959) "Physical objects as not reducible to perceptions" – an article in *Philosophy* (*34*, pp. 142–49). The engineering passage was taken from Rich (1973), *Environmental System Engineering*, pp. 113–14. The two subject-matter-biased passages were chosen with a number of criteria in mind. Firstly, the subject-matter of the passages should show some contrast between philosophy and engineering writings. Secondly, the topic should not have been previously studied by the testees. Thirdly, their difficulty level should be more or less the same as measured by the Fog Index. The two subject-matter-biased passages did conform to the three criteria set out above.

The neutral passage had 273 words, the philosophy passage 291 words, and the engineering passage 288 words. The first sentence in each passage was left intact to provide a context. Every seventh word was deleted to give 35 blanks in each.

(2) *Subjects.* A total of 146 first-year undergraduate students at the University of Hong Kong during the academic year 1979–80 were chosen. These comprised 91 students of Engineering and 55 students of Philosophy. The sample represented about one half of the total Engineering student population and about three quarters of the total population of students of Philosophy for that year.

(3) *Method and Design.* The cloze passages were given to the students of Philosophy and Engineering in two different sessions. The passages were arranged in the order of "neutral", "philosophy", and "engineering" for the students of Philosophy; and "neutral", "engineering", and "philosophy" for the students of Engineering, to offset any surprise factor during the session, when the subjects were confronted with a somewhat unfamiliar reading passage. The scripts were then scored for exact word answers by the author himself.

The first step in the analysis of the results was to establish whether the items measured the same or different underlying dimensions. To do this, the items of the three cloze passages were factor analysed using Principal Component Analysis. But before the data could be entered into the factor analysis one problem had to be surmounted. It is well-known among factor-analysts that a factor analysis on dichotomous variables (i.e. variables with only two possible values: right or wrong) would yield factors that are merely the functions of item difficulty levels. These are known as difficulty factors (Carroll, 1945, Horst, 1965, Lord and Novick, 1968, Gorsuch, 1971). Since the cloze items here are dichotomous, a solution must be found to eliminate this "difficulty bias". Guilford (1963) suggests a score transformation procedure called the G-coefficient (v. also Holley and Guilford, 1964 and 1966, Holley, 1966, and Gorsuch, 1971). One method of calculating such a G-coefficient is to create a score matrix which is the image of the original matrix. If the two matrices are combined, the p values (or difficulty level) of the items will all be .5. Thus the items are made to have the same difficulty level; and consequently, the factor analysis on the combined data matrix would not be biased by the difficulty level of the items.

The G-coefficient solution was therefore adopted and a computer program was written by the author to generate the G-coefficient matrix. It is called the "G-coefficient Generator". Principal component analyses were then performed on the three cloze passages. The data were first analysed with both the Engineering and the Philosophy groups combined. The groups were then split and analysed separately.

Results

Tables 1a, b and c below show the percentages of variance accounted for by each of the principal components in the combined-group and split-group data respectively. (The percentages of variance were derived from the eigenvalues of the factors.)

Tables 2a, b and c include the communalities of the variables in the principal component analyses in both the combined-and the split-group analyses.

It is clear from the figures in Tables 1a, b and c that, in all the principal component analyses, only one factor emerged as significant. No rotation is, therefore, required; and only the first factor will be interpreted.

Tables 3a, b and c contain the loadings of the items on the first factor for the three cloze passages in the combined—and the split-group data respectively.

Finally, all the items with significant loadings (a total of 78) were factor analysed. Again, one factor emerged which accounted for 50.2 % of the total variance in the matrix. The factor pattern remains the same across the three cloze passages.

An examination of the patterns of loading across all 9 matrices suggests that the factors are all bipolar. A series of canonical correlations was then performed to investigate whether the contrasting groups of items formed two distinct sub-scores. The two sets of variables (items) entered into the analyses were all the items having factor loadings above the .4 cut-off level on the one hand, and the sub-totals of significant items having positive loadings, and of significant items having negative loadings on the other. In this paper,

Table 1. *Percentages of variance accounted for in principal component analyses*

Factor	a – Combined Data			b – Philosophy			c – Engineering		
	NCL	PCL	ECL*	NCL	PCL	ECL	NCL	PCL	ECL
1	43.1	46.3	47.9	44.6	46.6	48.7	43.0	48.2	49.2
2	5.7	4.8	5.4	6.2	5.6	6.1	7.0	5.3	5.4
3	4.4	4.3	4.4	5.0	5.0	5.4	4.8	4.6	4.2
4	4.2	3.9	3.8	4.8	4.3	4.7	4.6	3.7	3.9
5	3.6	3.3	3.5	4.3	3.8	4.3	3.9	3.6	3.7
.	.	.	.	.	.	.	.	.	.
.	.	.	.	.	.	.	.	.	.
.	.	.	.	.	.	.	.	.	.

* NCL: Neutral Cloze Passage
PCL: Philosophy biased Cloze Passage
ECL: Engineering biased Cloze Passage

Table 2. *Communalities of the variables in the PCA*

	a – Combined Data			b – Philosophy			c – Engineering		
Items	NCL	PCL	ECL	NCL	PCL	ECL	NCL	PCL	ECL
1	.72	.45	.81	.79	.52	.78	.73	.64	.77
2	.57	.73	.48	.68	.88	.69	.53	.67	.62
3	.70	.56	.66	.76	.61	.71	.70	.57	.68
4	.60	.81	.47	.76	.84	.72	.55	.81	.77
5	.70	.94	.92	.66	.99	.98	.78	.92	.89
6	.93	.70	.52	.98	.90	.72	.90	.62	.43
7	.58	.56	.95	.54	.65	.93	.69	.57	.98
8	.66	.62	.60	.70	.61	.70	.76	.64	.63
9	.65	.60	.85	.75	.85	.70	.69	.59	.98
10	.76	.65	.70	.81	.67	.92	.77	.76	.62
11	.74	.81	.44	.79	.77	.64	.70	.88	.57
12	.76	.46	.97	.80	.80	.97	.55	.49	.97
13	.85	.89	.82	.92	.78	.84	.81	.98	.83
14	.80	.68	.60	.65	.67	.74	.80	.73	.66
15	.65	.65	.64	.76	.71	.77	.60	.68	.73
16	.66	.96	.70	.75	.99	.66	.52	.95	.81
17	.59	.64	.90	.59	.79	.93	.63	.63	.72
18	.71	.64	.56	.73	.66	.61	.71	.70	.66
19	.60	.62	.90	.66	.67	.93	.56	.54	.74
20	.78	.77	.62	.84	.82	.78	.78	.80	.56
21	.61	.46	.95	.70	.68	.93	.70	.54	.97
22	.91	.48	.63	.92	.71	.57	.91	.61	.78
23	.41	.98	.50	.69	.99	.65	.42	.98	.49
24	.75	.67	.92	.80	.74	.92	.76	.62	.79
25	.70	.84	.54	.64	.80	.59	.62	.68	.71
26	.73	.68	.55	.75	.80	.72	.74	.68	.52
27	.56	.61	.97	.51	.66	.98	.53	.72	.98
28	.75	.89	.76	.79	.88	.86	.76	.90	.75
29	.68	.61	.93	.72	.57	.92	.56	.80	.86
30	.74	.49	.71	.86	.65	.64	.70	.38	.78
31	.98	.84	.52	.98	.78	.64	.98	.92	.46
32	.98	.75	.65	.98	.71	.94	.98	.84	.68
33	.53	.78	.94	.57	.74	.97	.55	.92	.93
34	.60	.56	.38	.67	.72	.77	.67	.63	.44
35	.66	.61	.91	.70	.72	.97	.57	.72	.88

only the combined-group results will be included. Tables 4a, b and c contain the results of the canonical correlation for the three sets of combined-group data. It can be observed that, in all the three sets of results, two canonical variates are found. Moreover, in all cases, the two canonical variates include one for the positively-loaded item sub-total and another for the negatively loaded item sub-total. As expected, the canonical coefficient (i.e. the correlation with the canonical variate) of the sub-totals is perfect. The interesting thing, however, is that there is little overlapping between the two canonical variates, so that the items are clearly split into two groups according to their positive or negative loading on the first factor of the principal component analysis.

Discussion

The fact that in all 9 factor solutions only one significant factor emerges indicates that the three cloze passages are tapping one single dimension. This is true for both the

Table 3a. *First factors of the Principal Component Analyses for the neutral cloze passage (NCL) for the combined group data (1st column), the Philosophy student group (2nd column) and the Engineering student group (3rd column)*

Item		Factor 1		
1	is	−.84	−.87	−.82
2	is	−.35	−.07	−.48
3	which	.80	.83	.78
4	that	−.10	.08	−.20
5	into	−.40	−.60	−.28
6	pleasure	.96	.99	.95
7	kind	−.21	−.17	−.24
8	a	.80	.74	.84
9	of	−.21	−.31	−.16
10	if	−.85	.86	.85
11	them	.20	.16	.22
12	of	−.14	−.05	−.19
13	men	.91	.95	.89
14	the	−.34	−.51	−.23
15	and	−.17	−.13	−.19
16	when	−.74	−.81	−.70
17	the	−.69	−.66	−.71
18	whole	.79	.80	.89
19	opinion	−.50	−.53	−.49
20	been	−.87	−.87	−.87
21	without	−.55	−.35	−.67
22	religion	.95	.96	.95
23	unhappy	.43	.53	.36
24	a	−.85	−.86	−.85
25	recover	.43	.50	.39
26	tonic	.82	.80	.84
27	when	.22	.12	.28
28	be	−.86	−.86	−.85
29	without	−.37	−.22	−.45
30	things	.82	.92	.75
31	delights	.99	.99	.99
32	success	.99	.99	.99
33	the	−.56	−.67	−.48
34	and	−.72	−.64	−.76
35	his	.15	.14	.16

Table 3b. *First factors of the Principal Component Analyses for the philosophy passage (PCL) for the combined group data (1st column), the Philosophy student group (2nd column), and the Engineering student group (3rd column)*

Item		Factor 1		
1	are	.50	.59	.44
2	convinced	−.84	−.93	−.79
3	and	.61	.64	.58
4	that	.90	.90	.89
5	red	.97	.99	.95
6	if	−.81	−.93	−.74
7	conditions	−.45	−.49	−.44
8	we	.75	.76	.74
9	to	.72	.89	.62
10	to	.03	.58	.29
11	colour	−.88	−.80	−.93
12	talk	−.40	−.14	−.54
13	help	−.94	−.85	−.99
14	cloth	−.79	−.76	−.82
15	greyish	−.79	−.80	−.78
16	that	.98	.99	.97
17	the	−.04	.19	−.16
18	in	.76	.75	.76
19	or	−.10	−.42	.08
20	has	.06	−.14	.18
21	and	.40	.27	.46
22	it	.65	.71	.62
23	idiom	−.99	−.99	−.99
24	these	.31	.37	.27
25	some	−.04	.005	−.06
26	to	.82	.86	.79
27	and	.72	.50	.84
28	that	.94	.93	.94
29	hole	−.26	−.30	−.24
30	it	−.41	−.44	−.40
31	with	−.91	−.83	−.96
32	a	−.85	−.74	−.91
33	perceived	−.88	−.76	−.95
34	sensory	.45	.15	.62
35	look	.27	.14	.35

Table 3c. *First factors of the Principal Component Analyses for the engineering passage (ECL) for the combined group data (1st column), the Philosophy student group (2nd column), and the Engineering student group (3rd column)*

Item		Factor 1		
1	can	−.06	−.11	−.03
2	of	−.62	−.59	−.64
3	form	.80	.84	.77
4	the	−.28	−.54	−.12
5	through	.96	.98	.94
6	and	−.62	−.74	−.54
7	vegetation	−.97	−.95	−.99
8	the	−.28	−.22	−.31
9	of	−.92	−.80	−.99
10	fish	.81	.95	.73
11	may	.55	.57	.53
12	disappearence	.98	.98	.98
13	often	.89	.88	.90
14	either	−08	−.09	−.07
15	terms	.09	.18	.04
16	agreed	.80	.66	.89
17	and	−.61	−.46	−.70
18	nutrients	−.29	−.48	−.16
19	and	−.60	−.42	−.72
20	total	.68	.78	.62
21	body	.97	.96	.98
22	is	−.76	−.61	−.85
23	this	−.29	−.10	−.40
24	primary	.52	.41	.59
25	the	−.65	−.40	−.79
26	measured	.66	.78	.58
27	count	.98	.98	.99
28	quantity	.86	.88	.85
29	primary	.58	.49	.66
30	the	−.80	−.70	−.86
31	exposed	.06	.45	−.18
32	kept	.65	.95	.46
35	technique	.97	.98	.96
34	and	−.35	−.41	−.31
35	fluctuation	.95	.98	.93

Table 4. *Canonical correlations of the three cloze passages for the combined group data*

a – Neutral			b – Philosophy			c – Engineering		
Item	Canvar 1	Canvar 2	Item	Canvar 1	Canvar 2	Item	Canvar 1	Canvar 2
1	0	.20	1	0	.33	2	0	.31
3	.28	−.07	2	.23	−.02	3	.20	−.003
5	0	.34	3	0	.30	5	.10	−.002
6	.10	−.02	4	0	.17	6	0	.31
8	.28	−.07	5	0	.09	7	.07	−.001
10	.23	−.06	6	.25	−.03	9	0	.14
13	.18	−.04	7	.38	−.04	10	.19	−.003
16	0	.25	8	0	.26	11	.26	−.004
17	0	.28	9	0	.27	12	.05	−.001
18	.28	−.07	11	.21	−.02	13	.14	−.002
19	0	.32	12	.39	−.04	16	.19	−.003
20	0	.19	13	.14	−.01	17	0	.32
21	0	.31	14	.26	−.03	19	0	.31
22	.12	−.03	15	.26	−.03	20	.24	−.004
23	.40	−.10	16	0	.06	21	.09	−.001
24	0	.19	18	0	.24	22	0	.26
25	.40	−.10	21	0	.34	24	.28	−.004
26	.26	−.06	22	0	.28	25	0	.30
28	0	.19	26	0	.22	26	.24	−.004
30	.26	−.06	27	0	.26	27	.05	−.001
33	0	.31	28	0	.12	28	.16	−.002
34	0	.26	30	.38	−.04	29	.26	−.004
			31	.18	−.02	30	0	.25
			32	.22	−.02	32	.24	−.004
			33	.20	.02	33	.05	−.001
			34	0	.34	35	.10	−.002
Sub-score (open)	1	−.24		1	−.10		1	−.02
Sub-score (closed)	0	1		0	1		0	1

combined-and the split-group data. This is not surprising since studies involving more than one cloze passage have almost always come up with a "cloze factor" (*v.* Kingston and Weaver, 1963, Ohnmacht, Weaver and Kohler, 1970).

However, it must be observed that here we are not dealing with a g-factor situation. Jensen (1978) points out that in a typical g-factor situation the loadings on g should all be positive. This is not the pattern found in the factor solutions in this study, as the first factors are all bipolar (i.e. with both positively and negatively loaded variables). Thus, even though there is in all the factor solutions a large first factor, the variables are split into two groups polarized on two ends of one single dimension.

The interpretation of the first factors in the factor matrices should, therefore, be based on two contrasting characteristics, one being some common feature(s) among the positively loaded items, and the other being some common feature(s) among the negatively loaded items. If we examine the first factor in the combined data for the neutral cloze passage (Table 3a, Column 1) it can be seen that most of the significant negative loadings relate to items of a grammatical/structural nature (e.g. item 1: *is*, item 5: *into*, item 20: *been*) and that most of the significant positive loadings relate to lexical items (e.g. item 13: *men*, item 22: *religion*, item 26: *tonic*). It may be hypothesized that the two contrasting characteristics are related to a grammar/structure and lexis opposition. Nevertheless there are a number of items that cannot be fitted into such a contrast. For example, item 10 in the neutral passage *if*, which should be in the grammar/structure group, loads with the lexical group; and item 19 *opinion* which should be in the lexical group, loads with the grammar/structure group. The factor involved, therefore, cannot be simply the contrast between grammar/structure and lexis. If we examine the context of item 10, we find that the blank could be filled by anyone of a number of possible words (e.g. *as, when, because, since*); inversely, if we examine the context of item 19, we find that the expression "*in my opinion*" is a standard expression, and that there are few alternative answers. The two contrasting characteristics identified in the factor analyses, therefore, would seem to be the relative "openness" or "closedness" of the items. Since relative "openness" and "closedness" generally relate to grammar/structure and lexical items respectively, the two contrasting groups of items would be expected to fall into these two groups in this particular case.

The same contrast between "openness" and "closedness" is also found in the other two cloze passages. An interesting case in point is item 5 (*red*) in the philosophy passage. The answer *red* is found in the context of the sentence "Of course we say *that* grass is green and roses are *red*." It is obvious that the item has but one probable answer and, indeed, this item has the highest loading in the *closed* item group (.96). In fact, an examination of the sizes of the loadings in all the factor matrices reveals that the more open or closed an item is, the higher its loading in that group. Moreover, even with those items that do not have significant loadings, the sign (i.e. positive or negative) they have in their loading also corresponds to the "open" versus "closed" contrast.

There seem to be several factors determining the relative "openness" or "closedness" of an item. Firstly, there is the obvious factor of the English language system itself. Then, there is also the factor of the characteristics of particular groups of second/foreign language learners of English. For example, it is well known that non-native users of English in Hong Kong find prepositions in English very difficult to master, with the result that they are perceived as being quite like lexical items. And indeed, this phenomenon can be observed in the factor pattern in this study. Prepositions are very often grouped with "open" type items (e.g. item 31 in the philosophy passage and item 5 in the engineering passage). A third factor would be the context of language use, defined as familiarity with a certain type of language; for example, scientific English. In the engineering passage, for example, item 26 (*measured*) has a higher loading for Philosophy students (.78) than for Engineering students (.58). As the item belongs to the open item group, the implication is that students of Philosophy considered it more "open" than students of Engineering. In other words, the answer *measured* was more predictable to Engineering students than to students of Philosophy. In the same passage, item 31 (*exposed*) is grouped with the open item group (positive loading) for students of Philosophy, but with the closed item group (negative loading) for students of Engineering. As both *measured* and *exposed* are general technical vocabulary items, it seems that students of Engineering found them quite predictable because of their familiarity with technical writing in English, whereas the students of Philosophy, being less familiar with technical writing in English, found them relatively more open.

There is, therefore, only one single dimension being measured by the 3 cloze passages in this study (this is true for both the combined and the split group data). But the dimension is a complex one, including two contrasting poles of "openness" versus "closedness". The next question is whether there is only a single score for each of the cloze passages, or whether there should be two distinct sub-scores – one for each group of items – and what might be the relation between these two sets of sub-scores. To investigate this, the results from the canonical correlation analyses need to be examined.

The canonical correlation analyses reveal that the pairs of canonical variates identified in the 9 cloze scores can be defined by "openness" and "closedness" sub-scores (the correlation between these two sub-scores and the canonical variates being 1 in all cases). There are, therefore, two sets of consistent sub-scores in the 3 cloze passages here. The analyses further show that the two sub-scores are distinct.

Given that the items in the same cloze passage are split into two distinct groups, a further question would be the possible relationships between "open" and "closed" types of items across the three cloze passages. To investigate this problem, two sub-scores were derived for each of the cloze passages in the combined-group data. The sub-scores consisted of the unweighted sum of all the items having a loading above the .4 cut-off level in either the open group or the closed group. Six sub-scores were thus obtained from the three passages. A Principal Component Analysis was then performed. Table 5 below is the unrotated factor matrix of the Principal Component Analysis. It can be seen that the first factor is some sort of general factor, with all the variables having a moderate to high positive loading. Consequently, an oblique method of rotation was used (Direct Oblimin: v. Jensen 1978). Two factors were extracted for rotation to see whether the "open" versus "closed" contrast is present across cloze passages. Ten different angles between reference axes were used. The factor pattern from all the solutions remained the same; and the solution with the highest between-factor correlation is reported in Table 6 below. The interfactor correlation is .56, which means that the variance overlap between the two factors is 31.4%.

The results of the Principal Component Analysis just described suggest that the three cloze passages do measure some sort of overall language ability. However, it is not a

Table 5. *The unrotated factor matrix of the three pairs of open or closed sub-scores*

	Factor						
	1	2	3	4	5	6	h^2
Closed (NCL)	.55	.01	.42	−.59	−.38	.17	1
Open (NCL)	.70	−.10	−.15	−.22	.28	−.60	1
Closed (PCL)	.54	.35	−.31	.42	−.55	−.08	1
Open (PCL)	.44	−.38	.59	.55	.09	.01	1
Closed (ECL)	.43	.72	.11	.04	.46	.26	1
Open (ECL)	.55	−.48	−.49	−.02	.14	.45	1
Eigen-value	1.76	1.04	.88	.67			
% of s^2	29.3	17.3	12.9	11.1			

Table 6. *The oblique (Direct Oblimin) rotated factor matrix of the three pairs of open or closed sub-scores*

	Factor	
	1	2
Closed (NCL)	.36	.26
Open (NCL)	.56	.21
Closed (PCL)	.002	.64
Open (PCL)	.68	−.22
Closed (ECL)	−.45	1
Open (ECL)	.85	−.29

Correlation between factors: .56

simple *g*-factor solution, and there are possibly two underlying language abilities being measured, corresponding to an "openness" versus "closedness" opposition. Indeed, it may be pointed out that the "openness" versus "closedness" contrast may be a behavioural manifestation of the general underlying opposition between the "paradigmatic" and the "syntagmatic" relation in general linguistic theory.

Conclusion

It is difficult to say exactly what implications the findings in this study may have for the cloze procedure. What have been presented are initial results. More studies need to be carried out to find out whether the pattern observed here is indeed consistent across different samples of subjects and across different cloze passages. However, if scientific discovery is the attempt to identify systematic relationships in the seemingly random happenings of the world, then the results presented may well form the groundwork and starting point for something scientifically interesting. Whatever the possible implications of these results, the present study does open up the possibility of studying item statistics of cloze passages in a way which begins to be meaningful. The inability to do this in the past may have been the cause of the very inconsistent, and therefore scientifically not very interesting, results from previous studies of the cloze procedure.

The Use of Latent Trait Models in the Calibration of Tests of Spoken Language in Large-scale Selection-placement Programs

PATRICK E. GRIFFIN

Introduction

In programs developed for selection, screening, or placement according to language ability it is typical to have large numbers of candidates. Where the criterion skill involved is Spoken Language, the complexity of the task makes it difficult to construct valid, reliable, direct measures which can be routinely scored. The complexity of the task usually means that substitute or related skills are measured in tests of writing or reading skills, with perhaps an unstructured, impressionistic follow-up interview. The potential lack of validity in the written test and the lack of reliability in the interview simply negate the overall effectiveness of the combined exercise. The strength of one exercise does not compensate for the weakness of the other.

Validity is enhanced by directness of measure. Tests of spoken language therefore need to involve spoken language and would seem to require the interview format. Reliability is enhanced (but not assured) by routine scoring procedures. Hence the interview would need to be structured such that it could be scored routinely and objectively. The use of conversational or interview techniques also requires one-on-one approaches. The test therefore would need to be short to increase or maintain efficiency, but classical test analysis procedures warn us that short tests are notoriously unreliable. An alternative approach to test construction and calibration is required to break through the constraints imposed by the traditional test analysis techniques.

The problem of interview reliability may be reduced by the use of standardized interview items in which interviewers prompt with clearly defined stimuli designed to elicit a restricted range of acceptable responses. The responses should be such that immediate, routine scoring is possible. This can be achieved through the use of rating scales with acceptable responses scored on an ordered scale of acceptability.

Extensions of the Simple Logistic Model (SLM) commonly applied to dichotomously scored achievement tests can provide the solution to the dual problems of polychotomous responses (from the rating scales) and the necessary use of short sub-tests composed of structured interview items. Individual items, short tests composed of small groups of items, or whole item banks can be calibrated effectively using Latent Trait approaches. This paper will introduce the Latent Trait approach to analysis, sketch the procedures for the development of structured interview items and their collation into short sub-tests, and then demonstrate how a more recent approach can calibrate each of the sub-tests simultaneously to provide sensitive measures of spoken language ability, which can be argued to be both valid and reliable, without any loss of efficiency when compared with present methods of written test combined with unstructured interview.

Defining a System of Measurement

The argument here is that the current bases for the measurement of language ability can be expanded. At the same time, traditional measurement theory can be largely ignored, except where it is necessary to highlight some of the weaknesses associated with the type of setting envisaged for language testing.

We can use an analogy put forward by Choppin (1982) to establish the setting for rethinking the approach to the measurement of language abilities.

The way in which such physical measurements as temperature are obtained can serve as a model for the measurement of human abilities, including ability in spoken language. Consider the fact that the temperature of a substance is independent of the means of measuring the temperature. It does not matter which type of measuring device is used: if the device is sufficiently accurate a consistent reading should be obtained. Furthermore, all substances ·at the same temperature should register the same reading. These two points are worth considering further. Temperature is independent of the measuring instrument and the measuring instrument is independent of the substances being measured. The reading obtained is a result of the temperature of the substance and the gradations on the measuring instrument. It could be, and sometimes is, argued that measuring human abilities is very different from measuring physical entities. This is clearly true for abilities which do not lend themselves to a direct approach to measurement. We cannot use a ruler, thermometer or stopwatch to measure a person's linguistic ability. We can however define a range of tasks from the domain of language skills and observe performance. From these observations we can make inferences about ability. The measurement is indirect. The ability has to be treated as latent.

This should not prevent us from seeking an approach to measurement which contains the same desirable elements as the system used to measure physical entities. That is, the ability being measured should be independent of the measuring instrument, and the measurement should not depend on the person(s) being measured. Measurement instruments should be interchangeable. It should not matter which ability "thermometer" we use. A measurement system is required with specific properties:

(1) The measure obtained on the instrument should be independent of which substance (person, sample, population) is being measured. The measure obtained should only depend on the amount of trait or ability present.

(2) The instruments should be able to measure a large range of abilities. That is, the "gradations" should cover more than a narrow range but be sufficiently close together that some fine-tuned measures are possible. The instrument should not be affected by factors other than the trait it is designed to measure.

(3) The range of instruments designed to measure the trait should be interchangeable. It should be a matter of indifference which instrument is used to obtain the measure. Instruments capable of cross-calibration are required.

As a consequence of these three properties, the knowledge of a person's score on one test would make it possible to predict the score on another test. Traditionally this has been achieved by means of norm-referenced techniques using percentile ranks or standardized scores within the same sample or population. The reference population must be defined in order to interpret the score. Hence the measure obtained and the system of measurement fails on the first of the three measurement criteria. The use of percentile ranks means that the gradations between the score levels are not consistent across different samples or populations. Additional gradations such as age-norms, cultural indices or national norms need to be introduced and a separate percentile or gradation scale developed for each group even with the same instrument. Hence both the instrument and the measurement system fail to meet the second requirement of a measurement system. Clearly, interchangeability of instruments is only possible within defined populations and is not possible outside these defined groups. The norm-referenced system thus fails to meet the third criterion and does not provide a solution. A measurement system is required which approximates the techniques of physical measurement. The approach based only on the number of test items correct is simply not sufficiently powerful.

Latent Trait Models of Measurement

Since 1960 a number of developments in test models have taken place. Techniques of test construction can be adapted to develop cross-calibration forms, using the developments in one of the test models referred to as the generic class of Rasch models. In its simplest form, the Rasch (1960, 1980) model is based on the assumption that the interaction between a person and a test item is based on only two things: the ability of the person and the difficulty of the test item. These two interacting influences are termed parameters and a basic assumption underlying the model is that these parameters can be separated. The separability of the parameters is sometimes referred to as specific objectivity (Douglass, 1980).

Given this property it is possible to make individual ability independent of the measuring instrument, and the measuring instrument (or the difficulty levels of the items) becomes independent of the person or group to which the test is administered. This single property satisfies all three criteria of the required measurement system.

The model is used to estimate the probability or odds of a person's successful response to a test item. Unlike norm-referenced approaches to measurement it is also possible to express the ability and difficulty estimates in the same units, thus enabling direct comparisons between the ability of the person and the difficulty of the item. When ability is greater than difficulty the odds are that the person will be successful. When the difficulty is greater than ability the odds are that the person will be unsuccessful. The general mathematical form of the probability of success or failure is expressed as

$$P_r[X_{vi} = x/\beta_v, \delta_i, k, m] = \frac{e^{\sum\limits_{j=0}^{k} (\beta_v - \delta_{ij})}}{\sum\limits_{k=0}^{m_i} e^{\sum\limits_{j=0}^{k} (\beta_v - \delta_{ij})}}. \tag{1}$$

While this appears to be an extremely complex mathematical formula some explanation of its elements and some restriction placed on the type of test item can simplify it considerably. The subscript v represents a person; i represents an item; an X_{vi} can only have the scores of 1 or 0. For example, if on item number 16 person number 23 succeeds and person number 19 fails, then $X_{23,16} = 1$ and $X_{19,16} = 0$. The restriction to two responses (0.1) is a special case for dichotomously scored items. So, β_v is the ability of person v; δ_i is the difficulty of item i; m is the number of possible correct responses (for the dichotomous case m is always one); and K is the number of steps through which the ability level must pass in order to reach the score category as a proportion of m. This is zero for failure and 1 for a dichotomous item. Hence restricting the responses to 1 and 0 enables the model to be reexpressed as

$$P_r[X_{vi} = x/\beta_v, \delta_i, m] = \frac{e^{x(\beta_v - \delta_i)}}{\sum\limits_{x=0}^{m} e^{(\beta_v - \delta_i)x}} \qquad (2)$$

and since m can only be zero for an incorrect response and 1 for a correct response, the model further simplifies to

$$P_r[X_{vi} = x/\beta_v, \delta_i] = \frac{e^{x(\beta_v - \delta_i)}}{1 + e^{(\beta_v - \delta_i)}}. \qquad (3)$$

To those familiar with this system of measurement this is the basic Rasch model equation. The probability of success $(x = 1)$ or of failure $(x = 0)$ is restricted to the range 0 through 1.0. When the ability of the person equals the difficulty of the item $(\beta_v = \delta_i)$ the probability of success or failure is set at 0.50. That is to say, when the person and the item are evenly matched, the outcome of success or failure is equally likely. This very property means that, when we identify a set of tasks or test items which are deliberately ordered in increasing difficulty and which demonstrate, for a particular person, a trend of successes followed by a pattern of mixed success and then a trend of consistent failure, we have identified the region of ability for that person – the region of mixed success. The ability is in the region of the independent difficulties of the items. Furthermore, any set of calibrated items covering the same difficulty range should provide the same estimate of ability.

The unit of measurement commonly used is the "logit". It is defined as the natural logarithm of the odds of success, and is expressed as $\pi_x = \log_e (1 - p)/p$, where p is the probability of success as defined in the earlier equations. These measures can be obtained with simple computations using a hand calculator.

The model has its critics. Arguments against the application of the Rasch model are based fundamentally on the rigidity of assumptions, the arbitrariness of the scale and tests of fit (Goldstein, 1979). The model does make strong assumptions of specific objectivity and absence of guessing. However it has been shown to be quite robust as regards violations of these assumptions (Izard, 1981, Andrich, 1982). Objections to the arbitrary scale seem a little strong given that all measurements of latent human abilities are arbitrary, regardless of the measurement model. The test of fit of items to the model is being given considerable attention. The basic difficulty seems to be that there is no single sufficient test of fit. It is necessary to apply a series of tests. Objections to the use of Rasch model were based on the application of a single test and such objections are well founded but should not be directed at competent users. An excellent discussion of the tests of fit can be found in Douglass (1982). The measurement model does have limitations. It would be folly to pretend otherwise. However, within its limitations, it still makes a great deal of sense to utilize the separability of parameters it offers. The benefits of this property far outweigh any costs involved and greatly exceed the potential of conventional test construction and norming procedures.

Despite the complexity of the formulae presented earlier, the model is mathematically quite simple and convenient. Estimations of the separate parameters do not require large amounts of data. The model is also based on the "number correct". The only necessary and sufficient information for estimating the parameters is the number of items correct for each person and the number of persons correct on each item. It is these conditions which characterize the Rasch model. It is sometimes called the one-parameter model because, in its simplest form, only one item parameter is estimated. However this terminology is open to misunderstanding. It is possible to obtain more than one item parameter estimate using the Rasch model (Andrich, 1978, 1980, 1981, 1982, Douglass, 1982, Masters, 1981, 1982, Wright and Masters, 1982). The distinctive property of the Rasch model is the separability of the person and item parameters and the limitation of the necessary and sufficient information to the description of person and item scores. No other latent trait models possess these characteristics. No normative model provides the independence and specific objectivity of scores.

In the past 20 years sufficient work has been completed on the model to demonstrate that it can and does predict the behaviour of real people and real test items with consistency and accuracy. Other, more complex, models (Birnbaum, 1968, Samejima, 1969, or Lumsden, 1976) present persistent difficulties in obtaining estimates. Since the only information we can use is the person and item scores, models which do not allow the complete separation of the parameters have been shown to be over-parameterized (Andrich, 1982). It has also been assumed that the Rasch Model requires constant discrimination of items.

As a consequence of the application of Rasch calibration, each item can be represented by a characteristic curve which relates the probability of success $P(\theta)$ to the ability of the person (B_v). Examples are shown in the Fig. 1.

Using Fig. 1a as a basis, each of Figs 1b, 1c, and 1d demonstrate different properties of test items. The first thing to note is that each item has a maximum probability of success as ability reaches a certain level. The four curves start at zero probability and rise in a smooth curve to 1.0. However the point at which the curve begins to rise and the slope of the curves differ to some degree. The steeper the rising portion of the curve, the sharper the discrimination among persons of differing ability. As the rising portion of the curve moves to the right, it takes a greater ability level to increase the probability of success; that is, the more difficult the item, the greater the ability required to succeed. In the extreme case, where the curve rises vertically, as in Fig. 1e, the performance on the item is fully determined by the discrete ability of the person.

In such an instance the item would form part of a Guttman deterministic scale, first postulated in 1950. Such item sets are difficult to construct and sets of such items in one collection are rare. If the performance on a test item is fully determined by the ability of the person and the difficulty of the item, then the total score on a set of such items is also fully determined. It should be possible to reproduce the response pattern if the total score is known. The extent to which the score can be reproduced is known as the coefficient of reproducibility. Guttman conceded the difficulty of achieving perfect reproducibility but argued that the coefficient of reproducibility should be higher than 0.9, if the test was to be of practical value.

The Rasch model is based on similar ideas. But it is probabilistic rather than deterministic. The total score on the test is related to the ability of the person by a test characteristic curve similar in shape to that shown in Fig. 1a. Similar interpretations are made – the slope of the curve gives an indication of the extent to which the test separates persons of different abilities. The location of the rising portion of the curve indicates the

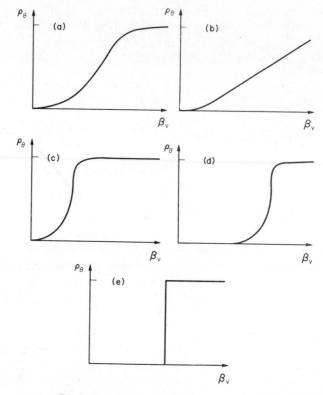

Fig. 1. *Variations in item characteristic curves*

general difficulty of the test. The non-linear relationship generally indicates the fact that scores based on the "number correct" from conventional test interpretations do not accurately reflect the ability levels.

For convenience the difficulty levels of the items are centred about zero. As Goldstein (1979) correctly pointed out in his criticism of the Rasch Model, it is an arbitrary scale, though it does possess proper measurement qualities – something that conventional (arbitrary) scoring procedures cannot provide – and the arbitrariness of the measure should be no more of a handicap than that of degrees used to measure temperature. Gradations may differ from one test to another, as may the position of the zero point. But each test constructed to measure the same trait can be cross-calibrated and ability measures can be equated just as Centigrade and Fahrenheit temperatures can be equated on to a single common scale. Individual items can also be mapped on to the common scale and it is this ability of the model which enables libraries or banks of test items to be developed. From such stores of items, short tests can be quickly developed to measure a trait, with accuracy, near a suspected level of ability. This item banking could provide language measurement specialists with almost global pools of test items which enable precise measurements to be made, in any one centre, which are directly comparable to ability estimates anywhere else. Detailed discussions of the calibration and equating procedures go beyond the scope of this paper but excellent descriptions may be found in papers by Wright and Stone (1979) and Wright and Masters (1982).

Rating Models

The Rasch model can be generalized to include more than one response category. It is in this generalization that the most promising development exists for the measurement of spoken language ability.

We may even introduce a third category – denoting a partly correct response. In fact many more categories may be introduced but for the purposes of this discussion we will add just one more.

Now the score X_{vi} can exist at three levels. Persons number 23, 19 and 5 can answer question 16 in three different ways. These could be represented as:

$$X_{23,16} = 2; \quad X_{19,16} = 1; \quad \text{and } X_{5,16} = 0.$$

The values 2, 1 and 0 represent the categories "fully correct", "partly correct" and "incorrect". The general form of the model can be written as:

$$P_r \left[X_{vi} = \frac{0}{\frac{1}{2}} / \beta_{v_1} \delta_{i_1} t_{x_1}, m = \frac{1}{2} \right] = \frac{e^{[\pi_x + x(\beta_v - \delta_i)]}}{\sum\limits_{k=0}^{2} e^{[\pi_k + k(\beta_v - \delta_i)]}}$$

where $\pi_x = 0$ if $x = 0$ and $\pi_k = \sum\limits_{k=0}^{k} t_k$, which for $x = 1$ or 2, $\pi_1 = -t_1$ and $\pi_2 = -(t_1 + t_2)$. These are threshold values of ability through which a person must pass if that person is to be given a score of "partly correct" or "fully correct" respectively. The restriction to only three levels (0, 1, 2) reduces the model to:

$$P_r \left[X_{vi} = \frac{0}{\frac{1}{2}} / \beta_{v_1} \delta_{i_1} t_{x_1}, m = \frac{1}{2} \right] = \frac{e^{[\pi_x + x(\beta_v - \delta_i)]}}{1 + e^{[-t_1 + (\beta_v - \delta_i)]} + e^{[-t_2 + 2(\beta_v - \delta_i)]}}.$$

All parameters are additive and completely separable, and thus fit the requirements that the two item parameters (d_i and t_i) can be estimated from three response categories. To be given a "partly correct" score the subject must exceed the "wrong" level but not proceed to the "correct" level. To be given the "fully correct" score the subject must surpass both the "wrong" and "partly correct" levels. This is the underlying notion of thresholds, levels at which the subject is closer to one score than another. There will be two thresholds t_1 and t_2 for three scoring levels each with a specific difficulty level δ_1, δ_2.

A constraint is placed on the model such that the difficulty of the item is only considered to be located between the two "correct" steps. So,

$$\delta_1 = \delta_{11} + t_1$$
$$\delta_2 = \delta_{22} - t_2 \quad \text{and so on, to } \delta_i = \delta_{ik} - t_k.$$

where t_k is the threshold value for the kth step on item i.

The model can be further simplified by imposing the constraints that t_1 and t_2 are equal across all items and that $\sum\limits_{k=0}^{k} t_k = 0$ or in this case, $t_1 = -t_2$. This step is not necessarily true in all circumstances (Andrich, 1982, Smith, 1982, Pedler, 1982) but the imposition does afford initial attempts at calibration some relief from variability of thresholds. The only difference between the items is the *location* of the item designated by the parameter δ_i. This is illustrated in the figure below which has been coded for convenience items 1 and 2.

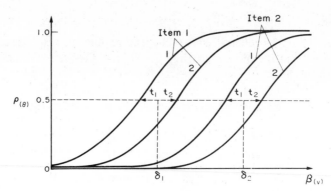

Fig. 2. *Characteristic curves and thresholds for rating scale items*

The item parameters δ_1 and δ_2 describe the location on the *ability variable* of the pair of operating curves for each item. Note now that we have two characteristic curves for each item and not one as was the case with the dichotomous items outlined earlier. Since $\sum_{k=0}^{k} t_k = 0$, then δ_i is located at the centre of each pair of curves. Since the location of each item can be determined, it is also possible to identify the location of each person on the *same variable*, by using a test characteristic curve, on which the raw score is mapped against ability.

Location and Dispersion of Item and Person Measures

The location of both the persons and the items on the ability continuum is based on some fairly stringent constraints. Firstly, the extension of the simple logistic Rasch model requires equal spacing of the curves and the summation of the threshold values to zero. Secondly, the position of the item difficulty or location parameters at the centre of the curve-pair ignores the possibility that there may be a "spread" or dispersion of the locations across the set of item curves. Under these constraints the model is analogous to a common constraint placed on statistics describing a range of score distributions; allowing the means to vary but restricting the distributions to a fixed standard deviation. Thirdly, and following from the notion of fixed dispersion, the model does not allow for a person's variability in performance across items; that is, if a person responds correctly to a difficult item it is probable but not certain that he will respond correctly to easier items. It is possible that only a partially correct score would be obtained for easier items. This response type adds to the total score and hence moves the person location further along the variable. But we are forced to ignore the variability within and among persons just as the model constrains variability within and among items.

To allow for a relaxation of these constraints and to take into account the variability ignored by the model we can turn to two recent developments in Rasch Model methodology. The first is a model which assumes that the response to any testing task is related to a set of cognitive processes (components) rather than an omnibus "ability" measure (Whitely, 1980). The items are assumed to be composed of more than one step, and each step has its own difficulty level (when holistically scored in a dichotomous manner). This allows the addition of further item parameters. The person components are also assumed to relate to different abilities and may be characterized by a set of parameters. Hence, more than one person and item parameter may be introduced. Providing that these are separable using only the descriptive data on items and persons, the measurement model fits within the generic class of Rasch models (Douglass, 1980). The second development assumes that sets of dichotomous items may be regarded as equivalent (in terms of measurements obtained) to a single rating item (Andrich, 1982). Given that the rating scale can be given a location parameter, so too should the sub-test of dichotomous items. Also, since an ability estimate can be determined from the test, both person and sub-tests can be located on the same scale. In this instance, however, there may be considerable variation within the sub-test and variation of a person's scores across sub-tests. The additional parameters which would allow for variation of person responses is given the symbol ε_v. The additional item parameter which allows for variation of item impact is given the symbol a_i. Andrich has successfully combined these to form the model:

$$P_r[X_{vi} = x/\beta_v, \delta_i, \varepsilon_v, a_i, m] = \frac{e^{[x(m-x)(\varepsilon_v - a_i) + x(\beta_v - \delta_i)]}}{\sum_{m=0}^{m} e^{[x(m-x)(\varepsilon_v - a_i) + x(\beta_v - \delta_i)]}}$$

The parameters can be estimated from the item and person scores as with other variations of the Rasch model and the person and item dispersion parameters are estimated from their raw score analogues. The parameters and the model satisfy the constraints of the generic Rasch model and thus satisfy the properties of a measurement model. The raw data is sufficient; the parameters are additive and separable, the instrument is independent of the trait and the measurement is independent of the person or group. This model clearly demonstrates the error in referring to the Rasch model as the single parameter model.

Andrich has demonstrated this version of the model using a set of sub-tests of dichotomously scored scholastic aptitude items. As we have already seen, it is desirable sometimes to have more than one score category. Hence the model can be further elaborated and applied to sets of short, ordered category or rating-scale test-items. Each sub-test can be considered as equivalent to a series of dichotomous items. A set of five two-step items could be considered equivalent to ten dichotomous or one-step items. This would yield ten item curves allowing for five location parameters each with one threshold value within each test. This information can provide the data to develop the notion of a series of sub-tests in which items are scored on a rating scale rather than as dichotomies. The data would fit the location–dispersion model and estimates of the four parameters can be obtained from the raw data. Each of these short tests can be equated and mapped on to the same underlying variable, thus locating both the items and the persons within a region on the scale. Masters (1982) has recently demonstrated this procedure.

The situation is then as follows:

(1) It is possible to develop a bank of items scored in more than one category for the correct response.
(2) Groups of these items measuring a common skill can be considered as homogeneous sub-tests measuring a skill or a component of a skill such as those measured in spoken language skills.
(3) Sets of sub-tests can be calibrated by means of the location dispersion model (or by stage-wise application of the Rasch Rating model).

(4) Point estimates and dispersion estimates of both persons and tests allow both persons and sub-tests to be mapped on to a single underlying variable.

(5) Calibration, administration of the sub-test and routine scoring enables a person to be placed with a dispersion space (or interval) on the skill continuum.

(6) The calibrated sub-tests can be administered as a group of items, or individually, to locate a particular person on the skill continuum.

(7) Tests of skills such as spoken language can be developed and administered individually using only a few questions (or sub-tests) to obtain an accurate placement of persons.

(8) The tests so calibrated can be shown to have both validity and reliability. Detailed discussions of these issues can be found in the Wright and Masters monograph (1982).

(9) Items, sets of items, or sub-tests can be exchanged once calibrated, so that a variety of centres can utilize the tests without interfering with the purpose of the tests or with the accuracy of the measures obtained.

The mathematical algorithms may appear to present some difficulty. Four basic methods have been developed to produce the item and person parameters for the dichotomous models. These are: PROX (Cohen, 1968, Wright and Masters, 1982, Izard and White, 1982); Pairwise Procedures (Choppin, 1982); Conditional Maximum Likelihood (Wright and Panchapakesan, 1969); and Unconditional Maximum Likelihood (Wright and Douglass, 1978). The Rating Scale model and the Dispersion model have also been developed to the operational stage by Masters (1981) and Andrich and Lynn (1981) respectively. A wide range of computer programs is available, particularly from the developers of the models. But each of the estimates of the parameters can be computed with no more than a simple worksheet and a hand calculator that does nothing more complex than finding the square root. The ease with which approximations of the parameters can be computed stems from the fact that the only information required is the person and item scores and dispersion values.

The simplicity of the rating scale affords the routine scoring methods which appear to be lacking in present forms of interview testing of spoken language. The combination of rating scales and the Rasch model affords an opportunity to obtain both ability and difficulty estimates, together with the independence of the parameters previously outlined. This means that a test produced in Hong Kong, for example, could be calibrated elsewhere, equated to the Hong Kong estimates and used anywhere in the world, provided that local colloquialisms were avoided. The validity of the tests can be supported by the cross calibration and the directness of the measures. There appears to remain only the step of actually producing the tests.

Developing Interview Tasks

Structured interview tests are not new, nor is the application of latent trait calibration to such tests. Rasch originally developed his model to assess reading ability of Danish school children. He used a verbal test.

Given the possibility of a points earned or a partial credit approach the first generalization of the Rasch model can be applied to sets of language tasks, each scored on a routine rating scale. The simplest of these could contain the ratings categories "wrong", "partly correct" and "totally correct". The first step of course is to develop the tests. Standard test development techniques suggest two promising approaches:

(1) The curriculum analysis approach
(2) The actuarial approach.

The curriculum analysis approach assumes that a detailed analysis of the spoken language components has been conducted. These components are translated into test specifications and the items developed from these. A full description of this approach to test construction can be found in Burrill's (1976) outline of procedures for developing standardized tests. The second approach may offer something to developers of language tests as well.

The actuarial approach to test construction, outlined by Cronbach (1970) demands that persons highly skilled in the desired attribute (e.g. spoken language) are identified and their observable characteristics noted (relevant of course to the trait in question). We would need to know how a native speaker would respond to a given situation, or use language effectively. Tests are then developed to measure the strength of these attributes. In the area of spoken language a combination of these two approaches would suggest that the items used to measure identified language skills are calibrated on articulate native speakers, articulate non-native speakers and a sample of persons with a partial and perhaps insufficient grasp of the language. The stimuli used to elicit spoken responses must be standardized. They would have to be written, pictorial or physical objects with standard instructions designed to elicit acceptable answers which could only fall within a very narrow range. Bruton and Gibbons (1976) have successfully demonstrated that the use of structured stimuli in interview situations can produce unanimity of correct responses from native speakers. Their method was to establish a simulated interview in which respondents acted a role. This could be simplified even further by presenting standard stimuli ranging from simple to complex and probing for interpretive responses.

A possible appropriate format for the one-to-one interview test has been developed for the measurement of mathematics skills (Dunn and Markwardt, 1970) and for Listening Skills (ACER, 1979). The format of the interview requires a flip-card set which presents the stimulus to the subject and the instructions and acceptable answers to the examiners. This is shown schematically in Fig. 3.

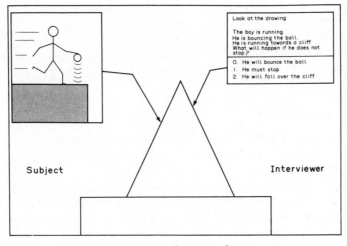

Fig. 3. *Structured interview format*

The responses in the figure are contrived. Field testing of the items is the only way to determine the precise type of instruction, stimulus and response required.

An Example Calibration

The example calibration below is from contrived data. Twenty-five items are answered by 70 students. The twenty-five items have been divided into five sub-sets each containing five items. Each item has five correct response categories. The student group has been divided into two groups. Group A answers 15 of the items as does Group B. This enables 5 common items to be used. The groups can contain 35 randomly allocated students, to enable the simulation of calibration of the test across two different populations. Each of the items is scored using the 0, 1, 2 rating scale to indicate "wrong", "partly correct" and "correct". Two trace lines are developed for each item. One for the partly correct level and one for the fully correct level. The location of the item can then be approximated using the centre of each pair of item curves. Each of the five items can then be mapped on to the ability variable and the location of the sub-test estimated from the mean of the five items; the dispersion can be estimated from the standard deviation of the difficulty values of the items in the sub-test. This enables the reordering of responses and categories such that we have five tests with ten response categories each. This is illustrated in Fig. 4 for one of the sub-tests.

This mapping of response curves illustrates that a fully correct score on one item, may be indicative of less ability than a partly correct score on another item. The positions of the curves can be estimated by scoring the data at each level and estimating each of the difficulty levels. The step is repeated with ten response categories per test. We thus have three tests, each of ten response categories for each student and those 30 response categories can be mapped on to the same variable. Ten of the response categories are common to the two groups, corresponding to the common items administered to both groups. The items have difficulty levels independent of the group to which they were administered so the arbitrary scale can be adjusted by moving the common group upwards

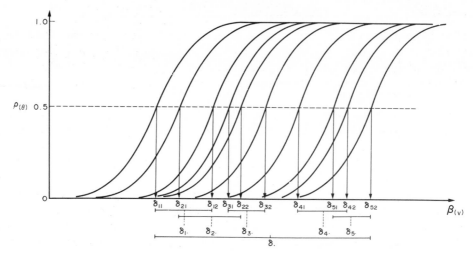

Fig. 4. *Characteristic curves for 5 item rating scale sub-test*

to match across groups. The same adjustment is then made to the non-common items of one-group and to all ability scores. Details of the equating method can be found in various papers of which Wright and Stone (1979), Morgan (1982) and Wright and Masters (1982) would be the easiest to follow.

The results of the calibration and equating of the sub-tests are presented below in graphic form. The tests increase in difficulty and have both a location and dispersion on the ability continuum.

It is also instructive to examine possible results for specific individuals. Their response patterns show that the administration of selected short tests can yield accurate placement on the ability scale. This has implications for the interview situation in which the test items measure language ability. After a short informal start to an interview, an examiner (who should of course be both trained and practiced in the use of the test materials) could readily select an appropriate subset of items. If these were collected together in the suggested flip-card form it would be merely a matter of turning to what was estimated to be an appropriate set of items. If the set proved to be too easy it would be a simple matter to adjust the selection appropriately.

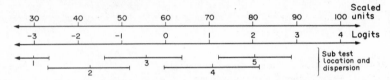

Fig. 5. *Location and dispersion of scaled and equated sub-tests*

This of course assumes that the tests have been developed and previously calibrated; that score sheets are available together with calibration tables. Such support materials would be the result of the field development of the test materials. With practice, the whole interview and placement, if necessary, should take a very short time indeed, and be free from the strains of the subjective interview format prevalent in some large-scale language testing programs.

Conclusion

The development of the item pool (or bank) can enable centres to vary the testing materials from session to session, to vary the composition of sub-tests, to change interviewers, and to save considerable time without loss of information but with a much more reliable and arguably more valid information source from which to judge the capability of individuals to cope with courses, employment or the like.

The developments of the latent trait models have much to offer language testing, in ways that workers in other fields of measurement of human abilities have discovered. This paper has suggested a shift in approaches to language skill measurement. The techniques outlined are not small-scale procedures, capable of development by individuals working alone. However there are a large number of people working in the same field in many different centres. Cooperation between centres and a serious coordinated attempt to develop standard instruments would yield a great return in terms of the facility of administration, accuracy of results, exchange of information and a relatively stable bank of language test-items capable of being used anywhere that a particular language is assessed.

Bibliography

Acheson, P. (1977) English for speakers of other languages: a survey of teacher preparation programs in American and British colleges and universities. In J. F. Fanselow and R. L. Light (Eds.) *Bilingual, ESOL and Foreign Language Teacher Preparation: Models, Practices, Issues.* Washington, D.C.: TESOL, pp. 69–81.

Alderson, C. (1979) The cloze procedure and proficiency in English as a foreign language. *TESOL Quarterly*, **13**, 219–223.

Alderson, J. C. and Hughes, A. (Eds.) (1981) *Issues in Language Testing*, ELT Documents 111. London: The British Council.

Alderson, J. C. and Urquhart, A. H. (1983) The effect of student background discipline on comprehension: a pilot study. In D. Porter and A. Hughes (Eds.) *Current Developments in Language Testing.* London: Academic Press, pp. 121–128.

Allen, D. (1982) *Oxford Placement Test.* London: Oxford University Press.

American Psychological Association (1974) *Standards for Educational and Psychological Tests and Manuals.* Washington, D.C.: A.P.A.

Anastasi, A. (1976) *Psychological Testing*, 4th ed. New York: Macmillan.

Anderson, J. (1976) *Psycholinguistic Experiments in Foreign Language Testing.* Queensland: University of Queensland Press.

Anderson, R. and Freebody, P. (1981) Vocabulary knowledge. In J. T. Guthrie (Ed.) *Comprehension and Teaching: Research Reviews.* Newark, Del.: International Reading Association, pp. 77–117.

Andrich, D. (1975) The Rasch multiplicative binomial model: application to attitude data. *Research Monograph 1.* University of Western Australia, Department of Education, Measurement and Statistics Laboratory.

Andrich, D. (1978a) A binomial latent trait model for the study of Likert-type attitude questionnaires. *British Journal of Mathematical and Statistical Psychology*, **31**, 84–98.

Andrich, D. (1978b) Scaling attitude items constructed and scored in the Likert tradition. *Educational and Psychological Measurement*, **38**, 665–680.

Andrich, D. (1978c) Application of a psychometric rating model to ordered categories which are scored with successive integers. *Applied Psychological Measurement*, **2**, 581–594.

Andrich, D. (1980) Using latent trait measurement models to analyse attitudinal data: a synthesis of viewpoints. In D. Spearritt (1982) (Ed.) *Improvement of Measurement in Education and Psychology.* Melbourne: Australian Council for Educational Research, pp. 89–126.

Andrich, D. (1981) Rasch's models and Guttman's principles for scaling attitudes. Paper presented at the Conference in Honour of Georg Rasch, University of Chicago.

Andrich, D. (1982) An extension of the Rasch model for ratings providing both location and dispersion parameters. *Psychometrika* **47**, 105–113.

Andrich, D. and Lyne, A. (1980) PIFIT: A Fortran VI program for testing person and item fit among populations in Rasch models. *Research Report 7*, University of Western Australia, Department of Education/Measurement and Statistics Laboratory.

Andrich, D. and Sheriden, B. E. (1980) RATE: a Fortran IV programme for analysing rated data according to the Rasch model. *Research Report 5*, University of Western Australia, Department of Education.

Archer, M. and Nolan-Woods, E. (1976) *Practice Tests for Proficiency.* Middlesex: Nelson.

ARELS (No date) *ARELS Oral Examination.* London: The Examinations Trust of the Association of Recognized English Language Schools.

Atkinson, P. (1981) *The Clinical Experience: the Construction and Reconstruction of Medical Reality.* Aldershot: Gower.

Australian Council for Educational Research. (1981) *ACER Listening Tests for 10-Year-Olds and 14-Year-Olds.* Melbourne: Australian Council for Educational Research.

Bachman, L. F. (1982) The trait structure of cloze test scores. *TESOL Quarterly*, **16**, 61–70.

Bachman, L. F. and Palmer, A. S. (1981) The construct validation of the FSI Oral Interview. *Language Learning*, **31**, 67–86.

Bachman, L. F. and Palmer, A. S. (1981) Basic concerns in test validation. In J. A. S. Read (Ed.) *Directions in Language Testing.* Singapore: RELC/Singapore University Press, pp. 41–57.

Bachman, L. F. and Palmer, A. S. (1981) Self-assessment of communicative competence in English. (Mimeo).

Bachman, L. F. and Palmer, A. S. (1982) The construct validation of some components of communicative proficiency. *TESOL Quarterly*, **16**, 449–465.

Balke-Aurell, G. (1977) *Validering av Språktest* (Validation of Language Tests). Stockholm: Personal-administrativa Rådet. (Mimeo).

Bates, M. and Dudley-Evans, T. (1982) *Nucleus General Science, Teacher's Manual*, Expanded New Edition. London: Longman.

Berkoff, N. A. (1982) Testing oral proficiency – a suggested new approach. *English Teachers' Journal (Israel)*, **27**, 33–36.

Birnbaum, A. (1968) Some latent trait models and their use in inferring an examinee's ability. In F. Lord and M. Novik (Eds.) *Statistical Theories of Mental Test Scores*. Reading, Mass.: Addison Wesley.

Bolus, R. E., Hinofotis, F. B. and Bailey, K. M. (No date). An introduction to generalizability theory in second language research. University of California, Los Angeles. (Mimeo).

Breen, M. P. and Candlin, C. N. (1980) The essentials of a communicative curriculum in language teaching. *Applied Linguistics*, **1**, 89–112.

Brennan, R. L. (1980) Applications of generalizability theory. In R. A. Berk (Ed.) *Criterion-Referenced Measurement*. Baltimore, Md.: Johns Hopkins University Press, pp. 186–232.

Brière, E. J. (1971) Are we really measuring proficiency with our foreign language tests? *Foreign Language Annals*, **4**, 385–391.

British Council (1977) *English for Specific Purposes: An International Seminar*. Bogotá, Colombia, 17–22 April. London: British Council.

Brown, J. D. (In press) A norm-referenced engineering reading test. In A. K. Pugh and J. M. Ulijn (Eds.) *Reading for Professional Purposes: Studies in Native and Foreign Languages*. London: Heinemann Educational.

Brown, J. D. and Bailey, K. M. (No date) An evaluation of a categorical scoring instrument for ESL compositions. University of California, Los Angeles. (Mimeo).

Bruton, A., Buckley, P. and Samuda, V. (1978) Getting it right: the oral testing situation. University of Lancaster. (Mimeo).

Bruton, C. and Gibbons, J. (1976) Language testing project: *testing oral production*. University of Lancaster, Department of Education. (Mimeo).

Burrill, L. (1976) The development of the standardised test. *Measurement Newsletter 24*. New York: The Psychological Corporation.

Buros, O. K. (1972) (Ed.) *The Seventh Mental Measurements Yearbook*. Highland Park, N. J.: Gryphon Press.

Buros, O. K. (1977) Fifty years in testing: Some reminiscences, criticisms, and suggestions. *Educational Researcher*, **6**, 9–15.

Canale, M. (1983) From communicative competence to communicative language pedagogy. In J. C. Richards and R. W. Schmidt (Eds.) *Language and Communication*. London: Longman, pp. 2–27.

Canale, M. and Swain, M. (1980a) Theoretical bases of communicative approaches to second language teaching and testing. *Applied Linguistics*, **1**, 1–47.

Canale, M. and Swain, M. (1980b) A domain description for core FSL: Communication skills. In *The Ontario Assessment Instrument Pool: French as a Second Language, Junior and Intermediate Divisions*. Toronto: Ontario Ministry of Education, pp. 27–39.

Candelier, H. P., Chaix, D., Coste, C., O'Neil, C. and Regourd, A. (1975 and 1976) *Report and Proposals for Establishing a Regional Inventory of Methods and Materials for Self-learning of Modern Languages in Europe*. Paris: UNESCO.

Candlin, C. N. and Edelhoff, C. (1982) *Challenges, Teacher's Guide*. London: Longman.

Carroll, B. J. (1978) *Guidelines for the Development of Communicative Tests*. London: Royal Society of Arts.

Carroll, B. J. (1980) *Testing Communicative Performance*. Oxford: Pergamon.

Carroll, J. B. (1945) The effect of difficulty and success on correlations between items or between tests. *Psychometrika*, **10**, 1–19.

Carroll, J. B. (1961) Fundamental considerations in testing for English language proficiency of foreign students. In H. B. Allen and R. N. Campbell. (Eds.) *Teaching English as a Second Language*. New York: McGraw-Hill (1972), pp. 313–20.

Carroll, J. B. (1968) The psychology of language testing. In A. Davies (Ed.) *Language Testing Symposium: A Psycholinguistic Approach*. London: Oxford University Press, pp. 46–69.

Carroll, J. B. and Sapon, S. M. (1959) *The Modern Language Aptitude Test, M.L.A.T. Manual*. New York: Harcourt Brace Jovanovich/The Psychological Corporation.

Carroll, L. (1876) *The Hunting of the Snark*. Reprinted (1967), M. Gardner (Ed.). Harmondsworth: Penguin.

Caulfield, J. and Smith, W. C. (1981) The reduced redundancy test and the cloze procedure as measures of global language proficiency. *Modern Language Journal*, **65**, 54–58.

Chihara, T., Oller, J. W. Jr., Weaver, K. and Chavex-Oller, M. (1977) Are cloze items sensitive to constraints across sentences? *Language Learning*, **27**, 63–73.

Choppin, B. (1978) *Item Banking and the Monitoring of Achievement*. Slough: National Foundation for Educational Research.

Choppin, B. (1982) The use of latent trait models in the measurement of cognitive abilities and skills. In D. Spearritt (Ed.) *The Improvement of Measurement in Education and Psychology*. Melbourne: Australian Council for Educational Research, pp. 41–63.

Clapham, C. M. (1975) *Test of English for Adult Learners*. University of Lancaster, Department of Linguistics.

Clark, J. L. D. (1972) *Foreign Language Testing: Theory and Practice*. Philadelphia, Pa.: Center for Curriculum Development.

Clark, J. L. D. (1975) Theoretical and technical considerations in oral Proficiency testing. In R. L. Jones and B. Spolsky. (Eds.) *Testing Language Proficiency*. Arlington, Va.: Center for Applied Linguistics, pp. 10–28.

Clark, J. L. D. (1978) (Ed.) *Foreign Service Institute Tests*. Educational Testing Service, Office of Education: Washington D.C.

Clark, H. and Clark, E. (1977) *Psychology and Language: An Introduction to Psycholinguistics*. New York: Harcourt Brace Jovanovich.

Cohen, A. D. (1980) *Testing Language Ability in the Classroom*. Rowley, Mass.: Newbury House.

Cohen, L. (1979) Approximate expressions for parameter estimates in the Rasch model. *British Journal of Mathematical and Statistical Psychology*, **32**, 113–120.

Communication Skills Unit (1980) *Intensive Grammar Programme*. University of Dar es Salaam, Tanzania.

Cooper, R. L. (1968) An elaborated language testing model. *Language Learning* (Special Issue), **3**, 57–72.

Corder, S. P. (1973) *Introduction to Applied Linguistics*. Harmondsworth: Penguin.

Cronbach, L. J. (1970) *Essentials of Psychological Testing*, 3rd ed. New York: Harper and Row.

Cronbach, L. J. (1971) Test validation. In R. L. Thorndike (Ed.) *Educational Measurement*, 2nd ed. Washington, D.C.: American Council on Education, pp. 443–507.

Cronbach, L. J. (1973) *Essentials of Psychological Testing*. New York: McGraw Hill.

Cronbach, L. J., Gleser, G. C., Nanda, H. and Rajaratnum, N. (1972) *The Dependability of Behavioral Measurements*. New York: Wiley.

Cummins, J. (1976) The influence of bilingualism on cognitive growth: a synthesis of research findings and explanatory hypothesis. *Working Papers on Bilingualism*, **9**, 1–43.

Davies, A. (1971) Language aptitude in the first year of the UK secondary school. *RELC Journal*, **2**, 4–19.

Davies, A. (1978 and 1979) Language testing. *Language Teaching and Linguistics Abstracts*, **11**, 145–159 and 215–231. Reprinted in V. Kinsella (1982) (Ed.) *Surveys*. Cambridge: Cambridge University Press.

Douglass, G. A. (1978) Conditional maximum-likelihood estimation for the multiplicative binomial response model. *British Journal of Mathematical and Statistical Psychology*, **31**, 73–83.

Douglass, G. A. (1982) Conditional inference in a generic Rasch model. In D. Spearritt (Ed.) *Improvement of Measurement in Education and Psychology*. Melbourne: Australian Council for Educational Research.

Douglass, G. A. (1982) Issues in the fit of data to psychometric models. *Educational Research and Perspectives*, **9**, 32–43.

Dunn, L. M. and Markwardt, F. C. (1970) *Peabody Individual Achievement Test (PIAT)*. Circle Pines, Minn.: American Guidance Service.

Ebel, R. L. (1961) Must all tests be valid? *American Psychologist*, **16**, 640–647.

Edwards, J. R. (1979) Judgements and confidence in reactions to disadvantaged speech. In H. Giles, and R. St. Clair, (Eds.) *Language and Social Psychology*. Oxford: Blackwell, pp. 22–44.

EST Clearinghouse Bibliography (1981) In *English for Specific Purposes 56*. Oregon State University, English Language Institute.

EST Clearinghouse Bibliography (1982) In *English for Specific Purposes 66*. Oregon State University, English Language Institute.

Ferguson, N. (1978) Test N. 73: instantaneous evaluation of speaking ability. *IRAL* **16**, 340–349.

Ferguson, N. (1980) *The Gordian Knot*. Geneva: CEEL.

Fitzpatrick, R. and Morrison, E. J. (1971) Performance and product evaluation. In R. L. Thorndike (Ed.) *Educational Measurement*, 2nd ed. Washington, D.C.: American Council on Education, pp. 237–270.

Fok, C. Y. Y. A. (1981a) Reliability of student self-assessment. Paper presented at the 1981 B.A.A.L. Seminar on Language Testing, Reading, England.

Fok, C. Y. Y. A. (1981b) Testing listening proficiency at the tertiary level. In J. A. S. Read (Ed.) *Papers on Language Testing*. Singapore: RELC/Singapore University Press, pp. 36–40.

Fok, C. Y. Y. A. (1982) Measuring reading achievement in a bilingual situation. *Working Papers in Linguistics and Language Teaching*, **5**, 1–21. University of Hong Kong, Language Centre.

Fowler, W. S. and Coe, N. (1978) *Nelson English Language Tests*. Middlesex: Nelson.

Genesee, F., Tucker, G. R. and Lambert, W. E. (1975) Communication skills of bilingual children. *Child Development*, **46**, 1010–1014.

Goldstein, H. (1979) Consequences of using the Rasch model for educational assessment. *British Education Research Journal*, **5**, 211–20.

Gorsuch, R. L. (1974) *Factor Analysis*. Philadelphia, Pa.: Saunders.

Gove, P. S. (1984) Navigation techniques for 16 + vocational students: assessment procedures and language skills development. In R. C. Williams, J. Swales & J. Kirkman (Eds.) *Common Ground: Shared Interests in E.S.P. and Communication Studies*. Oxford: Pergamon, pp. 159–168.

Green, P. (1974) Aptitude testing: an ongoing experiment. *Audio-Visual Language Journal*, **12**, 205–210.

Guilford, J. P. (1963) Preparation of item scores for the correlations between persons in a Q factor analysis. *Educational and Psychological Measurement*, **23**, 13–22.

Guilford, J. P. and Fruchter, B. (1978) *Fundamental Statistics in Psychology and Education*, 6th ed. New York: McGraw-Hill.

Guttman, L. (1950) The basis for scalogram analysis. In S. A. Stouffer (Ed.) *Measurement and Prediction*. Princeton, N.J.: Princeton University Press, pp. 70

Halliday, M. A. K. (1967) *Intonation and Grammar in British English*. The Hague: Mouton.

Hamilton, D. (1976) *Curriculum Evaluation*. London: Open Book.

Harley, B. and Swain, M. (1977) An analysis of verb form and function in the speech of French immersion pupils. *Working Papers on Bilingualism*, **14**, 31–46.

Harley, B. and Swain, M. (1978) An analysis of the verb system used by young learners of French. *Interlanguage Studies Bulletin*, **3**, 35–79.

Harley, B. (1982) *Age-related Differences in the Acquisition of the French Verb System by Anglophone Students in French Immersion Programs*. Unpublished doctoral thesis, University of Toronto.

Harris, D. P. (1969) *Testing English as a Second Language*. New York: McGraw-Hill.

Heaton, J. B. (1982) (Ed.) *Language Testing*. London: Modern English Publications.

Henner Stanchina, C. and Holec, H. (1977) Evaluation in an autonomous learning scheme. In *Mélanges Pédagogiques*, **11**, C.R.A.P.E.L., Nancy: Université de Nancy, pp. 73–84.

Holley, J. W. (1966) A reply to Philip Levy: in defence of the G index. *Scandinavian Journal of Psychology*, **7**, 244–246.

Holley, J. W. and Guilford, J. P. (1964) A note on the G index of agreement. *Educational and Psychological Measurement*, **24**, 749–753.

Holley, J. W. and Guilford, J. P. (1966) Note on the double centering of dichotomized matrices. *Scandinavian Journal of Psychology*, **7**, 97–101.

Horst, P. (1965) *Factor analysis of Data Matrices*. New York: Holt, Rinehart and Winston.

Howatt, A. (1974) The background to course design. In J. P. B. Allen and S. Pit Corder (Eds.) *The Edinburgh Course in Applied Linguistics*, vol. 3. London: Oxford University Press, pp. 1–23.

Hughes, A. and Woods, A. (1983) Interpreting the performance on the Cambridge Proficiency Examination of students of different linguistic backgrounds. In A. Hughes and D. Porter (Eds.) *Current Developments in Language Testing*. London: Academic Press, pp. 53–62.

Ingram, E. (1964) *English Language Battery*. University of Edinburgh, Department of Linguistics.

Izard, J. (1981) *The robustness of the Rasch model*. Melbourne: Australian Council for Education Research. (Mimeo).

Izard, J. F. and White, J. D. (1982) The use of latent trait models in the development and analysis of classroom tests. In D. Spearritt (Ed.) *The Improvement of Measurement in Education and Psychology*. Melbourne: Australian Council for Educational Research.

Jakobovits, L. A. (1970) *Foreign Language Learning: A Psycholinguistic Analysis of the Issues*. Rowley, Mass.: Newbury House.

Jensen, A. R. (1978) G: outmoded theory or unconquered frontier? Invited address given at the Annual Convention of the American Psychological Association in Toronto, August 29, 1978.

Johnson, F. C. and Wong Leung, C. K. L. (1981) The interdependence of teaching, testing, and instructional materials. In J. A. S. Read (Ed.) *Directions in Language Testing*. Singapore: RELC/Singapore University Press, pp. 277–302.

Johnson, K. and Morrow, K. (1981) *Communication in the Classroom*. London: Longman.

Johnson, K. (1982) *Communicative Syllabus Design and Methodology*. Oxford: Pergamon.

Jones, R. L. (1975) Testing language proficiency in the United States Government. In R. L. Jones and B. Spolsky (Eds.) *Testing Language Proficiency*. Arlington, Va.: Center for Applied Linguistics, pp. 1–9.

Jones, R. L. (1977) Testing: a vital connection. In J. K. Phillips (Ed.) *The Language Connection: From the Classroom to the World*. ACTFL Foreign Language Education Series 9, Skokie, Ill.: National Textbook Co., pp. 237–365.

Jones, R. L. (1978) Interview techniques and scoring criteria at the higher levels. In J. L. D. Clark (Ed.) *Direct Testing of Speaking Proficiency: Theory and Practice*. Princeton, N.J.: Educational Testing Service, pp. 89–102.

Jones, R. L. (1979a) Performance testing of second language proficiency. In E. J. Brière and F. B. Hinofotis (Eds.) *Concepts in Language Testing: Some Recent Studies*. Washington, D.C.: TESOL, pp. 50–57.

Jones, R. L. (1979b) The oral interview of the Foreign Service Institute. In B. Spolsky (Ed.) *Advances in Language Testing. Series 1: Some Major Tests*. Washington, D.C.: Center for Applied Linguistics, pp. 104–115.

Jones, R. L. (1981) Assessing second language proficiency: where are we and where are we going? In J. E. Redden (Ed.) *Proceedings of the 1980 Southern Illinois Language Testing Conference*. Southern Illinois University Occasional Papers on Linguistics 8, pp. 103–115.

Jones, R. L. and Spolsky, B. (Eds.) (1975) *Testing Language Proficiency*. Arlington, Va.: Center for Applied Linguistics.

Kelly, A. U. (1977) *The Curriculum, Theory and Practice*. London: Harper and Row.

Kerlinger, F. N. (1964) *Foundations of Behavioral Research: Educational and Psychological Inquiry*. New York: Holt, Rinehart and Winston.

Kirk, R. E. (1968) *Experimental Design: Procedures for the Behavioral Sciences*. Belmont, Calif.: Brooks/Cole.

Klein-Braley, C. (1983) A cloze is a cloze is a question. In J. W. Oller, Jr. (Ed.) *Issues in Language Testing Research*. Rowley, Mass: Newbury House, pp. 218–228.

Krashen, S. D. (1982) *Principles and Practice in Second Language Acquisition*. Oxford: Pergamon.

Labov, W. (1970) The study of language in its social context. *Studium Generale*, **23**, 30–87.

Lado, R. (1961) *Language Testing: The Construction and Use of Foreign Language Tests*. London: Longman.

Lado, R. (1978) Scope and limitations of interview-based language testing: are we asking too much of the interview? In J. L. D. Clark (Ed.) *Direct Testing of Speaking Proficiency: Theory and Application*. Princeton N.J.: Educational Testing Service, pp. 113–128.

Lambert, W. E. and Tucker, G. R. (1972) *Bilingual Education of Children*. Rowley, Mass.: Newbury House.

Lange, D. L. and Clifford, R. T. (1980) *Testing in Foreign Languages, ESL and Bilingual Education, 1966–1979: a Select, Annotated ERIC Bibliography*. Language in Education: Theory and Practice 24, Arlington, Va.: Centre for Applied Linguistics.

Lee, Y. P. and Low, G. D. (1982) Are communicative tests really worth the effort? Paper presented at the TESOL International Convention, Honolulu, Hawaii, May 1982.

Lewis, E. G. and Massad, C. E. (1975) *The Teaching of English as a Foreign Language in Ten Countries*. Stockholm: Almqvist and Wiksell.

Littlewood, W. (1981) *Communicative Language Teaching*. Cambridge: Cambridge University Press.

Low, G. D. (1982) The direct testing of writing in a second language *System*. **10**, 247–257.

Low, G. D. and Lee, Y. P. (1982) Classifying tests of language use: the dimension of test directness. *Journal of Applied Language Study*, **1**, 16–28.

Lord, F. M. and Novick, M. R. (1968) *Statistical Theories of Mental Test Scores*. Reading, Mass.: Addison-Wesley.

Lumsden, J. (1977) Person reliability. *Applied Psychological Measurement*, **4**, 477–482.

Madsen, H. S. and Jones, R. L. (1981) Classification of oral proficiency tests. In A. S. Palmer, P. J. M. Groot and G. A. Trosper (Eds.) *The Construct Validation of Tests of Communicative Competence*. Washington, D.C.: TESOL, pp. 15–30.

Masters, G. (1980) *A Rasch model for rating scales*. Doctoral dissertation, University of Chicago.

Masters, G. (1982) A Rasch model for partial credit scoring. *Psychometrika*, **47**, 149–174.

McCallum, G. P. (1979) *Practice Tests for Michigan Certificate English*. Middlesex: Nelson.

Morgan, G. (1982) The use of the Rasch latent trait measurement model on the equating and analysis of classroom tests. In D. Spearritt (Ed.) *The Improvement of Measurement in Education and Psychology*. Melbourne: Australian Council for Education Research.

Morrison, D. M. and Lee, N. (1984) Simulating an academic tutorial: a test validation study. Paper presented at the International Symposium on Language Testing, University of Hong Kong, Dec 18–21 1982 (this volume).

Morrison, N. K. (1982) *SPSS-11: The SPSS batch system for the DEC PDP-11*, 2nd Edition, New York: McGraw-Hill.

Morrow, K. (1977) *Techniques of Evaluation for a Notional Syllabus*. Reading: Centre for Applied Language studies.

Morrow, K. (1979) Communicative language testing: revolution or evolution? In C. J. Brumfit and K. Johnson (Eds.) *The Communicative Approach to Language Teaching*. London: Oxford University Press, pp. 143–157.

Moys, A., Harding, A., Page, B. and Printon, V. J. (1980) *Modern Language Examinations at Sixteen Plus: A Critical Analysis*. London: Centre for Information on Language Teaching and Research.

Munby, J. L. (1978) *Communicative Syllabus Design*. Cambridge: Cambridge University Press.

North, S. P. and Rea, P. M. (1980): Course design: theory and practice. In *Language for Education*. University of Dar es Salaam, Tanzania: Communication Skills Unit.

Odell, L. (1977) Measuring changes in intellectual processes as one dimension of growth in writing. In C. R. Cooper and L. Odell (Eds.) *Evaluating Writing*. Urbana, Ill.: National Council of Teachers of English, pp. 107–132.

Ohnmacht, F. W., Weaver, W. W. and Kohler, E. T. (1970) Cloze and closure: a factorial study. *The Journal of Psychology*, **74**, 205–217.

Oller, J. W. Jr. (1973) Cloze tests of second language proficiency and what they measure. *Language Learning*, **23**, 105–118.

Oller, J. W. Jr. (1979) *Language Tests at School: A Pragmatic Approach*. London: Longman.

Oller, J. W. Jr. and Perkins, K. (Eds.) (1978) *Language in Education*. Rowley, Mass.: Newbury House.

Oller, J. W. Jr. and Perkins, K. (Eds.) (1980) *Research in Language Testing*. Rowley, Mass.: Newbury House.

Oller, J. W. Jr. and Streiff, V. (1975) Dictation: a test of grammar-based expectancies. *English Language Teaching Journal*, **30**, 25–36.

Ontario Ministry of Education (1980) *The Ontario Assessment Instrument Pool: French as a Second Language, Junior and Intermediate Divisions.* Toronto: Ontario Ministry of Education.

Oskarsson, M. (1980) *Approaches to Self-assessment in Foreign Language Learning.* Oxford: Pergamon.

Palmer, A. S. and Bachman, L. F. (1981) Basic concerns in test validation. In J. C. Alderson and A. Hughes (Eds.) *Issues in Language Testing.* ELT Documents 111. London: The British Council, pp. 136–151.

Palmer, A. S., Groot, P. J. M. and Trosper, G. A. (Eds.) (1981) *The Construct Validation of Tests of Communicative Competence.* Washington, D.C.: TESOL.

Pedler, P. (1982) Independence, dependence and local correlation. Paper prepared for the Seminar on Educational and Psychological Measurement, University of Western Australia, August 2–4.

Pendergast, T. M. (1983) Pair practice in the language laboratory: the MEDIATEC. *Osaka Gaikokugo Daigaku Eibei Kenkyu* **13.**

Perry, F. A. (1976) The systems approach to basic English language training in The Canadian armed forces. *System,* **4,** 178–181.

Pimsleur, P. (1966) *Language Aptitude Battery.* New York: Harcourt Brace Jovanovich.

Powers, D. and Swinton, S. (1980) *Factor Analysis of the Test of English as a Foreign Language for Several Language Groups.* Princeton, N.J.: Educational Testing Service.

Rasch, G. (1960) *Probabilistic Models of Some Intelligence and Attainment Tests.* Coper Lagon: Danmarks Paedagogiste Institut. Reprinted (1980), University of Chicago Press.

Rea, P. M. (1980) Formative assessment of student performance: the role of self-appraisal. Paper presented at the 14th TESOL International Convention, San Francisco, March 4–9.

Read, J. A. S. (Ed.) (1981) *Directions in Language Testing.* Singapore: RELC/Singapore University Press.

Reading and Thinking in English, Discovering Discourse (1979) Teacher's Edition. London: Oxford University Press.

Reading and Thinking in English, Concepts in Use. (1980) Teacher's Edition, London: Oxford University Press.

Reves, T. (1980) The group-oral test: an experiment, *English Teachers' Journal (Israel),* **24,** 19–21.

Richards, J. C. (1976) The role of vocabulary teaching in the English syllabus. In G. H. Wilson (Ed.) *Curriculum Development and Syllabus Design for English Teaching.* Singapore: RELC, pp. 99–117.

Richterich, R. and Chancerel, J-L. (1980) *Identifying the Needs of Adults Learning a Foreign Language.* Oxford: Pergamon.

Robinson, G. (1976) Foreign language research in Australia: implications for American teachers. Paper presented at the ACTFL Annual Meeting, New Orleans, 24–26 November.

Robinson, P. (1980) *English for Specific Purposes.* Oxford: Pergamon.

Samejima, F. (1969) *Estimation of Latent Ability Using Response Pattern of Graded Scores.* Psychometrika, Monograph Supplement 17.

Sang, F. and Vollmer, H. J. (1980) Modelle Linguistischer Kompetenz und ihre Empirische Fundierung. *Quantitative Linguistics,* **6,** 1–84.

Savignon, S. J. (1972) *Communicative Competence: An Experiment in Foreign Language Teaching.* Philadelphia, Pa.: Center for Curriculum Development.

Savignon, S. (1983) *Communicative Competence: Theory and Classroom Practice.* Reading, Mass.: Addison-Wesley.

Schulz, R. A. (1977) Discrete-point versus simulated communication testing in foreign languages. *Modern Language Journal,* **61,** 91–101.

Shavelson, R. J. and Webb, N. M. (1981) Generalizability theory: 1973–1980 *British Journal of Mathematical and Statistical Psychology,* **34,** 133–166.

Shaw, A. M. (1975) *Approaches to a Communicative Syllabus in Foreign Language Curriculum Development.* Unpublished doctoral thesis, University of Essex.

Shaw, A. M. (1977) Foreign language syllabus development: some recent approaches. *Language Teaching and Linguistics Abstracts,* **10,** 217–233.

Shoemaker, D. M. (1980) Improving achievement testing. *Educational Evaluation and Policy Analysis,* **2**(6), 37–49.

Skehan, P. (1982) *Language Aptitude.* Unpublished doctoral thesis, University of London.

Smith, R. M. (1982) Validating individual response patterns. Paper prepared for the Seminar on Educational and Psychological Measurement, University of Western Australia, August 2–4.

Spaan, M. and Douglas, D. (1981) A search for EFL proficiency test validation criteria. University of Michigan, English Language Institute. (Mimeo).

Spolsky, B. (1967) Do they know enough English? In *Selected Conference Papers of the Association of Teachers of English as a Second Language.* New York: National Association for Foreign Student Affairs.

Spolsky, B. (1976) Language testing: art or science. In G. Nickel (Ed.) *Proceedings of the Fourth International Congress of Applied Linguistics,* vol. 3. Stuttgart: Hochschulverlag, pp. 215–234.

Spolsky, B. (1968) Language testing – the problem of validation. *TESOL Quarterly,* **2,** 88–94.

Stanley, J. C. and Hopkins, K. D. (1972) *Educational and Psychological Measurement and Evaluation.* Englewood Cliffs, N.J.: Prentice-Hall.

Stansfield, C. (1976) Teachers' attitudes towards publishers' tests. In D. P. Benseler (Ed.) *Second Language Teaching 76*, Corvallis, Or.: Pacific Northwest Council on Foreign Languages, pp. 112–114.

Stevenson, D. K. (1983) Foreign language testing: all of the above. In C. J. James (Ed.) *Practical Applications of Research in Foreign Language Teaching*. Lincolnwood, Ill.: National Textbook Company, pp. 153–203.

Stevenson, D. K. and Riewe, U. (1982) Teachers' attitudes towards language tests and testing. In T. Culhane, C. Klein-Braley and D. K. Stevenson (Eds.) *Practice and Problems in Language Testing: Proceedings of the Fourth International Language Testing Symposium of the Interuniversitäre Sprachtestgruppe*. Colchester: University of Essex, Department of Language and Linguistics, pp. 146–155.

Sutcliffe, D. (1982) *British Black English*. Oxford: Blackwell.

Swain, M. (1981a) Bilingual education for majority and minority language children. *Studia Linguistica*, **35**, 15–32.

Swain, M. (1981b) Immersion education: applicability for non-vernacular teaching to vernacular speakers. *Studies in Second Language Acquisition*, **4**, 1–17.

Swain, M. and Lapkin, S. (1982) *Evaluating Bilingual Education: A Canadian Case Study*. Clevedon, Avon: Multilingual Matters.

Szamosi, M., Swain, M. and Lapkin, S. (1979) Do early immersion pupils 'know' French? *Orbit*, **49**, 20–23.

Taba, H. (1962) *Curriculum Development, Theory and Practice*. New York: Harcourt, Brace and World.

Taylor, W. C. (1953) Cloze procedure: a new tool for measuring readability. *Journalism Quarterly*, **30**, 415–33.

Thorén, B. (1967) *10.000 ord for tio års engelska*. Lund: Gleerups.

Thorndike, R. and Lorge, I. (1944) *The Teacher's Word Book of 30,000 words*. New York: Columbia University, Teachers' College.

Trim, J. L. M., Richterich, R., van Ek. J. A. and Wilkins, D. A. (1973) *Systems Development in Adult Language Learning*. Strasbourg: Council of Europe. Reprinted (1980) Oxford: Pergamon.

Upshur, J. A. (1971) Productive communication testing: progress report. In G. E. Perren and J. L. M. Trim (Eds.) *Applications of Linguistics*. Cambridge: Cambridge University Press. pp. 435–441.

Upshur, J. A. (1979) Functional proficiency theory and a research role for language tests. In E. J. Brière and F. B. Hinofotis (Eds.) *Concepts in Language Testing: Some Recent Studies*. Washington, D.C.: TESOL, pp. 75–100.

Valette, R. M. (1977) *Modern Language Testing*, 2nd ed. New York: Harcourt Brace Jovanovich.

Valette, R. M. and Disick, R. S. (1972) *Modern Language Performance Objectives and Individualization*. New York: Harcourt Brace Jovanovich.

van Ek, J. A. (1975) *Systems Development in Adult Language Learning: The Threshold Level*. Strasbourg: Council of Europe. Reprinted (1980) Oxford: Pergamon.

van Ek, J. A. and Alexander, L. G. (1977) *Systems Development in Adult Language Learning: Waystage*. Strasbourg: Council of Europe. Reprinted (1980) Oxford: Pergamon.

van Naerssen, M. M. (1978) ESL in medicine: a matter of life and death. *TESOL Quarterly*, **12**, 193–203.

Vollmer, H. J. (1981) Why are we interested in general language proficiency? In J. C. Alderson and A. Hughes (Eds.) *Issues in Language Testing*. ELT Documents 111. London: British Council, pp. 152–175.

von Elek, T. (1977) *Invandrarnas färdigheter i svenska* (The Swedish Proficiency of Migrants). Report 4. University of Göteborg, Language Teaching Research Center.

von Elek, T. (Ed.) (1978) *Försök med alternativa modeller för undervisningen i svenska för invandrare inom AMU*. (Experiments with Alternative Course Designs in the Teaching of Swedish to Migrants at Labour Market Schools.) Report 5. University of Göteborg, Language Teaching Research Center.

von Elek, T. (1981) *Självbedömning av färdigheter i svenska som andra språk*. (Self-Assessment of Swedish as a Second Language.) Working Paper 31. University of Göteborg, Language Teaching Research Center.

Wangsotorn, A. (1981) Self-assessment of language proficiency. In J. A. S. Read (Ed.) *Directions in Language Testing*. Singapore: RELC/Singapore University Press, pp. 240–260.

Weaver, W. W. and Kingston, A. J. (1963) A factor analysis of cloze procedure and other measures of reading and language ability. *Journal of Communication*, **13**, 252–261.

Weir, C. J. (1984) The Associated Examining Board's test in English for Academic Purposes (T.E.A.P.): towards a framework of categories for the description of communicative test events. In R. C. Williams, J. Swales & J. Kirkman (Eds.) *Common Ground: Shared Interests in E.S.P. and Communication Studies*. Oxford: Pergamon, pp. 145–157.

Whitely, S. E. (1980) Multicomponent latent trait models for ability tests *Psychometrika*, **45**, 479–494.

Widdowson, H. G. (1977) Discussion in *English for Specific Purposes, An International Seminar*. Bogotá, Colombia, 17–22 April. London: British Council.

Widdowson, H. G. (1978) *Teaching Language as Communication*. London: Oxford University Press.

Wilds, C. P. (1975) The oral interview test. In R. L. Jones and B. Spolsky (Eds.) *Testing Language Proficiency*. Arlington, Va.: Centre for Applied Linguistics, pp. 29–44.

Wilson, G. H. (Ed.) (1976) *Curriculum Development and Syllabus Design for English Teaching*. Anthology Series 3. Singapore: RELC/Singapore University Press.

Woehike, P. L. and Chai, S. H. (1979) The predictive ability of standardised tests of EFL. South Illinois University, Carbondale. (Mimeo).

Wright, B. D. and Panchapakesan, N. (1969) A procedure for sample-free item analysis. *Educational and Psychological Measurement*, **29**, 23–48.

Wright, B. D. and Douglass, G. A. (1977a) Conditional versus unconditional procedures for sample-free item analysis. *Educational and Psychological Measurement*, **37**, 47–60.

Wright, B. D. and Douglass, G. A. (1977b) Best procedures for sample-free item analysis. *Applied Psychological Measurement*, **1**, 281–294.

Wright, B. D. and Masters, G. N. (1982) *Rating Scale Analysis: Rasch Measurement*. Chicago: Mesa Press.

Wright, B. D. and Stone, M. H. (1979) *Best Test Design*. Chicago: Mesa Press.

Zettersten, A. (1977) A report on experiments in English vocabulary testing in Denmark, Finland, Norway and Sweden. In A. Zettersten (Ed.) *Papers on English Language Testing in Scandinavia*. Anglica et Americana 1. University of Copenhagen, Department of English.

Zettersten, Arne (1979) *Experiments in English Vocabulary Testing*. Copenhagen: LiberHermods Malmö.